Explaining Social Institutions

Explaining Social Institutions

Edited by
Jack Knight and Itai Sened

Ann Arbor
THE UNIVERSITY OF MICHIGAN PRESS

First paperback edition 1998
Copyright © by the University of Michigan 1995
All rights reserved
Published in the United States of America by
The University of Michigan Press
Manufactured in the United States of America
⊗ Printed on acid-free paper

2001   2000   1999   1998   4   3   2   1

A CIP catalog record for this book is available from the British Library.

Library of Congress Cataloging-in-Publication Data

Explaining social institutions / edited by Jack Knight and Itai Sened.
          p.   cm.
     Includes bibliographical references and index.
     ISBN 0-472-10588-4 (alk. paper)
     1. Social institutions.   I. Knight, Jack, 1952–   .   II. Sened,
Itai.
HM131.E956   1995
306 — dc20   95-16975
                                                                   CIP

ISBN 0-472-08576-X (pbk. : alk. paper)

Contents

Introduction

Jack Knight and Itai Sened

Institutional analysis has reemerged as a central focus of social science research in the last several years. This analysis has taken many forms, both in terms of substantive concerns and of methodological approaches. The essays collected in this volume are contributions to an area of this analysis that has particularly flourished in the last fifteen years: the study of the political economy of social institutions. The analysis of institutions in terms of the rationality of social actors who interact through them has developed in a variety of fields: political science (Riker 1980; Shepsle 1979; Shepsle and Weingast 1987); economic history (North 1981, 1990); sociology (Coleman 1990; Hechter 1990); philosophy (Lewis 1969; Ullman-Margalit 1977; Sugden 1986); and organizational theory (Miller 1992). These efforts have significantly enhanced our understanding of the role of institutions in economic and political life.

Until recently, the main focus of this work has been on the effects of institutional arrangements on social outcomes: What are the effects of electoral rules on political competition (Cox 1987, 1990)? What impact do property rights have on the efficiency of allocation of resources (Libecap 1989; Sened and Riker 1992)? How does the organization of property rights and mechanisms of taxation affect the political development of the state (Levi 1988)? How can different norms of cooperation resolve collective action problems (Taylor 1987; Ostrom 1990; Heckathorn 1993)? How does internal organization affect the success of economic firms and political bureaucracy (North 1990)?

Less attention has been paid to questions of emergence and change. This has led to gaps and weaknesses in our understanding of these institutions. A main source of the problem with many of these accounts is their reliance on the unwarranted premise that describing what an institution does explains either why it exists or how it emerged. However, the fact that an institution has a particular effect may merely be a by-product or only a part of the explanation of both emergence and continued existence.[1] A closer attention to questions of institutional origin is a prerequisite for comprehensive explanations of maintenance and stability, on the one hand, and emergence and change, on the other. The contributors to this volume attempt in a variety of ways to address these questions.

In order to better situate these essays in the overall literature on the political economy of social institutions, we begin with a brief overview of this field. Studies of the rationality of social institutions take many forms. The explanations offered by these studies can be characterized according to two criteria: (1) the institutional effects invoked to explain maintenance and stability and (2) the mechanism for institutional change (Knight 1992).

Institutional Effects. Traditional accounts of social institutions treat the process of institutionalization as a problem of collective action. According to these accounts, social institutions provide groups of individuals with the means of resolving collective action problems and provide benefits for collective activity. On these accounts, institutional maintenance and stability are primarily explained by the capacity of institutions to produce collective goods or benefits for social groups (Ostrom 1990). The collective benefits may be efficiency (in terms of allocation or employment of scarce resources), social optimality (the maximization of social benefits), minimization of transaction costs, stability, or the satisfaction of some other functional need.

Some versions of this approach merely assume that social institutions produce efficient or socially optimal outcomes (Buchanan and Tullock 1962). Other versions allow for the possibility that suboptimal institutions may emerge, but retain the basic conception of collective benefits and seek to explain these inefficiencies by failures within the community or the institutions (Ostrom 1990). On either account, however, the continued ability of an institution to provide one of these collective benefits is invoked to explain its ongoing stability.

A number of recent studies have given greater emphasis to the distributional consequences of social institutions (Knight 1992; Miller 1992; Sened 1990). On this account the primary explanation for why social institutions take the particular forms that they do is to be found in the ways that these institutions distribute the benefits of collective activity. The ongoing maintenance and stability of an institution are explained by the ability of the institution to provide distributional advantage to those who have the power and/or authority to change it.

Institutional Change. Theories of institutional change can be distinguished by the form of change on which they focus. Evolutionary theories generally rely on one of the mechanisms originally formulated by classical theory: spontaneous emergence, market-coordinated exchange, or social selection (Smith 1976; Hume 1978). Theories of intentional design generally adopt a contractarian approach, explaining institutions as the intentional product of free and voluntary exchange in the political market (Buchanan and Tullock 1962; Umbeck 1981). Complicating this conceptual distinction is the fact that a number of recent theories either explicitly or, more often, implicitly combine aspects of both approaches: for example, intentional design at the microlevel that is subject to some competitive selection process (either the market or some other competitive mechanism) at the macrolevel.

Evolutionary accounts of institutional change employ a collective benefits focus to explain a variety of institutional forms. Theories that focus on the evolutionary development of socially efficient institutions explain basic social conventions (Lewis 1969), norms (Axelrod 1986; Coleman 1990), law (Posner 1980), property rights (Schotter 1981; Demsetz 1967), and various forms of social and economic organization (Williamson 1975, 1985; Brennan and Buchanan 1985). Evolutionary theories that allow for the emergence of institutions that are less than socially efficient include explanations of social conventions and norms (Sugden 1986; Young 1993), property rights (Barzel 1989; Libecap 1989; North 1990), and forms of economic organization (Coase 1960; Nelson and Winter 1982).

Several of these theories, especially those explanations of a society's network of conventions and norms, are based on the spontaneous-emergence argument that has received its most systematic contemporary formulation by Hayek (1967). Hayek's theory of cultural evolution establishes the basic framework for these "spontaneous order" explanations. First, the "invisible hand" mechanism: social institutions are the unintended social consequence of individual action. Second, the arbitrariness of the resultant set of institutions: since individuals lack the knowledge to design socially optimal institutions of their own making, the spontaneous order can take any one of several different forms. Third, a process of social selection: the collectively beneficial nature of the emerging order is determined by a competitive selection mechanism.[2]

Other theories, mainly those that seek to explain property rights or other economic institutions, rely on market competition as a mechanism (Alchian 1950; Demsetz 1967). A direct descendant of Smith's invisible-hand thesis, Alchian's argument relies on competitive pressures of the market to select socially beneficial economic organization. In its purest form the argument requires no particular intentionality on the part of individual economic actors. One purpose of Alchian's original article was to suggest that economic analysis need not rely on the claim that economic actors actually make the sophisticated utility-maximization calculations prevalent in rational-actor models. Due to the competitive pressure of the market, the resulting equilibrium consists of a socially efficient set of economic organizations whose behavior appears "as if" they were utility maximizers. The market selects out the most efficient forms of organization and production. In this way it guarantees social efficiency even without any intention by the actors to achieve it.

Many recent accounts that invoke the market-selection logic modify the pure evolutionary argument by synthesizing competitive selection with intentional attempts to create rights or forms of organization through market exchange. Prominent examples are those that employ Coase's (1960) theory of transaction costs for an explanation of the structure of economic exchange (Williamson 1975, 1985; North 1990). Individual economic actors seek to order their exchanges to minimize the costs of these transactions. For these private orderings to become institutionalized for the community as a whole, there must be some means of generalizing them. Here, the competitive pressure of the market comes into play, selecting those orderings that are best at minimizing costs.

Theories of intentional design have primarily been invoked to explain the creation of political institutions. Here, we need to distinguish the transaction-costs-based theories that synthesize intentional and evolutionary elements from those theories based purely on intentional efforts to develop institutional arrangements. Two strands can be distinguished. In the first, the creation of basic political rules—either constitutions (Riker 1988; Tsebelis 1990) or legislative rules and principles (Shepsle and Ordeshook 1982; Shepsle 1986)—is attributed to a "founding" body. In the second strand, the establishment of political institutions and rights is the responsibility of an established government. The nature of these rights is explained as the product of competition among state officials and private-interest groups (Bates 1989; North 1990). Issues of distribution are explicitly acknowledged in these intentional theories, usually as an explanation for the suboptimality of political institutions. These accounts maintain a primary focus on collective benefits and coordination. Implicit in them is the fundamental idea that inefficiency and suboptimality are somehow the product of state intervention in an otherwise relatively efficient world.

Concomitant with the explicit emphasis on the distributional consequences of social institutions has been the introduction of bargaining as a mechanism of institutional change. Bargaining models have been employed in theories of both evolutionary and intentional institutional change. They have formed the basis of explanations of the evolutionary emergence of social conventions and norms (Knight 1992), as well as of the intentional creation of property rights (Sened and Riker 1992; Ensminger 1992), bureaucratic organizations (Miller 1992), and constitutions (Heckathorn and Maser 1987). Such explanations invoke the relative bargaining power of relevant social actors as a way of identifying both why a particular institutional rule was established and why such rules subsequently changed.

The chapters in this volume represent some of the most important recent work in the analysis of social institutions. They reflect the considerable diversity in both method and substantive focus that can be found in the rational choice, or political economy, approach to institutional analysis. The chapters are evenly divided in their substantive focus. Four of the chapters in this volume — those of Douglass North, Randall Calvert, and Jack Knight and the chapter by Avner Greif, Paul Milgrom, and Barry Weingast — concentrate on issues related mainly to the evolution of informal social institutions, that is, institutions that emerge and are maintained without the support of explicit enforcement by the state. The other four chapters — those of William Riker, Jon Elster, Norman Schofield, and Itai Sened — focus primarily on issues related to the intentional design of formal institutions, that is, institutions that are reinforced by the legal authority of the state.

The chapters are also evenly divided in terms of their methodological emphasis. While all of the chapters investigate the implications of an assumption of rational decision making for the development of social institutions, they differ in the extent to which they rely on formal mathematical models to develop their arguments. Three of the chapters — those of North, Riker, and Elster — rely on the more informal logic of social choice and strategic analysis to ground their studies of institutional creation and change. One chapter — that of Knight — employs a simple game-theoretic model as a heuristic device to illustrate a set of arguments about the underlying logic of various general theories of evolutionary institutional change. Four of the chapters — those of Calvert, Schofield, Sened, and Greif, Milgrom, and Weingast — use more mathematically complex models to formally derive the main conclusions of their analyses.

In addition, these chapters as a group demonstrate how rational-choice accounts of institutional emergence and change can address many features of social life that critics have previously suggested are lacking in such explanations.[3] These chapters represent attempts to incorporate power, social context, history, community values, ideology, social norms, and deliberative debate into a broad rational-choice framework. To better highlight the variety of issues to be found in these chapters, we will briefly preview in the remainder of this section the main focus of each.

Douglass North presents five fundamental propositions that he suggests are central to explaining institutional change. In doing so, he reiterates previous themes and recommends new directions for institutional analysis. He begins by reasserting his long-developed concern with the central importance of transaction costs for explanations of the creation of economic and political institutions. Then, in addressing the question of the evolution of institutions over time, he emphasizes the problem of path dependence, asserting that despite all of the acknowledgments that institutional change is characterized by path dependence, we actually know very little about the causal mechanisms for such dependence. Similarly, he cautions us about our lack of understanding of the role that political markets play in the evolution of institutions. He suggests that one of the main reasons that we have not gone further in our understanding of these questions is that the model of "rational" choice presently employed in our models is inadequate to the task of capturing the cognitive dimensions of choice. In the remainder of the chapter, North suggests a research agenda that he thinks is the most promising direction for institutional analysis: a transaction-costs approach to institutions and a cognitive-science approach to rational choice.

Avner Greif, Paul Milgrom, and Barry Weingast exemplify in their chapter how formal game-theoretic models and historical evidence can be combined to investigate institutional emergence and change. Like North, their substantive concerns are the institutional foundations of markets and the role of the state in the enforcement of contracts and property rights. These substantive concerns raise an important set of theoretical issues about how social institutions afford social actors the opportunity to coordinate behavior and to enhance the credibility of commitments for future actions. Their particular focus in this chapter is the emergence of merchant guilds in the late medieval period. They argue that merchant guilds emerged in order to allow trade centers to commit to the security of alien merchants. By interpreting historical evidence in light of a repeated-game model, they show that the merchant guild developed the theoretically required attributes, secured merchants' property rights, and evolved in response to crises to extend the range of its effectiveness, contributing to the expansion of trade during the late medieval period. They also elaborate on the relationship between their theory and the monopoly theory of merchant guilds and contrast it with repeated-game theories that provide no role for formal organization.

Randall Calvert argues that our explanations of social institutions would be better served if we rethink how we conceptualize the relationship between individual choice and institutional structure. Employing a game-theoretic approach, he challenges those rational-choice studies of institutions that portray institutions as constraints imposed upon actors as "rules of the game." He suggests rather that institutions are themselves simply agglomerations of behavior and expectations, unless we posit that they are exogeneously enforced, in which case there must always be a higher institution that remains to be explained. On his account, a coherent general analysis of institutions and their effects must treat the choice of individual actions and the structure of institutions as parts of the same individual-choice process. Calvert presents a simple model based on a prisoner's-dilemma game, with random matching, imperfect information, and communication that illustrates the existence of endogeneous "rules of the game" through increasingly structured equilibria that involve communication processes and differentiated roles. He demonstrates how, in some situations, more highly structured equilibria, which he conceives of as formal institutions, can support cooperation, while less structured ones, conceived of as informal norms, cannot. He concludes with some observations of the major implication of the model: all of these institutional features, both formal and informal, consist simply of equilibrium expectations and behavior.

Jack Knight calls attention to the relationship between modeling and theory building, insisting on the need for greater care in making the move from the initial development of rational-choice models of social institutions to the subsequent interpretations of these models offered as part of theories of institutional emergence and change. He argues that rational-choice explanations of social institutions have often failed to take adequate account of the implicit assumptions that are made in the transition from model to interpretation to theory and explanation. In this chapter he analyzes contemporary theories of spontaneous emergence and evolutionary change. Three distinct accounts are considered: theories of the evolutionary emergence of social conventions, market-based theories of exchange and selection through competition, and a bargaining theory that explains the emergence of institutions in terms of the asymmetries of power in a society. Knight employs a simple game-theoretic model to illustrate how the different theories identify quite distinct mechanisms as the primary explanation for the generation of institutional solutions to problems of social interaction. In doing so he highlights the different ways that important features of the social context in which social interactions occur enter into the process of institutional emergence and change. In addition, he emphasizes the diversity to be found in the theories of institutional change that have been grounded in an assumption of rational decision making.

William Riker investigates the framing of the United States Constitution as a case study of the more general phenomena of intentional institutional creation. In his analysis he emphasizes a number of factors that should guide studies of formal institutional design. First, he demonstrates the importance of predecessor institutions for the establishment of new institutions. In the case of the U.S. Constitution, Riker shows how the framers relied on the existing structure of state governments, particularly the three-branch arrangement, in the design of the new federal system. Second, he addresses the problem of internal consistency in political institutions and, in so doing, highlights the importance of political entrepreneurs in the development of formal institutions. By internal consistency he has in mind a situation in which the various provisions of a constitution are all aimed at achieving goals in an ordered way. He argues that the only circumstance in which internal consistency can be guaranteed is when there is a transitive social ordering of goals. Here, Riker reminds us that social choice theory suggests that in a social group of any significant size the probability of achieving such transitivity approaches zero. However, he then argues that internal consistency remains an achievable goal if the basic task of institutional design is left to a single individual. Riker uses the example of Madison and the U.S. Constitution to illustrate the effect a single political entrepreneur can have on the process of formal institution building.

Jon Elster also uses the U.S. Constitutional Convention as a case study for the process of formal institutional design. Elster has a quite different theoretical question in mind, however. In this chapter he investigates the ways that different types of arguments might influence negotiations over the substance of formal constitutional provisions. To do so, he contrasts two distinct types of speech acts: arguing and bargaining. While the former focuses on normative principles as a source of persuasion, the latter relies on the power differentials among the actors to effectuate a resolution of the conflict. The particular issue that Elster analyzes is the debate over the representation of the states in the Senate. The relevant puzzle here is that although the large states argued for proportional representation in both houses of the Congress, the framers established proportionality in the House and equal representation in the Senate. Elster investigates the debates over this decision to assess the relative importance of bargaining power, as well as three forms of principled argument: justice, efficiency, and a principle of representation. In doing so, he offers some insights into how we might incorporate the analysis of both arguing and bargaining into other instances of intentional institutional design.

Itai Sened suggests a new approach to the study of institutions that treats the role of authorities in the evolution of institutions more explicitly. Using a noncooperative game-theoretic model, he specifies conditions under which governments would grant and enforce property rights. With the model he provides an analytical framework for the study of the evolution of individual rights at two levels. First, he explains why property rights are granted and enforced by central governments. Second, he provides a rationale for the emergence of more fundamental institutions in Western democracies. Such institutions include those that guarantee freedom of speech, "the right to know your rights," and the right to petition for new rights.

Norman Schofield closes the volume with a social-choice theoretic analysis of democratic institutions. He addresses a familiar question concerning the stability of the outcomes of collective decision making in democratic institutions. He begins by reviewing the existing social-choice results: the results generally indicate that the outcomes of voting can be highly unstable. However, Schofield points out that these results are best developed for the case of direct democracy. He then goes on to argue that a more appropriate analysis would incorporate the fact that democratic institutions are not generally direct decision-making arrangements, but rather are mechanisms of representative voting. Thus, Schofield concludes that we cannot offer an unequivocal answer to the question of democratic stability until we have a fully developed theory of representative democratic institutions. In the remainder of the chapter he presents a model of representative democracy that addresses such details as the nature of the electoral system, the motivations of the politicians, and the effects of political parties. Schofield argues that his model will allow us to better address the question of the representativeness of democratic institutions.

We believe that a general picture emerges from this collection of essays; a conception that provides insights into how to study the ways in which networks of social conventions, norms, and formal institutions structure everyday life.

Institutions structure social interactions by establishing rules with which social actors comply in making strategic choices concerning their future action. They structure social interactions through a combination of (1) information provided about the choices of social actors and (2) a threat of sanctions to be imposed by other actors in the event of noncompliance. Information about future actions of those with whom we interact is relevant to all institutions. Such information serves to directly alleviate some of the uncertainty present in social interactions. The threat of sanctions may seem primarily relevant to institutions that are characterized by external enforcement, but informal sanctions may arise to punish non-compliance even in the case of self-enforcing institutions.

The key to understanding the importance of social institutions lies in the role that they play in the formation of social expectations and beliefs. The problem here is one of establishing expectations about the actions of the other players in the game; the formation of such expectations is a prerequisite for making a rational choice. Each player must formulate expectations about the actions of other players before making his own choice, but his choice will affect the choice made by the other players, affecting the original expectations of the former about the latter, and so on. This obvious infinite regression in expectation formation can only be avoided in those cases where the expectations of the players come to rest at an equilibrium. Only in such cases can we say that the players' expectations are rational.

It is here that institutions enter the strategic calculation. They do so by providing information about the choices of the other players. Institutions structure the choices of agents toward the achievement of equilibrium outcomes. They provide actors with a rational basis for formulating expectations about the actions of others. The information provided by institutions helps actors formulate the expectations necessary to make decisions that maximize their payoffs, given the actions of the other actors.

Informal institutions structure social interactions through the information they provide concerning future actions of agents, decreasing the uncertainty faced by the players in the game. The information provided by informal rules alters the expectations that players attach to the possible strategies of other actors with whom they are involved in interactions. These expectations delimit the strategies that must be considered by the players in the game. Yet, while institutions often restrict the range of strategies available to actors, only in rare cases do they constrain the set to one alternative. How much the set is constrained depends on various factors related to the subject matter of the rule and the conditions at the time of its creation. The institution may establish general parameters for the interaction by excluding some strategies, but, in most cases it will still allow for considerable flexibility in the choice of strategies within that framework.

Although information provision is the main force for compliance in these institutions, informal sanctions often develop to lend additional force to these constraints. One might ask: if these institutions are self-enforcing, why would we see any violations? There are two main reasons. First, there may be slippage in the socially shared knowledge of these institutional rules. This could come from lack of knowledge of these rules on the part of members of the community, or from differences in the interpretation of the substantive content of the rules. Second, since institutional rules usually affect the distribution of the benefits of social outcomes, it is likely that there will be actors who want to change these institutional arrangements. Efforts to change such rules will begin with individual or collective violations that will be resisted by those who benefit from the rules. The basic effect of informal sanctions is to diminish the value of noncompliant behavior.

This mechanism is similar to that characteristic of externally enforced institutions: sanctions affect the costs of choosing particular strategies. This then leads us to the question of formal social institutions. The informal networks of social conventions, rules, and norms provide the framework in which social interactions take place. Without the information they provide about the actions of those with whom we interact we would be unable to perform the most trivial tasks of social life. However, this information, even with the informal sanctions that reinforce it, is often not enough to assure social order. In such cases, enforcement mechanisms are invoked to govern social institutions.

If some agents control the means of enforcement, it is very plausible for other members of society to expect that these agents will use these means to enforce those institutional outcomes that maximize their utility. This, in and of itself, provides "focal points" (Schelling 1960) for those involved in social interactions that help them develop more concrete expectations about the way the game will be played, and, therefore, about the strategies that will maximize each agent's utility. The transparent utility-maximizing behavior of rational agents who control the maintenance and the evolution of institutional structures allows other members of society to develop clear and stable expectations about the strategies of these agents and the strategies that other agents may employ to accept or challenge these institutions (Ainsworth and Sened 1993).

More generally, formal institutions emerge when agents in society—usually called "political entrepreneurs" (Frohlich, Oppenheimer, and Young 1971)—find ways to make society accept rules that make these entrepreneurs better off. Those rules may benefit the entire society or only a small minority—that is, they need not necessarily improve the welfare of society as a whole. The point is that political entrepreneurs use existing institutions, force, money, and other means to maintain or change institutions in order to guarantee for themselves benefits that these institutions allow them to receive, regardless of whether or not these institutions benefit society as a whole or any sizable majority of the agents affected by the institutional change or lack thereof.

An example that is often cited in the literature is the provision of public goods. A political entrepreneur—whether a government or an individual legislator—can provide public goods to agents in society, such as property rights or more benign public policies, and collect a share of the benefits he helped those agents to obtain by collecting taxes or obtaining other forms of political support, such as votes in a general election. Changing institutions to provide a public good to a segment of society can often be costly to society as a whole, and particularly damaging to interests in society. Yet whether or not political entrepreneurs work to achieve such institutional changes or to stop them from happening will depend not on comprehensive welfare benefit/cost analyses, but on whether or not they perceive a tangible benefit to themselves in doing so (Sened and Riker 1992).

This conception of the role of institutions in social life brings us to the question of the convergence of social expectations. There are actually two important issues at stake. First, in some general sense, a complete explanation of any existing institution should somehow argue that, given the state of affairs as described by the model, there is no room for institutional change or there are good reasons to slow or stop such evolution from happening. This may be the case because those involved in the game have institutionalized the environment so as to take advantage of all possible resources, or because the power structure is such that those who are in power are as content with the existing institutions as they can possibly be and those who are discontent simply do not have the power to change them.

The second, more fundamental, question of convergence is a theoretical one. Starting from any possible "state of nature," do we expect to converge to a specific, well-defined set of social institutions, either formal or informal? Traditional neoclassical economists have argued for years that we should eventually expect convergence to the set of most efficient institutions. We believe that this proposition will not withstand careful scrutiny for two reasons. First, as we discussed earlier, we see no obvious reason to expect that the institution that maximizes the payoffs of those who control the means to make institutional changes will maximize the welfare of society as a whole (Knight 1992). The second reason not to expect institutional convergence has to do with the notion of path dependence (North 1990). At any stage of the history of institutional evolution we expect games to have a multitude of equilibria. Each one of these equilibria could emerge at that stage as the equilibrium institutional solution. This is true for formal as well as informal institutions. Yet the institutional equilibrium that emerges at each stage of the institutional evolution has a significant effect on the evolution of institutional structures in the future. Therefore, we should not expect the final institutional structure to converge to any specific form. There is growing evidence that institutions that evolve in similar environments do not converge to particular institutional structures. One advantage of the contemporary study of social institutions is precisely that it allows us to explain this puzzling diversity (Libecap 1989).

Finally, most of the technical literature on the evolution of institutional structures takes a very deterministic approach to the study of the problem, inasmuch as it relies on the notion that rational agents—which we all assume—will do "the right thing at the right time" to maximize their utility, allowing us to derive fairly precise predictions with regard to the final outcomes of these games. We have already noted above that, given the multitude of possible equilibria, the predictive set may be quite big, but we want to insist on the view that nondeterministic aspects of human interactions should not be dismissed offhand. This is in part due to the natural fortunes and misfortunes of individual agents and entire communities. The nondeterministic aspect of the evolution of institutions is also related to the ingenuity of those who construct the institutions. Forming institutions is an art, not a science. Some formers may be more skillful than others at this craft, and students of institutions can only make educated guesses in this direction.

NOTES

1. For a detailed critique of the problems that such a premise presents for explanations of social institutions, see Knight 1992.

2. In his various works Hayek offers differing accounts of the nature of this selection mechanism, but among them is the Humean mechanism that has been the basis for many recent formalizations of spontaneous order: "the emulation by others of rules which secure successful behaviour" (1967, 34–35).

3. For criticisms of the rational-choice approach to the study of social institutions, see Oberschall and Leifer 1986; Zald 1987; and March and Olsen 1989.

Five Propositions about Institutional Change

Douglass C. North

The five propositions about institutional change are:

1. The continuous interaction between institutions and organizations in the economic setting of scarcity, and hence competition, is the key to institutional change.
2. Competition forces organizations to continually invest in skills and knowledge to survive. The kinds of skills and knowledge individuals and their organizations acquire will shape evolving perceptions about opportunities, and hence choices, that will incrementally alter institutions.
3. The institutional framework provides the incentives that dictate the kinds of skills and knowledge perceived to have the maximum payoff.
4. Perceptions are derived from the mental constructs of the players.
5. The economies of scope, complementarities, and network externalities of an institutional matrix make institutional change overwhelmingly incremental and path-dependent.

Explanation

Proposition 1. The study of institutions and institutional change necessitates as a first requirement the conceptual separation of institutions from organizations. Institutions are the rules of the game and organizations are the players. The interaction between the two shapes institutional change.

Institutions are the constraints that human beings impose on human interaction. They consist of formal rules (constitutions, statute law, common law, and regulations) and informal constraints (conventions, norms, and self-enforced codes of conduct) and their enforcement characteristics. These constraints define (together with the standard constraints of economics) the opportunity set in the economy.

Organizations consist of groups of individuals bound together by some common objectives. Firms, trade unions, and cooperatives are examples of economic organizations; political parties, the Senate, and regulatory agencies illustrate political organizations; religious bodies and social clubs are examples of social organizations. The opportunities provided by the institutional matrix determine the kinds of organizations that will come into existence; the entrepreneurs of organizations induce institutional change as they perceive new or altered opportunities. They induce it by altering the rules (directly, in the case of political bodies, or indirectly, by economic or social organizations pressuring political organizations); or by altering, deliberately and sometimes accidentally, the kinds and effectiveness of enforcement of rules or the effectiveness of sanctions and other means of informal constraint enforcement.

Informal constraints will be altered as organizations, in the course of interaction, evolve new, informal means of exchange and hence develop new social norms, conventions, and codes of conduct. In this process "obsolete" informal constraints will gradually wither away to be replaced by new ones.

Proposition 2. New or altered opportunities may be perceived to be either a result of exogenous changes in the external environment that alter relative prices to organizations or a consequence of endogenous competition among the organizations of the polity and the economy. In either case the ubiquity of competition in the overall economic setting of scarcity induces entrepreneurs and the members of their organizations to invest in skills and knowledge. Whether it is learning by doing on-the-job or the acquisition of formal knowledge, the key to survival is improving the efficiency of the organization relative to that of rivals.

While idle curiosity is surely an innate source of acquiring knowledge among human beings, the rate of knowledge accumulation is clearly tied to payoffs. Secure monopolies, be they organizations in the polity or in the economy, simply do not have to improve to survive. However, firms, political parties, or even institutions of higher learning faced with rival organizations must strive to improve their efficiency. When competition is "muted" (for whatever reason), organizations will have less incentive to invest in new knowledge and in consequence will not induce rapid institutional change. Stable institutional structures will be the result. Vigorous organizational competition will accelerate the process of institutional change.

Proposition 3. There is *no implication* in the foregoing proposition (proposition 2, explained in the preceding paragraph) of evolutionary progress or economic growth—only of change. The institutional matrix defines the opportunity set, be it one that makes the highest payoffs in an economy income redistribution or one that provides the highest payoffs to productive activity. While every economy provides a mixed set of incentives for both types of activity, the relative weights (as between redistributive and productive incentives) are crucial factors in the performance of economies. The organizations that come into existence will reflect the payoff structure. More than that, the direction of their investment in skills and knowledge will equally reflect the underlying incentive structure. If the highest rate of return in an economy comes from piracy, we can expect that organizations will invest in skills and knowledge that will make them better pirates. Similarly, if there are high returns to productive activities, we will expect organizations to devote resources to investing in skills and knowledge that will increase productivity.

The immediate investment of economic organizations in vocational and on-the-job training will obviously depend on the perceived benefits; but an even more fundamental influence on the future of the economy is the extent to which societies will invest in formal education, schooling, the dissemination of knowledge, and both applied and pure research, which will mirror the perceptions of the entrepreneurs of political and economic organizations.

Proposition 4. The key to the choices that individuals make is their perceptions, which are a function of the way the mind interprets the information it receives. The mental constructs individuals form to explain and interpret the world around them are partly a result of their cultural heritage, partly a result of the local everyday problems they confront and must solve, and partly a result of nonlocal learning. The mix among these sources in interpreting one's environment obviously varies as between, for example, a Papuan tribesman on the one hand and an economist in the United States on the other (although there is no implication that the latter's perceptions are independent of his or her cultural heritage).

The implication is that individuals from different backgrounds will interpret the same evidence differently; they may, in consequence, make different choices. If the information feedback on the consequences of choices were "complete" then individuals with the same utility function would gradually correct their perceptions and over time converge to a common equilibrium. However, as Frank Hahn has succinctly put it, "There is a continuum of theories that agents can hold and act upon without ever encountering events which lead them to change their theories." (Hahn 1987, 324) The result is that multiple equilibria are possible due to different choices by agents with identical tastes.

Proposition 5. The viability, profitability, and indeed survival of the organizations of a society typically depend on the existing institutional matrix. That institutional structure has brought them into existence, and their complex web of interdependent contracts and other relationships has been constructed on it. Two implications follow. Institutional change is typically incremental and is path-dependent.

Institutional change is incremental because large-scale change would harm existing organizations and therefore is stoutly opposed by them. Revolutionary change will only occur in the case of "gridlock" among competing organizations that thwarts their ability to capture gains from trade.

The direction of the incremental institutional change will be broadly consistent with the existing institutional matrix and governed by the kinds of knowledge and skills that the entrepreneurs and members of organizations have invested in. That is, institutional change will be path-dependent.

Discussion

Let me justify each of the five propositions.

Proposition 1. The study of institutions has been bedeviled by ambiguity about the meaning of the term. It is not possible to develop a theory of institutional change that mixes up the players and the rules of the game. Institutions are the rules of the game and organizations are the players, and they require different modelings to understand the way they operate and interact. Modeling institutions is modeling the man-made constraints on human interaction that define the incentive structure of the society. Modeling organizations is theorizing about the structure, governance (including the constraints defining the incentive structure internal to the organization), and policies of purposive entities.

While individuals are the actors, it is typically individuals in their capacities as part of organizations that make the decisions that alter the rules of the game or gradually evolve new informal constraints in the process of human interaction.

Proposition 2. This proposition restates the fundamental postulate of economics and specifically applies it to the organizations of an economy. It bears emphasis, however, that the stock of knowledge the individuals in a society possess is the deep underlying determinant of the performance of economies and societies; changes in that stock of knowledge are the key to the evolution of economies. The rise of the Western world was ultimately a consequence of the kinds of skills and knowledge (not only "productive knowledge" but, notably, knowledge about military technology) that were deemed valuable to medieval political and economic organizations. The key point is that learning by individuals and organizations is the major influence on the evolution of institutions.

Proposition 3. The institutional matrix reflects the bargaining strength of those able to make or change the rules. Their perceptions with respect to the gains to be made by redistributive versus productive policies will shape the rules of the game and the resultant opportunity set. That opportunity set, in turn, will shape perceptions about the kinds of skills and knowledge that will pay off. Throughout most of history to date the players have more often than not perceived the game as one where the highest rewards accrued to military conquest, exploitation (such as enslavement), formation of monopolies, and so forth; in consequence, the kinds of skills and knowledge invested in have been aimed at furthering such policies. In contrast, the perception that there is a high payoff to investment in skills and knowledge that make the individual, organization, and economy more productive will result in long-run economic growth.

Proposition 4. Where do the perceptions that individuals possess come from? Neoclassical theory simply skips this step under the assumption that people know what they are doing. This may be true in evaluating opportunity costs at the supermarket; but it is wildly incorrect when it comes to making more complicated choices in a world of complex problems and incomplete information, and in which subjective models are used to analyze problems and interpret that incomplete information.

What we mean by rationality requires explicit specification for social scientists in general, but particularly for those who employ rational-choice models. If we are going to employ the choice-theoretic approach we must be explicit about just how people arrive at the choices they make. Explicit specification entails defining the subjective models people possess to interpret information and defining the information they receive.

Proposition 5. Why can't economies reverse their direction overnight? This would surely be a puzzle in a world that operated as neoclassical theory would have us believe. That is, in a neoclassical world, abrupt, radical change should immediately result from a radical change in relative prices or performance. Now, it is true that on occasion accumulated pressures do produce an abrupt change in institutions akin to the punctuated equilibrium models in evolutionary theory. However, the overwhelming majority of change is simply incremental and gradual. We take this for granted, but why do we take for granted something that is inconsistent with the theory we employ? Revolutions are extraordinary, and even when they do occur often turn out over time to be far less revolutionary than their initial rhetoric would suggest.

Path dependence could mean nothing more than that yesterday's choices are the initial starting point for today's. Path dependence appears to be a much more fundamental determinant of long-run change than that, however. The difficulty of fundamentally altering paths is evident, and suggests that the learning process by which we arrive at today's institutions constrains future choices. The institutional structure builds in a set of constraints, with respect to downstream changes, that biases choices.

A Research Agenda

With these five propositions about institutional change we can lay out a specific agenda for the study of institutions that is different from game-theoretic or spatial-political modeling of institutions. The focus here is a transaction-cost approach to institutions and a cognitive-science approach to rational choice. While the former—the transaction-cost approach—is at least partly complementary to game-theoretic approaches, the latter suggests a distinct departure from much of the current rational-choice theory. Let me discuss each approach in turn.

Game theory can define the conditions that will provide a hospitable environment for the solution to the more complex political and economic exchanges essential to economic growth. Therefore, game theory is an essential tool in helping us specify the problems of cooperation that are at stake. It does not, however, tell us how to achieve such results. My concern is with *how* such cooperation came about and *why* such cooperation has not occurred in other settings. How institutions evolve and the specific ways they affect transaction and transformation costs are, I believe, the areas on which research should focus.

Understanding how institutions evolve entails a far greater understanding of the interrelationship between institutions, learning, and organizations than we now possess. The assertion made in North (1990, chap. 9) is that the institutional framework not only dictates the opportunity set that defines the kind of organizations that will come into existence but also creates the incentives that will shape the kind of knowledge and skills that the organizations will invest in. Just what kinds of skills and knowledge will lead to sustained economic growth, and what kind to stagnation? Since the human capital "revolution" of the 1960s, the answer to the first query has been investment in education—both formal and on-the-job training. There is clearly a relationship between investment in education and economic growth (unfortunately third world countries have frequently misdirected educational investment into higher education rather than putting it into primary education, which has a much higher social rate of return). An emphasis on formal education reflects the view that there is complementarity between physical and human capital: educational investment is essential in order to realize the potential of modern technology. Richard Easterlin's presidential address to the Economic History Association in 1980 reflected the widespread optimism that education was the solution for economic growth (Easterlin 1981). While investment in education may be a necessary condition, however, it is clearly insufficient, as the recent evidence from third world countries and particularly the Eastern European economies will attest. Easterlin's own data (and his discussion) point to poor countries such as Romania and the Philippines that have had long histories of educational investment above the threshold level that he thought would make a difference but have not seen sustained growth; the former Soviet Union had both high levels of formal education and a skilled labor force. Equally important, then, are the incentives that lead economic and political organizations to invest in productive institutions.

The issue has crucial modern-day policy implications. How do we get institutions that will produce sustained economic growth? Will they come about automatically if we get the "prices right"? The implications of my five propositions provide little support for such a view. The nature of path dependence, the characteristics of political markets, and the mental constructs of the players all suggest fundamental obstacles to successful economic growth.

We simply are ignorant about path dependence. One of the most fundamental of historical regularities is the persistence through time of patterns of human interaction that appear to be the deep underlying source of performance. Historians have, for the most part, taken this persistence for granted rather than made it the subject of research. Brian Arthur (1989) and Paul David (1985) called our attention to this phenomenon in technological change and linked it to the increasing-returns characteristics of the technologies that produce path dependence. By implication they have suggested that the same forces may be operative in overall societal or economic path dependence. However, institutional path dependence does not, I believe, result from increasing returns in the same way as technological change does. Nor do small chance events typically alter the path of institutional change in the way that Arthur and David suggest occurs with technologies. I have suggested that network externalities, complementarities, and economies of scope are the source of institutional path dependence.[1] What is at stake here is much more than simply today's choices being influenced by the current institutional matrix derived from the past. Instead, there is something about the way that the institutional framework has evolved that constrains choices to shape the long-run direction of economies. I believe that the informal constraints of norms, conventions, and codes of conduct that have deep-seated cultural antecedents are particularly important as sources of path dependence. There has been some suggestive research on cultural values, behavioral beliefs, and economic performance, but we are just beginning such research.[2]

How institutions affect transaction and transformation costs takes us to issues of credible commitment. While Shepsle (1991) has correctly pointed out that credible commitment is not a panacea for the problems of development, the reduction of uncertainty in economic and political exchange is perhaps the central historical issue influencing economic growth. In addition, I believe it to be a central issue in creating the conditions that would foster the growth of the economies of central and eastern Europe today. The uncertainty arising from the lack of credible commitment does manifest itself in predictable ways—specifically in the nonexistence of markets that require impersonal exchange, such as capital markets, and the biasing of economic activities into relatively inefficient molds that can circumvent the consequent problems. The result is either no exchange or exchange with high transaction and/or transformation costs.

How can institutions make credible commitment possible? In the case of economic institutions—property rights—impartial enforcement through a judiciary and other governmental agencies can create credible commitment. How does one get the property rights established to begin with, however, and how does one carry out impartial enforcement? The polity is the issue. Suggested solutions have varied from disarming governmental discretion to establishing norms of behavior that shift the locus of enforcement from government to the participants. Yet the first is imperfect, at best. If the government has the coercive power to enforce property rights, it also has the power to act in the interest of factions—to use Madison's felicitous term. Yet disarming government as Madison attempted to do is far from ideal, as the history of the Fifth Amendment—the takings clause—will attest. In addition, we simply don't know how to achieve the second, even though we do observe a variety of informal norms that do just that.

A transaction-cost approach to political markets suggests the sources of the difficulty in making credible commitment in such markets. Transaction costs are the costs associated with the measurement and enforcement of agreements. In economic markets such costs consist of the measurement of the physical and property rights dimensions to goods and services and of the performance of agents. While such measurement can frequently be costly, the physical dimensions have objective characteristics (size, weight, color, etc.) and the property rights dimensions are defined in standard legal terms. Competition plays a critical role in reducing enforcement costs and the judicial system provides coercive enforcement. Even so, economic markets throughout history and in the present world are frequently very imperfect, beset by high transaction costs and defined by institutions that produce incentives that work against economic efficiency. In fact, creating institutions that provide low-cost transacting in economic markets is the key to creating productive economies, but it is the polity that defines and enforces the property rights.

Political markets are far more prone to inefficiency. It is extraordinarily difficult to measure what is being exchanged, and, in consequence, to enforce agreements. What is being exchanged are promises for votes. The observable dimensions of the promises are agreements between constituents and their representatives (in a democracy), between the representatives, between representatives and the executive, and so on. The new political economy has provided us with elaborate models of the way institutions structure Congress and its committees to reduce measurement and enforcement costs in such settings (Weingast and Marshall 1988). However, the transaction costs between constituents and representatives and between representatives and agents enacting the policies are far greater. The powerful role played by competition in the economic marketplace is far less effective here. The constituents' only weapon is periodic elections at which the representative can be held accountable and the opposition candidate has the incentive to promulgate his or her deficiencies. This is a very dull instrument, however, as congressional elections will attest. For a variety of simple, easy-to-measure, and important to constituent well-being policies, something like the rational-choice model of the new political economy has explanatory value. Transfer payments fit this criterion. However, the crucial issues that influence the long-run performance of economies and polities are complex, subject to contradictory theories that cannot be resolved with the information available, even if the constituents did have the incentives to invest in information.[3] Ideological stereotypes take over and provide the basis for choices in such contexts, which leads me to rational-choice models.[4]

We will never come to grips with effective modeling choices—and particularly choices in the polity—until we seriously undertake an exploration of the information the mind receives and how the mind interprets this information. Surely this subject should be at the top of the research agenda for scholars who believe institutions are important, since there are no institutions needed in a world of substantive rationality. The very existence of institutions as real constraints on choices is a contradiction of simple rational-choice models. Institutions exist to reduce uncertainty in human interaction precisely because of the limited information we possess to evaluate the consequences of the actions of others and the limits of the models we possess to explain the world around us. As Simon has pointed out,

> If we accept values as given and constant, if we postulate an objective description of the world as it really is, and if we assume the decisionmaker's computational powers are unlimited then two important consequences follow. First, we do not need to distinguish between the real world and the decisionmaker's perception of it: he or she perceives the world as it really is. Second, we can predict the choices that will be made by a rational decisionmaker entirely from our knowledge of the real world and without a knowledge of the decisionmaker's perceptions or mode of calculation (we do, of course, have to know his or her utility function). (Simon 1986, 210)

Values are not constant; there is no objective description of the world as it really is; and while cognitive science research reveals that the mind is an extraordinarily adaptive and creative instrument, its computational powers are severely limited.

There is more to the rationality issue. Part of the explanation of path dependence must come not only from the way institutions bind alternatives, but also from the way perceptions equally limit the choice set. The complex interaction between institutions and the mental constructs of the players together shape downstream developments. Surely the past seventy years in which Communist ideology has shaped the economic and political policies of much of the world should be convincing evidence of the power of ideological perceptions to influence choices.

Let me conclude with a specific research agenda.

1. Cognitive science has come a long way in modeling how the mind and brain receive, store, process, and interpret informa-

tion but there has not, to the best of my knowledge, been significant research on the role that institutions play in that process. That is, cognitive scientists have been preoccupied by research exploring the way in which the mind and brain attempt to "make sense" out of the environment. Making sense consists of learning from experiences that generate the mental models that individuals possess and that therefore are the sources of the choices that individuals make. Different experiences will generate different mental models and hence different choices. However, there is a complex (and little understood) interplay between the cultural heritage that is the source of much early learning, the formation of consequent mental models, and the particular institutions that will result. If we accept the proposition that institutions exist to reduce uncertainty in human interaction, they are clearly an extension of the mental constructs the human mind develops to interpret the environment of the individual. Clearly there is a connection; research on the nature of that connection would be a major step in understanding more about the formation of institutions.[5]

2. Analyzing political markets in a transaction-cost framework that takes into account the incomplete information and mental constructs of the players and the path-dependent pattern of institutional evolution would begin to give us a handle on the persistence of the poor political and economic performance that characterizes most economies throughout history and the present day. The concentration of the talent of the new political economy on the U.S. polity is not only a misallocation of resources but has blinded most of the players to the limitations of rational-choice models. A brief glimpse into the polities of third world countries would be salutary medicine.

3. We need to learn how norms of behavior come about and disappear and what their relationship is to cultural beliefs. We must also learn how they interact with formal rules and influence economic performance.

4. The research on path dependence must not only specify what it is about institutions that constrains downstream choices but how institutions and mental constructs of the players interact in that process.

Progress on this research agenda will not only provide us with an enormously improved framework for better understanding history but will also provide a solid base for policy making in the reconstruction of

Eastern European economies — an ongoing activity that provides depressing testimony to our ignorance of these issues.

NOTES

I am indebted for improvements on an earlier draft of this essay to the participants of the economic history workshop at Stanford and particularly Paul David and Avner Greif, to my colleagues at Washington University, Lee Benham, Art Denzau, Thrainn Eggertsson, and Jack Knight, and to Elisabeth Case for editing the essay.

1. In a wide-ranging paper, David (1988) imaginatively explores a variety of sources of path dependence.

2. For a recent review of some of this literature with interesting hypotheses about the relationship between cultural beliefs and economic performance, see Greif 1991.

3. For an excellent study in political/economic history that is a telling indictment of the rational-choice assumptions and most of the consequent political economy models, see Anne Kreuger's (1991) study of the political economy of sugar in the United States between 1934 and 1987.

4. For an early discussion of ideology and voting, see Downs 1957. For an elaboration of the argument presented in this essay, see North 1991.

5. In an important essay Ronald Heiner (1983) does make the connection between the way the mind attempts to solve problems and the existence of institutions. For an excellent synthesis of the cognitive-science literature, see Holland et al. 1986 and specifically for the parallel distributed-processing literature, see Clark 1989.

Coordination, Commitment, and Enforcement: The Case of the Merchant Guild

Avner Greif, Paul Milgrom, and Barry R. Weingast

One of the central questions about the institutional foundations of markets concerns the power of the state. The simplest economic view of the state as an institution that enforces contracts and property rights and provides public goods poses a dilemma: a state with sufficient coercive power to do these things also has the power to withhold protection or confiscate private wealth, undermining the foundations of the market economy. In the particular case of medieval cities, these threats were sometimes realized, discouraging trade by foreign merchants to the mutual disadvantage of the ruler and the merchants. It is our thesis that merchant guilds emerged with the encouragement of the rulers of trading centers to be a countervailing power, enhancing the ruler's ability to commit, and laying an important institutional foundation for the growing trade of that period.

European economic growth between the tenth and the fourteenth centuries was facilitated by the "Commercial Revolution of the Middle Ages" — the reemergence of Mediterranean and European long-distance trade after an extended period of decline (e.g., Lopez 1976). For this commercial expansion to be possible, institutions had to be created to mitigate the many kinds of contractual problems associated with long-distance trade. Assessing the significance of these institutions requires a subtle analysis. Indeed, the effectiveness of institutions for punishing contract violations is sometimes best judged like that of peacetime armies — by how little they must be used. Thus, in reading the historical record to determine whether a major role of merchant institutions was to ensure contract compliance, the number of instances of enforcement is not a useful indicator. Instead, we must ask: What were the things that threatened, and on occasion thwarted, efficient trading? Can the powers and organizational details of merchant institutions be explained as responses to those threats? Did failures of enforcement trigger major changes in these institutions?

A comprehensive analysis of a contract-enforcement institution must consider why the institution was needed, what sanctions were to be used to deter undesirable behavior, who was to apply the sanctions, how the sanctioners learned or decided what sanctions to apply, why they did not shirk from their duty, and why the offender did not flee to avoid the sanction. Some analyses meeting these criteria have been developed. One is Greif's (1989, 1993a) analysis of the contractual relations between merchants and their overseas agents in eleventh-century Mediterranean trade. To reap the benefit of employing overseas agents, an institution was required to enable the agents to commit to acting on behalf of the merchants. One group of merchants known as the "Maghribi traders" managed their agency relations by forming a coalition whose members ostracized and retaliated against agents who violated their commercial code. Interrelated contractual arrangements motivated merchants to participate in the collective retaliation against agents who had cheated, while close community ties assured that each member had the necessary information to participate in sanctions when necessary.[1] Similarly, Milgrom, North, and Weingast (1990) have argued that the use of merchant courts in the Champagne fairs during the twelfth and the thirteenth centuries can be analyzed as an institution that created proper incentives for gathering information, honoring agreements, reporting disputes, and adhering to the judgments of the merchant courts. Moreover, by centralizing certain record-keeping functions and effectively permitting only merchants in good standing to remain at the fairs, this institution also achieved significant transaction-costs economies relative to other feasible enforcement institutions.

The cited papers provide consistent analyses of institutions used to overcome contractual problems among individual merchants active in long-distance trade. Individual merchants, however, were not the only important parties; the rulers of the trading centers where the merchants met and brought their goods were an important independent force. Trading centers needed to be organized in ways that secured the person and property of the visiting merchants. Before a trading center became established, its ruler might be inclined to pledge that alien traders would be secure and that their rights would be respected. Once trade was established, however, the medieval ruler faced the temptation to renege on that pledge, failing to provide the promised protection or abusing the merchants' property rights by using his coercive power. In the age prior to the emergence of the nation-state, alien merchants could expect little military or political aid from their countrymen. Without something tangible to secure the ruler's pledge, alien merchants were not likely to frequent that trading center—an outcome that could be costly for both the ruler and the merchants. That rulers recognized the importance of this problem is well reflected in the words of the English king, Edward the First, who noticed in 1283 that because alien merchants' property rights were not properly protected, "many merchants are put off from coming to this land with their merchandise to the detriment of merchants and of the whole kingdom."[2]

Based on the theory of repeated games, one might conjecture that since trade relationships between a specific merchant and ruler consist of a potentially long sequence of trading visits, the rulers' commitment problem could be overcome by either a *bilateral reputation mechanism* in which a merchant whose rights were abused ceased trading, or a *multilateral reputation mechanism* in which the cheated merchant and his close associates ceased trading. Yet, the historical records indicate that, by and large, the ruler-merchant relations were governed by neither bilateral nor informal multilateral arrangements. On the contrary, ruler-merchant relations were governed by administrative bodies rooted outside the territory of the ruler that held certain regulatory powers over their member merchants in their own territory and supervised the operation of these merchants in foreign lands. What roles could these administrative bodies theoretically play in overcoming the ruler's commitment problem? What roles did they in fact play?

To investigate these questions, we utilize historical records to develop a series of game-theoretic models corresponding to different institutional arrangements. The theoretical analyses indicate that although some trade is possible even without supporting organizations, sustaining an efficient level of trade is more demanding. Without administrative bodies capable of coordinating and sometimes compelling merchants' responses to a ruler's transgressions, trade could not expand to its efficient level. The corresponding historical analysis then suggests that during the late medieval commercial revolution, a specific institution—the *merchant guild*—developed the necessary attributes to enforce agreements with rulers, thus overcoming the commitment problem and enabling trade expansion. Merchant guilds exhibited a range of administrative forms, from subdivision of a city administration to an intercity organization. Yet these forms all shared the common function of ensuring the coordination and internal enforcement required to surmount the commitment problem by permitting effective collective action. We emphasize two points at the outset. First, that our argument concerns merchant guilds and not craft guilds.[3] Second, we define merchant guilds according to their function rather than their "official," late medieval name. Hence, as we discuss below, our theory applies to a wider range of medieval merchant organizations than those labeled as merchant guilds.

The evaluation of merchant guilds as supporting efficient trade is complementary to the view more common among economic historians that merchant guilds emerged to reduce negotiation costs, to administer trade and taxation, to extract privileges from foreign cities, and to shift rent in their own city.[4] While the existence of merchant guilds could affect the distribution of rents in addition to enhancing the security of agreements, the unadorned theory of merchant guilds as cartels presents a puzzle: If the purpose of the guilds was to create monopoly power for the merchants and to increase their bargaining power with the rulers, why did powerful rulers during the late medieval period cooperate with alien merchants to establish guilds in the first place? What offsetting advantages did the rulers enjoy? The puzzle is resolved if the guild's power enabled trade to expand to the benefit of merchants and rulers alike.[5]

While this paper emphasizes the function of the merchant guild in facilitating trade between political units during the late medieval period, it also sheds light on the changing nature of guilds over time and the complex nature of guilds at any point in time. Although certain features of the merchant guild enabled it to advance trade during the late medieval period, these same features were, in some cases, utilized during the premodern period to restrict trade. Furthermore, even during the late medieval period some merchant guilds had quasi-monopoly rights in their own territories. These rights were part of the relations between rulers and local merchants. Since our paper concentrates on the relations between ruler and *alien* merchants, such rights are not considered here. It is interesting to note, however, that our theory suggests that a merchant guild's monopoly rights in its home locality may have been instrumental in advancing trade between different localities. This type of monopoly rights generated a stream of rent that depended on the support of other members and so served as a bond, allowing members to commit themselves to collective action in response to a ruler's transgressions.[6]

The paper proceeds as follows. Section 1 reports the relevant history. It describes the serious problems trading centers and merchants faced in providing security for merchants and their goods, demonstrates that the guild structure had the features required to resolve the problem, and recounts milestones in the evolution of the guild among German traders and the related expansion of trade. The second section formalizes the analysis. Its game-theoretic model allows us to explore the incentives of traders and cities and explain why a guild organization could sometimes successfully support an efficient level of trading activity when a simple reputation mechanism could not. The third section concludes by considering subsequent history—the transformation and decline of the merchant guild associated with the rise of the state—and suggests other applications of the theoretical framework.

1. The Commitment Problem and the Role of Merchant Guilds

Institutions and Commitment

Long-distance trade in late medieval Europe was based upon the exchange of goods brought from different parts of the world to central cities or fairs located in geographically or politically favorable places. Yet the presence of gains from trade and locations suitable for conducting exchange does not imply that exchange could occur without an institutional environment in which the merchants and their property were secure. The concern that rulers felt to provide security, reflected in the words of Edward I quoted above, should be understood against a background of events like the following one that occurred in Boston, England, in, or shortly before, 1241. A Flemish merchant accused an English trader of not repaying a commercial loan. This resulted in

> an uproar on all sides and the English merchants assembled to attack the Flemings, who retired to their lodging in the churchyard. . . . The English threw down the pailings, broke the doors and windows and dragged out Peter Balg [the lender] and five others, whom they foully beat and wounded and then set in the stocks. All the other Flemings they beat, ill-treated and robbed, and pierced their cloths with swords and knives. . . . Their silver cups were carried off as they sat at table, their purses cut and the money in them stolen, [and] their chests broken open and money and goods, to an unknown extent, taken away.[7]

Such disorders were not peculiar to England, but mark the history of long-distance medieval trade. For example, the commercial relations between Byzantine and the Italian city-states were often hindered by insecurity during the twelfth century. The Genoese quarter in Constantinople was attacked by the Pisans in 1162. At least one merchant was killed, while the other Genoese merchants had to escape to their ship, leaving all their valuables behind them. In 1171 the Venetians attacked and destroyed the same Genoese quarter. About ten years later a mob destroyed all of the Italian quarters in Constantinople during the "Latin massacre" of 1182.[8]

In light of the theory of repeated games, one might conjecture that a ruler's commitment problem could be solved by a *bilateral reputation mechanism* in which individual merchants whose person and property were not protected by a local ruler would refuse to return with their goods in the future. The ruler, while perhaps reaping short run gains from ignoring a merchant's rights, stood to lose the future stream of rents from the cheated merchant's trade.[9] As we demonstrate formally in section 2, this intuition is misleading. At the level of trade that maximizes the total net value of trade—that is, at the *efficient volume of trade*—a bilateral reputation mechanism cannot resolve the commitment problem. In our formal theory, the reason is that, at the efficient volume of trade, the value of the stream of future rents to be collected by the ruler from an individual marginal merchant is almost zero, and therefore smaller than the value of the goods that can be seized or the cost of the services that can be withheld. The same conclusion would hold even at lesser volumes of trade if the frequency of visits by an individual trader were low. As long as ruler-merchant relations are governed by only a bilateral reputation mechanism, our theory holds that trading volume cannot expand to its efficient level.

The preceding discussion, as well as the formal model below, allows only one kind of sanction for cheated merchants: the withdrawal of trade. Military action might seem to be another important alternative. In the late medieval period, however, defensive technology was superior to offensive, and the costs and risks of offensive military action at distant ports limited its credibility as a sanction for trade violations.[10]

A possible means for increasing the punishment is a multilateral response by all the merchants to transgressions against any subgroup of merchants. Indeed, the history of the relations between trade centers and alien merchants presents several examples of multilateral retaliations against rulers who had reneged on their contractual obligations. For example, circa 1050 the Muslim ruler of Sicily imposed a 10-percent tariff (instead of the 5-percent tariff specified in the Islamic law) on goods imported to Sicily by Jewish traders. The traders responded by imposing an embargo and sending their goods to the rival trade center, Tunisia. The embargo was effective, and after a year the Sicilian ruler relented and removed the tariff.[11]

The above examples suggest that a *multilateral reputation mechanism* might be able to surmount the commitment problem without the aid of any formal organization. In each case, merchants imposed a collective punishment of the city that included participation by merchants who had not been directly injured. Several of the cited offenses were offenses *against an entire group of merchants*. In medieval trade, however, a city could also discriminate among merchants, abusing or not protecting them selectively. For example, a city could confiscate the belongings of some traders or withhold legal protection from them without directly harming other alien merchants. Indeed, the Sicilian rulers increased the tariff only to Jewish traders; and during two attacks on the Genoese quarter in Constantinople, other Italian merchants were not harmed. This suggests two interconnected reasons why, without a supporting organization, a multilateral reputation mechanism might be insufficient to surmount the commitment problem at the efficient level of trade. The first involves contract ambiguities and asymmetric information, while the second reflects the distinct incentives among different traders generated by a multilateral response.

Long-distance premodern trade took place in a highly complex and uncertain environment. Unanticipated events and multiple interpretations of existing agreements were always possible under these circumstances, implying that the definition of a "contract violation" was often ambiguous. Information asymmetry, slow communication, and different interpretations of facts among merchants imply that without an organization that coordinated responses, it was not likely that all the merchants would respond to the abuse of any group of merchants. As demonstrated formally in section 2, if the fraction of merchants who detect and react to an abuse against any group of merchants is only proportionate to the number abused, then a multilateral reputation mechanism is ineffective at the efficient volume of trade. It is ineffective for the same reason that a bilateral reputation mechanism is ineffective: a threat by a group of marginal traders to withdraw their trade is barely significant, once trade has expanded to its efficient level.

To permit an efficient expansion of trade in the medieval environment, there was a need for an organization that would supplement the operation of a multilateral reputation mechanism by coordinating the responses of a large fraction of the merchants. Only when a coordinating organization exists can the multilateral reputation mechanism potentially overcome the commitment problem. In our formal model, when a coordinating organization exists there is a subgame perfect equilibrium at which traders come to the city (at the efficient level of trade) as long as a boycott has not been announced, but none of them come to trade if a boycott has been announced. The ruler respects merchants' rights as long as a boycott has not been announced, but abuses their rights otherwise. Thus, when a coordinating institution exists, trade may plausibly expand to its efficient level.

Although the behavior described forms a perfect equilibrium, the theory in this form remains unconvincing. According to the equilibrium strategies, when a coordinating institution organizes an embargo, merchants are deterred from disregarding it because they expect the ruler to abuse violators' trading rights. But are these expectations reasonable? Why wouldn't a city *encourage* embargo breakers rather than punishing them? As verified in section 2, this encouragement is potentially credible. During an effective embargo, the volume of trade shrinks and the value of the marginal trader increases; it is then possible for bilateral reputation mechanisms to become effective. That is, there may exist mutually profitable terms between the city and the traders that the city will credibly respect. This possibility limits the potential severity of an embargo and, correspondingly, potentially hinders the ability of any coordinating organization to support efficient trade. To support the efficient level of trade, a multilateral reputation mechanism may need to be supplemented by an organization with the ability to both coordinate embargo decisions and enforce them by applying sanctions on its own members.

Evidence of the Role of Formal Organizations

The discussion has so far focused on two issues: a demonstration that guaranteeing the security of alien merchants and their goods was problematic in medieval Europe and that both historical evidence and theoretical reasoning suggest that a simple reputation mechanism could not completely resolve the problem. In this section, we identify more direct evidence that merchants and rulers recognized the need to provide believable assurances of security for traders and their goods, that they negotiated trading arrangements that often included a role for formal organizations, that these organizations served an important coordination and enforcement role, and that trade expanded in cities that negotiated these agreements. Notice that this pattern of facts is inconsistent with at least the simplest cartel theories of guilds, which predict that guilds will form only after trade relations are already established and will limit entry and price competition, leading to smaller quantities being traded.

That medieval rulers and merchants recognized the need to secure alien merchants' property rights before trade expansion could occur is borne out repeatedly in the historical record. Christian traders, for example, did not dare to trade in the Muslim world unless they received appropriate securities. Similarly, throughout Europe itself, merchants did not trade in locations in which they did not have security agreements. The Italians began traveling to other European cities and to the Champagne fairs and the Germans began traveling to Flanders, England, and the Slavic East only after negotiating appropriate safety agreements.[12]

Safety agreements allowing the merchants some measure of internal organization appear crucial to trade expansion. The Genoese trade with North Africa provides an instructive illustration. Prior to 1160, the Genoese trade with North Africa never exceeded 500 lire. In 1161, the Genoese legate, Otobonus d'Albericis, and the local ruler of North Africa, Abd almumin, signed a fifteen-year agreement securing the property rights of the Genoese. Genoese trade then more than doubled, to 1057 lire, and remained at this higher level in later years. Moreover, the agreement focused on security issues. Though it specified a 2-percent reduction in the 10-percent custom, it was hardly concerned with the distribution of gains from trade. Given that the expected gains from goods that reached North Africa were, on average, more than 26 percent during this period, it is highly unlikely that the custom reduction accounted for the expansion of trade that followed.[13]

Merchants from other trading cities had similar experiences. For example, the Catalan merchants' trade expanded "within only a few months" after they received, in 1286, privileges and the right to have a consul in Sicily.[14] The trade of the German merchants in Bruges expanded after they received privileges and the right to have a *Kontor* (establishment or office).[15] The Italian trade with Flanders flourished only after they were allowed to establish local organizations, called *nations*.[16]

There also exists indirect evidence that the parties recognized the importance of an institutionalized commitment to security, rather than mere promises. Muslim rulers provided European traders with *aman*—a religious obligation to secure the merchants' rights. Some cities in England went so far as to elect an alien merchant as mayor. Yet, it seems that a specific institution—the *merchant guild*—was the most common successful institution. The core of the merchant guild was an administrative body that supervised the overseas operations of merchant residents of a specific territorial area and held certain regulatory powers within that territorial area. In England, for example, the merchants of a town were granted the right to establish a society of merchants that retained specific commercial privileges in the internal and external trade of the town and usually had representation in the trade centers where its members traded. On the European continent, many towns were controlled by the mercantile elite, who organized a merchant guild to advance their interests. In some Italian and German towns the merchant guilds were virtually identical with the town's government itself, while in some Italian cities the merchants' operations were supervised by the city.[17]

Guilds provided merchants with the leadership and information-transmission mechanisms required for coordinated action. In the examples we have studied, it was the guild that decided when to impose a trade embargo and when to cancel it.[18] The trade center usually provided the guild with the right to obtain information about disputes between its members and that center's authorities or between its members and other traders. The guild's regulations facilitated the collection and transmission of information among its members.[19]

Though the term *merchant guild* was not used in Italy, the Italian cities served the same functions on behalf of their resident merchants. The city's role in coordinating embargo decisions is well reflected in the relationships between Genoa and Tabriz, a vital city on the trade route to the Persian Gulf and the Far East. In 1340 Tabriz's ruler confiscated the goods of many Genoese traders. Genoa responded by declaring a *devetum* (a commercial embargo) against Tabriz. In 1344, however, Tabriz's ruler sent ambassadors to Genoa promising an indemnity for everything that had been taken from the Genoese and favorable treatment in the future. As a consequence, the *devetum* was removed and the Genoese traders flocked to Iran. However, the ruler of Tabriz did not keep his promise to protect their rights and the Genoese traders were robbed and many of them were killed. The material damage reached two hundred thousand lire, an immense sum. When the ruler later invited the Venetians and Genoese to trade, he "could not give them the guarantees they required, . . . [hence] the Italian merchants, eager as they were to recover their prosperous trade in Persia and to reopen the routes to India and China, felt it was unsafe to trust a mere promise."[20] As discussed below, however, it was the Genoese traders as a whole who could not trust a "mere promise"; an individual Genoese trader might still be able to trust the ruler of Tabriz while the *devetum* was in force.

An incident that occurred during the Genoese embargo of Tabriz confirms the historical importance of enforcement within the merchant group and the fact that merchant guilds assumed this enforcement role. In 1343, during the *devetum* against Tabriz, a Genoese merchant named Tommaso Gentile was on his way from Hormuz to China. Somewhere in the Pamir plateau he became sick and had to entrust his goods with his companions and head back to Genoa by the shortest way. That way, however, passed through Tabriz. When knowledge concerning his journey through Tabriz reached Genoa, Tommaso's father had to justify this transgression with the "Eight Wisemen of Navigation and the Major [black] Sea," that is, the superior colonial board of Genoa.

These officers accepted the thesis of an act of God, and acquitted Tommaso from every penalty, inasmuch as he had gone through Tabriz without merchandise.[21]

The merchant guild's strategy of conditioning future trade on adequate past protection, the use of ostracism to achieve security (rather than privileges or low prices), and the relationship between acquiring information, coordination, and the ability to boycott, are reflected again in the agreement made in 1261 between the Flemish merchants from Ghent, Ypres, Douai, Cambrai, and Dixmude who purchased English wool. "For the good of the trade," they decided that

> if it should happen that any cleric or any other merchant anywhere in England who deals with sales of wool deals falsely with any merchant in this alliance, . . . by giving false weight or false dressing of the wool or a false product, . . . and if they do not wish to make amends, we have decided that no present or future member of this alliance will be so bold as to trade with them. . . .[22]

To make this threat of boycott functional, they "decided that there will be in each of these cities one man to view and judge the grievances, and to persuade the wrongdoers to make amends."[23]

The credibility and force of a coordinating organization's threat to embargo crucially depended on the ruler's ability to undermine an embargo by offering special terms to embargo violators. In theory, the marginal gains from additional trade rise during an embargo. Both this fact and the fact that guilds needed to take special measures to prevent shipments to the embargoed city are confirmed by the historical evidence. For example, in 1284, a German trading ship was attacked and pillaged by the Norwegians. The German towns responded by imposing an embargo on Norway. The export of grain, flour, vegetables, and beer was prohibited. According to the chronicler Detmar, "there broke out a famine so great that (the Norwegians) were forced to make atonement." The temptation for an individual merchant to smuggle food to Norway in this situation is clear. To sustain the embargo, the German towns had to post ships in the Danish Straits.[24] The fact that the success of a trade embargo crucially depended on obtaining the support of virtually all of the merchants involved was also clear to the cities on which embargo was inflicted. When, in 1358, the German towns imposed an embargo on Bruges, the city attempted to defeat the embargo by offering merchants from Cologne extensive trading privileges.[25]

Placing ships in a strait and imposing fines are specific ways to overcome the distinct incentives problem. The evidence, however, suggests that the credibility of the threat to carry out an embargo was, in many cases, sustained by a different means. Credibility was established by endowing guilds with the ability to impose commercial sanctions upon their member merchants. In England and other regions in Europe a local guild usually had exclusive trade privileges in its own town, typically including monopoly rights over retail trade within the town, exclusive exemption from tolls, and so forth, as well as the right to exclude, under certain circumstances, members from the guild.[26] These guilds were therefore able to provide their members with streams of rents in their hometowns. Receiving these rents, however, could have been made conditional on following the recommendations, rules, and directives of the guild. Hence these rents could serve to tie a member to the guild and to ensure solidarity among the guild's members by making change of residence costly.[27]

The Flemish regulations of 1240 illustrate the role of the stream of rents in providing the appropriate incentives: a merchant who ignored the ban imposed by the guild on another town was expelled, losing his rent stream.

> If any man of Ypres or Daouai shall go against those decisions [made by the guild] . . . for the common good, regarding fines or anything else, that man shall be excluded from selling, lodging, eating, or depositing his wool or cloth in ships with the rest of the merchants. . . . And if anyone violates this ostracism, he shall be fined 5s. . . .[28]

Evolution of Guild Organizations

Perhaps the best example of the guild's contribution to fostering the growth of trade is the evolution and operation of the institution that governed the relations between the German merchants, their towns, and the foreign towns with which they traded. To achieve the coordination and enforcement that were required for the reputation mechanism to operate effectively, a means was needed to influence the behavior of merchants from different towns. This led to the rise of an interesting form of guild—the German Hansa.[29] Several extensive studies have mined the abundant historical records of the Hansa and enable us to examine its evolution in light of our theoretical analysis.

Our analysis of the evolution of the guild in northern Europe emphasizes episodes during which conflict occurred and trade was affected. In purely theoretical terms, conflict can be explained as an equilibrium phenomenon when information about the behavior of the parties is imperfect,[30] as it surely was in the periods we are studying.

The episodes we study, moreover, are ones in which conflict was followed by institutional change, and it seems implausible to model these as equilibrium outcomes. Instead, we shall regard the episodes themselves as disequilibrium outcomes and the resulting changes as adaptations to changing circumstances or as improvements based on accumulated experience.

Specifically, we focus on the development of the German Hansa. For historical reasons, membership in the basic organizational unit that coordinated the activities of German merchants abroad—the *Kontor*—was not conditional upon residency in one particular town. Any German merchant who arrived in a non-German city could join the local *Kontor*. A *Kontor* performed the same function as the guild in coordinating the responses of the German merchants in disputes with the town; however, it lacked the ability to punish merchants in the towns where they resided, weakening its ability to enforce sanctions against its members. If our theory is correct, the differences between the German *Kontore* and other guilds should have made the *Kontore* less effective and should have led to changes in or the dissolution of that form of merchant organization. The history of the contractual relations between the city of Bruges, the local *Kontor,* and the German towns provides a clear illustration of the evolution of merchant organization.

In 1252, a *Kontor* of German merchants obtained extensive trading privileges from Bruges, and a permanent settlement followed.[31] The *Kontor* was led by six aldermen elected by the German merchants present in the town. Two of the aldermen were from Rhenish towns, two from Westphalian-Wendish towns, and two from Prussian-Baltic towns, reflecting the range of origins of the participating German merchants.[32] The trading privileges given to the alien merchants in Bruges were continually abused, and eventually riots broke out, endangering both people and property. The situation is described in a document dated 1280 reporting that "it is unfortunately only too well known that merchants traveling in Flanders have been the objects of all kinds of maltreatment in the town of Bruges and have not been able to protect themselves from this."[33] Along with most of the other alien traders who operated in Bruges, the German merchants retaliated in 1280 by transferring their trade to Aardenburg. After two years of negotiation, a new agreement was reached and the *Kontor* returned to Bruges.

Seemingly successful, the embargo failed to guarantee the property rights of the German merchants, as Bruges simply ignored its agreement with them.[34] It should be noted, however, that Bruges did respect the rights of other alien merchants who frequented the city. Our analysis points to the reason for that discrimination. The embargo was not imposed by the German merchants alone, but by all alien merchants in Bruges, including the important and well-organized Italian and Spanish *nations*. While the lesson for Bruges from that episode was to respect the rights of those well-organized groups, it became clear to the city that the German merchant organizations were different. The *Kontor* proved incapable of enforcing its decisions upon its members. Because the *Kontor* encompassed only the German merchants actually present in Bruges—rather than all of the potential German traders who might want to trade during a boycott—its threat of sanctions was not credible. For a time, German merchants had to accept inferior treatment.

Another embargo, from 1307 to 1309, was thus required to force Bruges to respect its contractual agreements with the Germans, and in this embargo, only they participated. What had changed between 1280 and 1307 was the ability of the German traders from different towns to coordinate their responses and enforce their embargo. A milestone occurred in 1284 when the Wendish German towns imposed an embargo on Norway. Merchants from the city of Berman refused to cooperate in the embargo, and the other German towns excluded Berman's merchants from all German *Kontore*. The German towns had achieved the coordination needed to expel one of their members. The importance of the achievement is indicated by the fact that the act of expelling a city came to be referred to by a special word, *Verhansung*.[35]

After 1307, the ability of the German merchants to coordinate their actions and to enforce their decisions on individual merchants and towns was rather advanced, thus guaranteeing adherence by Bruges to its contractual obligations. Bruges respected the charters agreed upon in 1307 and 1309, and consequently trade in Flanders flourished and expanded for the next fifty years.[36] As our theoretical analysis indicates, once the ability of the German *Kontor* to coordinate and enforce their decisions upon their members was well developed, the contract-enforcement problem could be resolved and trade expanded.

It was not until the middle of the century, when the cost of providing security around Bruges rose drastically, that a new level of cooperation among the German towns was required to force Bruges to provide the security required to support efficient trade. Hansa relations with Bruges deteriorated around 1350, mainly because Bruges was not ready to compensate the Germans for their damages in Flanders from the war between England and France. The Hansa responded by strengthening its internal organization. In 1356 the German Hansa held its first diet. It was decided that the *Kontor* of Bruges should be operated according to the decisions of the diet. Apparently recognizing the need for coordination among towns, the *Kontor* accepted this decision. The prominent historian of the Hansa, Dollinger, has emphasized the importance of this change. "In law, and not only in fact, the towns, acting through the general diet were establishing their authority over their merchants in foreign ports."[37]

A Hanseatic embargo of Bruges followed in 1358. It was announced that any disobedience, whether by a town or an individual, was to be punished by perpetual exclusion from the Hansa. Bruges attempted to defeat the embargo by offering trade privileges to individual cities, including both non-Hanseatic ones like Kampen and a Hanseatic one, Cologne. Our theory suggests that by offering these privileges it hoped to undermine the effectiveness of the new leadership. While the non-Hanseatic cities accepted the city's terms, Cologne refused to cooperate. The embargo proved a success and, in 1360, Bruges came to terms with the Hansa. This time, reflecting the parties' more complete understanding of the range of circumstances under which the city would have to provide services, the privileges were written, "in much detail as to prevent any one-sided interpretations."[38]

The institution of the German Hansa was now crystallized. It was a nexus of contracts between merchants, their towns, and foreign cities that advanced exchange. The Hansa's leadership served to coordinate and enforce cooperation between German merchants and towns—a cooperation that served the interests of all sides. The trade of northern Europe prospered for generations under the supremacy of the Hansa. Although the trade embargo of 1360 was not the last, later trade disputes seemed to center around distributive issues such as the provision of trade privileges. Commitment for security was no longer an issue.

It is illuminating to contrast the development of the Hansa among German towns with the rather different organization among the Italian merchants. The solid internal political and commercial organization of the Italian cities and their prominence in trade enabled them to overcome the coordination and internal-enforcement problems. Collective action among the merchants from Italian cities was ensured, and because none of the cities were "marginal players" in the ports where they traded, coordination among the cities was unnecessary.[39] In contrast, the German *Kontor* was a local organization in a trading center that lacked the ability to enforce its decisions upon its members, who came from various German towns. As noted, the German towns were small and, before the establishment of the Hansa, most were relatively insignificant in large trading centers like Bruges.

The historical analysis presented in this section supports our hypothesis that the medieval merchant guild was an institution that overcame the ruler's commitment problem and facilitated trade expansion. Although the merchant guilds exhibited a range of administrative forms—from subdivision of a city administration (such as that of the Italian city-states) to the intercity organization (of the Hansa)—their functions were the same: to ensure the coordination and internal enforcement required to surmount the commitment problem by permitting effective collective action. The actions taken by rulers and traders, their strategies as reflected in their regulations, and the expansion of trade that followed the establishment of guilds all confirm the importance of this role of the guild organization.

2. The Formal Model

Our theoretical modeling is kept intentionally simple and directed to analyzing the potential of various plausible mechanisms for overcoming the ruler's commitment problem. Each of the mechanisms we consider might feasibly permit commitment by the ruler at some levels of trade; our focus is on the growing need for more sophisticated mechanisms as the level of trade rises and approaches the efficient level.

We model the basic environment in which trade took place as having two kinds of players: a city and individual merchants. The merchants, identical and large in number, are identified with the points on the interval $[0,\bar{x}]$. The city—a potential trading center—has the following trading technology: If the number of traders passing through the city in a single period is x, the gross value of trade in that period is $f(x)$. In addition, we suppose that there is a cost of $c > 0$ per unit of value traded incurred by the city for the services it provides and a cost $\kappa > 0$ per unit of value incurred by each trader, so that the net value of trade is $f(x)$ $(1 - c - \kappa)$. We assume that trade is profitable, that is, $c + \kappa < 1$. We also assume that f is nonnegative and differentiable, that $f(0) = 0$, and that f achieves a maximum at some unique value $x^* > 0$, which we call the *efficient volume of trade*. In our model, the city funds its services and earns additional revenues by charging a toll or tax of $\tau \geq c$ per unit of value passing through its ports, so that its total tax revenues are $\tau f(x)$. If it provides the services contracted for, then its net revenue for the period is $f(x)(\tau - c)$. If the city breaches its contract by failing to provide services to a fraction ϵ of the traders, it saves costs of $\epsilon c f(x)$, so its payoff for the trading period is $f(x)[\tau - c(1 - \epsilon)]$.[40] Traders who are not cheated each earn profits, net of costs, tolls, and taxes, of $(1 - \tau - \kappa)f(x)/x$. Traders who are cheated pay taxes and incur costs κ but receive no revenues; they each earn $-(\tau\Sigma + \kappa)f(x)/x$.

All of this is repeated period after period, and the players' payoffs from the whole repeated game are the discounted sum of the periodic payoffs, using discount factor δ. Thus, the city's payoff when the trading volume is x_t in period t is given by

$$\Sigma_{t=0}^{\infty} \delta^t f(x_t)[\tau - c(1 - \epsilon_t)] \tag{1}$$

and the payoffs of the individual traders are determined similarly as the discounted sum of their periodic payoffs.

The specification of the model captures the idea that merchants are substitutes as far as the ruler is concerned and each of them is relatively "small." The historical observation that rulers could discriminate between traders is captured through the specification of the ruler's strategy. We abstract away from the issue of competition among alternative trade centers, since an essence of medieval trade was that it was based on exchange of goods brought by traders from several regions to a specific trading place. Thus, by and large, the threat of a group of traders from a specific region permanently switching to an alternative potential trade center without the cooperation of traders from other regions was not credible.

The historical records also indicate, as discussed above, that merchants were most likely to trade abroad when they perceived their rights to be secure. The specification of the merchants' payoffs is based on this observation. The specification of the ruler's payoff reflects the fact that a ruler could gain either from abusing rights or from allowing his subjects to do so. While the model equates the gains from abusing rights as the protection costs saved, one can alternatively think of gains from abuse as reflecting gain from ruler's confiscation of merchants' goods. The ruler's and the merchants' payoffs are specified to allow a conceptual and analytical distinction between issues of distribution and efficiency. We treat the tax rate as given and hence abstract away from examining the process through which the gains from trade are allocated. Any loss to the merchants above the agreed-upon rate of taxation, however, is defined to be an abuse. Analytically, this specification implies that any first-best is characterized by the level of trade x^* in every period and no cheating by the city. Different first-best utility allocations are achieved by setting different tax rates τ. Technically, this conclusion reflects our assumption that some value is being lost when the ruler fails to provide protection, which reflects events such as those that took place in Boston, as described earlier: failure to provide protection led to a destruction of goods and loss of value. Whatever the merchants were willing to pay the ruler, namely all issues of transfer, is modeled here as part of the tax.

Game 1. Informationally Isolated Traders—Bilateral Reputation Mechanism

Our first model represents the situation of traders who travel alone or in small groups with no social or economic organization, so that they remain unaware of how the city has treated other merchants. Although this model is surely too extreme to be fully descriptive, it highlights the difficulties faced by individual traders negotiating with the city on their own.

In this game, a trader must decide whether to bring his goods to the city in each period, knowing only the history of his own decisions and his own past treatment by the city. A strategy for the trader is a sequence of functions mapping the trader's personal history into decisions about whether to offer his goods for trade in that period. Similarly, the city must decide who to cheat under various conditions. A strategy for the city is a sequence of functions identifying a (measurable) subset of the current traders for the city to cheat as a function of who shows up to trade currently and the full past history of the game.

Readers familiar with either the economics of reputations or the theory of repeated games will recognize that the repetition of the interactions between the city and the individual traders creates the possibility for reputations to be created that enforce good behavior by the city. The idea is that a trader who is cheated once might refuse to return to the city in future periods, leading to a loss of profits for the city. The effectiveness of this threat depends on both the frequency of trade and the periodic value of the individual merchant's trade to the city. If the frequency of trade is sufficiently high and the volume sufficiently low, so that the value of the repeat business of any individual trader to the city is high, the simple reputation mechanism can be effective for providing incentives to the city to protect individual rights. In our model, however, when the volume of trade rises to the efficient level, the value of repeat business falls to zero, so the usual conclusions of the Folk Theorem of repeated games do not apply.

PROPOSITION 1. *No Nash equilibrium of game 1 can support honest trade ($\epsilon \equiv 0$) at the efficient level ($x_t \equiv x^*$), regardless of the levels of c, τ, κ, or δ.*

Proof. Suppose there were such an equilibrium and consider the payoff to the city if it deviates from the equilibrium strategy and cheats a fraction ϵ of the first-period traders. In the initial period, its payoff is $f(x^*)[\tau - c(1 - \epsilon)]$. In subsequent periods, the informational assumptions of the model imply that the play of at most ϵ traders is affected. Consequently, at least $1 - \epsilon$ traders come to the city in each future period, and the city's payoff from treating them honestly is, in present-value terms, at least $\gamma(\tau - c)f[x(1 - \epsilon)]$ where, for convenience, we define $\gamma = \delta/(1 - \delta)$. So the city's total payoff from cheating a fraction ϵ of the traders in the first period and adhering to the purported equilibrium thereafter is at least:

$$f(x)\tau - c(1 - \epsilon)] + \gamma(\tau - c) f [x(1 - \epsilon)], \tag{2}$$

and this expression coincides exactly with the actual payoff when $\epsilon = 0$—that is, when the city adheres to the purported equilibrium. The derivative of expression 2 with respect to ϵ at $\epsilon = 0$ and $x = x^*$ is:

$$cf(x^*) - \gamma(\tau - c)x^*f'(x^*) = cf(x^*) > 0, \tag{3}$$

because $f'(x^*) = 0$. This establishes that the city has a profitable deviation, that is, the specified behavior is not consistent with Nash equilibrium. □

No mechanism based only on sanctions by those who are cheated can support honest trading at the efficient level, x^*, because when trading is conducted at that level, the marginal trader has zero net value to the city. By cheating a few marginal traders, the city loses nothing in terms of future profits, but saves a positive expense in the present period. To support the efficient level of trading, some kind of collective action among merchants is needed.[41]

We have stated the proposition in terms of Nash equilibrium because this is a negative result and we want to emphasize that, even with the most inclusive of noncooperative equilibrium concepts, there is no way to support the efficient volume of trade. For our later positive results, we will utilize stronger, more convincing equilibrium concepts.

Game 2. Informational Isolated Small Groups of Traders—An Uncoordinated Multilateral Reputation Mechanism

While information in medieval times was slow to diffuse by modern standards, it was nevertheless available. In particular, if a specific merchant was ever abused, even in the absence of any organization for information diffusion, some of his peers were likely to learn it. For example, the traders cheated in Bruges might become known to others from the same hometown or to their traveling companions. Can this process of limited, uncoordinated information diffusion enable the ruler to commit himself at the efficient level of trade?

To examine this issue, suppose that an incident in which the city cheats a group of traders always becomes known to a larger group of traders. Formally, whenever a set T of traders is cheated, there is a set of traders $\hat{T} \supset T$, each of whom learns of the event. We assume that there is some constant K $(1 \leq K < \infty)$ such that if the number of traders cheated is $\mu(T)$, then the number who learn about the event, $\mu(\hat{T})$, is no more than $K\mu(T)$: if few traders are cheated, then proportionately few discover that the event has occurred. In game 2, traders make their decisions to bring goods based on what they know of their own and the city's past behavior, including whatever they may know about how the city has cheated others. Potentially, an incident of cheating may then lead to a withdrawal of trade by a group that is many times larger than the group that was cheated. Even if this potentiality could be realized, however, it would not be sufficient to support an efficient volume of trade.

PROPOSITION 2. *No Nash equilibrium of game 2 can support honest trade ($\epsilon_t \equiv 0$) at the efficient level ($x_t \equiv x^*$), regardless of the levels of c, τ, κ, or δ.*

The proof is essentially the same as for the first proposition, except that the bound on the number who decline to trade in the future is multiplied by K. In particular, expression 3 is replaced by $cf(x^*) - \gamma K(\tau - c)x^*f'(x^*) = cf(x^*) > 0$.

Violations against a few merchants that are noticed by proportionately few cannot be deterred by a threat of retaliation by just those with firsthand knowledge.

The real situation faced by the traders is considerably more complicated than we have modeled in games 1 and 2. One important missing element concerns informal and word-of-mouth communication. Although we allowed that some traders were informed when the city cheated another trader, we also assumed that traders know nothing about who else is currently trading. This assumption was a device to rule out endogenous communication among the traders in the game, by which one trader might infer that another was cheated because someone did not show up to trade. In theory, this kind of communication can be significant.[42] No doubt, both word-of-mouth and some inferences of this kind could take place, but we have built our formal model to disallow them on the assumption that they were of minor importance for enforcing contract compliance. To the extent that informal communications and indirect inferences could provide effective information, the need for organized communication and coordination is reduced.

Game 3. Guild with Coordinating Ability

We have now seen that it is impossible for the city and the traders to sustain an efficient level of trade based only on sanctions applied by small groups. Given the historical evidence of the existence of organizations that governed the relationships between the traders and the city, it is natural to examine whether these could contribute to trade expansion.

How the guild ought to be modeled is a serious issue. In our view, a crucial characteristic that separates formal institutions like guilds from informal codes of behavior is the creation of specialized roles such as those of the guild's aldermen. Determining how the guild selects its aldermen, what private interests those merchants may have, and how the guild manages the principal-agent problem of controlling the aldermen is a serious and complex issue that merits close analysis. Nonetheless, including such a model here would only obscure the main point of this paper. So, we set these issues aside for future research and model the guild here as a mere automaton. By assigning different information and behavioral rules to the guild, we can evaluate its contribution to trade expansion.

In this subsection, we examine the role of the guild as an organization for communication and coordination. In our formal model, if the city cheats a set of traders, T, then the guild is assumed to discover the event and announce a boycott with probability $\alpha(T) \geq \mu(T)$. This specification means that the more merchants who were abused, the more likely the guild is to conclude that some abuse has occurred. On the other hand, it does not imply that the guild has information superior to that available to the merchants under the uncoordinated reputation mechanism examined in game 2.

In this game, the guild makes boycott announcements mechanically and without any means of enforcement. Traders learn the guild's announcement in each period, but they are not forced to heed it. It simply becomes part of the information that is available to them and to the city. Otherwise, this game is the same as game 1. Despite the guild's lack of enforcement ability, the mere change in information alters the set of equilibria.

PROPOSITION 3. *Suppose that* $\tau + \kappa \leq 1$ *and*

$$c \leq \gamma(\tau - c). \tag{4}$$

Then, the following strategies form a Markov perfect equilibrium of game 3:[43] The city does not cheat unless a boycott is announced by the guild leader; after a boycott is announced, it cheats any trader who offers to trade. Traders offer to trade in a given period if and only if no boycott has been announced.

The formal proof is by direct verification. The condition (4) is just the condition that what the city stands to gain by cheating a trader, which is proportional to $cf(x^*)$, be less than the average future profits from each trader, which is $\gamma(\tau - c)f(x^*)$. With group enforcement, *average* trading profits rather than marginal profits determine the city's incentives. It is this fact that accounts for the continued effectiveness of group sanctions even at the efficient level of trade.

As remarked earlier, the equilibrium strategies contain a counter-intuitive element: that the city cheats any trader who offers to trade during a boycott. It is the traders' unanimous expectation that the city will behave this way that causes them all to honor the boycott. However, why should the city not welcome traders during the boycott, rather than cheating them? Since we are looking at a Markov perfect equilibrium, the city can be expected to cheat embargo-breaking traders only if it is actually in the city's interest to do so once the embargo has been announced. Given the specified strategies, if y traders violate the boycott and offer their goods, the city expects a payoff of $(\tau - c)f(y)$ in the current period, and zero in future periods, if it acts honestly. If it cheats, it expects $\tau f(y)$ in the current period and zero in the future, so cheating is, indeed, optimal.

Although the strategies described in proposition 3 do constitute an equilibrium, the expectations and behavior that they entail seem implausible. The equilibrium requires, for example, that no matter how desperate the city may be for renewed trade relationships once a boycott has been announced, it must nevertheless cheat anyone who ventures to trade with it. In addition, the traders must expect that behavior. By the equilibrium logic, the city does this because it expects the boycott to take full hold in the next round anyway, so it anticipates that any cooperation it may offer will be fruitless.

This equilibrium behavior does not match the historical facts very well, and it is of doubtful import even as theory, because it supposes that the city and potential embargo breakers play the equilibrium with the lowest possible value for themselves. Similar criticisms have been leveled at the equilibria of other repeated-game models, notably by Farrell and Maskin (1989), Bernheim and Ray (1989), Pearce (1987), and Abreu and Pearce (1991). None of the alternative solution concepts that these authors suggest apply directly to our model, but all suggest that it is more reasonable to suppose that some cooperation may be achieved between traders and the city even after a boycott is announced. As an example, we emphasize the possibility that mutually profitable *bilateral* agreements between the city and individual traders may be reached even during a boycott. It will be apparent from the logic of the arguments that any other kind of cooperation would lead to qualitatively similar conclusions.

Let us therefore suppose that if some traders agree to trade with the city despite the embargo, they cannot rely on the threat of a group boycott to enforce their own claims against the city. What, then, can enforce honest behavior by the city during the boycott? We feel that it is the threat by a cheated trader to withdraw his own future trade. Proposition 1 established that the efficient level of trade x^* could not be supported by such an equilibrium, but it leaves open the possibility that some inefficiently low level of trade can be supported. We are therefore led to ask: what is the highest level of exchange, x', that can be supported in this way?

PROPOSITION 4. *Assume that f is concave. Consider the strategies in which the city cooperates in each period with just those traders that it has never before cheated and consider that each trader offers to trade in each period if and only if he has not been cheated before. These strategies constitute a subgame perfect equilibrium of game 1 when the volume of traders is x and the taxes are τ if and only if for all $y \leq x$*

$$0 \geq cf(y) - \gamma(\tau - c)yf'(y). \tag{6}$$

A sufficient condition is that (i) $0 \geq cf(x) - \gamma(\tau - c)xf'(x)$ and (ii) the elasticity $e(x) = d\ell nf(x)/d\ell n(x)$ be a decreasing function of x.

Proof. It is obvious that the traders' strategies are best replies from any point in the history of the game to the strategy of the city, so we need consider only the optimality of the city's strategy.

Beginning with x current traders, consider the subgame achieved after $x - y$ traders depart, when there are $y \leq x$ traders remaining. By cheating a fraction ϵ of the y current traders, the city's payoff will be $g(\epsilon;y) = [\tau - (1 - \epsilon)c]f(y) + \gamma f[y(1 - \epsilon)](\tau - c)$. A necessary condition for the optimality of $\epsilon = 0$ is $\partial g(\epsilon;y)/\partial \epsilon \leq 0$ at $\epsilon = 0$. An easy calculation verifies that this is just the same as condition (6), so the latter condition is necessary for all y.

By the optimality principle of dynamic programming, it is sufficient to show that there is no subgame in which the city would do strictly better by setting $\epsilon > 0$ in the initial period and then adhering to its equilibrium strategy thereafter, given the strategies of the others. If f is concave, then for all y, $g(\epsilon;y)$ is concave in ϵ, so a sufficient condition is that for all y, $\partial g(\epsilon;y)/\partial \epsilon \leq 0$ at $\epsilon = 0$, which is again equivalent to (6), proving sufficiency.

The elasticity can be rewritten as $e(x) = xf'(x)/f(x)$. The condition (6) is that $e(y) \geq c/[\gamma(\tau - c)]$ for all $y \leq x$, which follows from $e(x) \geq c/[\gamma(\tau - c)]$ and the hypothesis that $e(\cdot)$ is decreasing. $\qquad\square$

Let x' be the largest solution of (6). The equilibrium described by proposition 4 suggests an interesting interpretation of the levels of trade x' observed during boycotts and explains why some merchants continued to trade but others did not. According to the theory, additional traders, beyond the number x', would be cheated by the city and would be unable to exact retribution for their losses. Alternatively, if we think of the level of trade $x < x^*$ during the boycott as being determined by factors outside the model (such as existing alliances or other interests), then condition (6) implies that the minimum tax rate necessary to deter cheating is less the lower x is. This confirms the intuition that an embargo breaker may be able to negotiate an unusually attractive deal, both because the value of trade per trader $(f(x)/x)$ is higher when x is small and because the minimum tax rate τ necessary to prevent cheating is lower for small x.

Proposition 4 implies that in the absence of a strong guild—one that can enforce the boycott on its members—the guild cannot credibly threaten to reduce the city's income to less than $f(x')$. This threat may or may not be sufficient to support honest trade, depending on the parameters γ, τ, and c. That is, a boycott with leaks may or may not be enough to deter the city from violating its agreement. If this kind of boycott is not enough, then there may be mutual gains to be had by strengthening the guild and enabling it to make a more powerful threat. In particular, a guild with the ability to enforce its boycott decision on all the merchants may be able to assure trade expansion.

The force of any potential boycott depends not only on $f(x')$ and $f(x^*)$, but also on the net rate of profit, $\tau - c$, earned by the city. Incentives for honest behavior by the city are stronger when the taxes and tolls are high, because the city than has more to lose from a boycott. A strong guild can make it feasible to offer lower taxes and tolls while still promoting honest behavior by the city that, in a richer model, could lead to additional advantages in terms of increased value of trade.

Game 4. The Guild with Coordination and
Enforcement Abilities

The final variant is a game in which the guild has the ability to enforce
compliance from the individual traders. We offer no formal analysis of
this case. It is obvious that the only role of enforcement by the guild
against member merchants in our formal model is to prevent trade during boycotts. Accordingly, the results are the same as in proposition 3,
but now the traders participate in the boycott because they are required
to do so, rather than because they expect participation to serve their
individual interests.

3. Discussion

All models in economics are stylized to highlight particular points, and
ours are no exception. Our game models treat all merchants as small and
perfect substitutes for one another; they abstract from the costs of run-
ning a guild and the problems of enforcing good behavior on the part of
guild leaders; they omit the issues of competition among different trading
centers and they do not delve into how organized merchants actually enforce sanctions against their own members. Although the models' narrow
focus highlights the need for cohesiveness among merchants and gives
what we think is a convincing account of many details of the historical record, the omitted features are also important for understanding the history
of merchant guilds. Merchant guilds were primarily an urban rather than
a rural phenomenon. That may be accounted for by the costs of organiz-
ing merchants over large geographic areas. Guild membership also extended gradually. In Germany, large cities took the lead in forming intercity guilds. This pattern, too, seems to reflect the costs and other barriers
to forming large organizations, and the potential for success for small
guilds is surely an important part of the dynamics of guild development.

Although our models treat merchants as homogeneous in their commercial affairs with the city, their geographic diversity was the very basis
for the trade. There were exports of timber and Sengalese gold from
North Africa, silk, spices, drugs, flax, and wine from the Middle East
and Byzantium, luxury furs, cheese, butter, fish, and iron from Scandina-
via and Russia, grains from Germany, wine from France and Spain,
textiles from Flanders, wool, copper, dried fish, and goat- and sheep-
skins from England, and so on.

When groups of merchants are close substitutes for one another,
competition among them can undermine the joint action needed to enforce rights obtained from rulers of trading centers. The pattern of guild

membership along product lines that the theory implies is nearly identical to the patterns implied by a theory of the merchant guild as an instrument of monopoly, so it is important to emphasize how the other predictions of the theories differ.

Our theory predicts that rulers will *encourage* the establishment of merchant guilds with specific rights and an effective organization. Such encouragement would not be expected if the sole purpose of the guilds was to shift some of the fixed gains of trade from rulers to merchants unless the encouragement itself reflected the merchants' ability to coerce the rulers to shift rent in their favor. The evidence reveals that even when merchants could not coerce rulers by the threat of embargo and even when the privileges provided to the merchants did not entail any shift in the rent, rulers did grant merchants various rights,[44] including the right to organize, to hold courts and assemblies, to elect their own consuls, and to participate on juries when merchants were being tried. Our theory predicts that establishment of these guild rights will lead to trade expansion, but a cartel theory of guilds suggests that guilds will form to reduce trade in goods in order to drive up relative prices. The evidence cited earlier supports the conclusion that, at least during the late medieval period, guilds led to trade expansion. While it is likely that the merchant guilds sought to advance the merchants' interests in many ways, including by negotiating for rights to control prices, these rent-seeking activities cannot account for the patterns we have identified.

Of special interest for our theory is the richness and complexity of the guild system. The guild functioned as a nexus of contracts, weaving separate agreements with the individual merchants and the cities where its members traded into a system whose parts were mutually supporting. Exclusive (but not necessarily monopolistic) trading arrangements with the city allowed the guilds to organize merchants, and other rights helped them to keep informed about disputes and to help the city enforce good behavior by merchants. The guilds contracts with the merchants were fundamental to allowing them to enforce their agreements with the city and with other merchants, including those from towns that tried to smuggle goods past their embargoes. The Hansa, effectively involving intercity contracts, further strengthened the merchants' hands in enforcement.

As centuries passed and trade gave impetus to political integration, larger political units emerged, taking upon themselves the functions that the merchant guilds had previously performed. The political, commercial, and military relations among rulers enabled each to commit to the safety of the alien merchants frequenting his realm. Illustrative are such acts as those of the English kings, who made agreements and enforced embargoes to provide the English Merchants of the Staple and the Merchant Adventurers with security in their dealings with the Hanseatic league. As the state system evolved, the need for the merchant guilds to secure merchants' rights declined.[45]

Merchant guilds, however, did not necessarily disappear, and some guilds became fiscal instruments that hindered trade expansion in the emerging states. Other guilds consolidated their political power and, after securing their members' rights, turned to limit the rights of their competitors. For example, the German Hansa of the late medieval period was a new political entity aimed at preserving the property rights of German merchants. Although its establishment enabled northern European trade to flourish, once organized, the Hansa's concern was not efficiency but profitability. In its constant efforts to preserve trade rights and supremacy, the Hansa crushed the advance of other traders' groups without consideration of their comparative efficiencies. Thus, a merchant guild that had facilitated trade in the late medieval period was transformed into a monopolistic organization that hindered trade expansion during the premodern period.[46]

Up to this point, we have focused exclusively on the role of the merchant guild in a particular time and place, but we believe that the principles that applied then help to explain the emergence of other organizations in other places and times. Our analysis explains why a powerful party might find it advantageous to help weaker powers organize themselves into entities that can exert countervailing power, in order to allow itself to commit to certain mutually beneficial arrangements. For example, prior to the Revolution, the French kings developed an elaborate system to help secure their borrowing and thereby enhance their ability to borrow.[47] The ingredients of this system—using the officer corps both to aggregate loans and to help borrowers coordinate, and relying on the Parliaments to authorize the legality of royal edicts—suggests an attempt by the kings to create organizations capable of collective action to enforce the king's fiscal promises. Similarly, part of Britain's financial and military success following the Glorious Revolution in 1688 involved creating the Bank of England. This organization seems to have had the necessary attributes identified by our theory, for instance, the ability to announce the initiation of a credit boycott and to punish lenders who attempted to lend to the government.[48] The theoretical ideas introduced in this paper provide a promising new framework for analyzing these events and institutions.

NOTES

An earlier version of this chapter was prepared for the conference on "Economic Policy in Political Equilibrium," June 14–16, 1990. We thank Yoram

Barzel, Douglass North, Jean-Laurent Rosenthal, and Nathan Sussman for helpful discussions, Esther-Mirjam Sent and Joshua Gans for editorial assistance, and the National Science Foundation for financial support. The participants at the conference on "Markets and Organizations" organized by the Center for Economic Research at Tilburg, and seminar participants at the University of California at Berkeley, Boston University, Indiana University, the University of Illinois at Urbana–Champaign, Harvard University, the Hebrew University, Stanford University and Tel-Aviv University contributed helpful comments.

Grateful acknowledgment is made to the University of Chicago Press for permission to reprint this chapter, which first appeared as "Merchant Gilds" in *Journal of Political Economy* 102, no. 4 (1994): 745–76.

1. For an analysis of the institution that governed agency relations in twelfth-century Genoa, see Greif 1993b. For game-theoretical and comparative historical analysis of the evolution and functioning of various trading institutions among the twelfth-century Genoese and the eleventh-century Maghribi traders from the Muslim world, see Greif 1992c.

2. *English Historical Documents,* vol. 3, 420. The recognition that unprotected alien merchants would not come to England is also expressed in the *Carta Mercatoria* of 1303. See *English Historical Documents,* vol. 3, 515.

3. Economists have long associated the latter with the monopolization of a given craft within a specific town. For a recent economic analysis of craft guilds, see Hickson and Thompson 1991. See also, Gufstafsson 1987.

4. See, for example, Thrupp 1963; Gross 1980; and North and Thomas 1973.

5. De Roover (1965) asserts that the guild's role "was, of course, to provide collective protection in foreign lands, to secure trade privileges, if possible, and to watch over the strict observance of those already in effect" (111). While his intuition carried him a long way, it did not explain how the guilds could provide protection and assure observance of rights by local rulers in foreign lands where the ruler had a preponderance of military force.

6. This is not to argue, however, that this function was necessarily the main reason for these local monopoly rights.

7. *Curia Regis,* 121, m.6, published by Salzamn (1928).

8. See Day 1988. For additional examples, see also Kedar 1976, 26 ff.; Lane 1973, 34; and De Roover 1965.

9. Clearly, there was a limit to the security a ruler could provide the merchants. Accordingly, we have detailed above instances where rights were abused in major cities or trade centers in which the relevant ruler had a relatively high level of ability to secure rights.

10. Parker (1990, 7) comments that "After the proliferation of stone-built castles in Western Europe, which began in the eleventh century . . . [I]n the military balance between defence and offense, the former had clearly become predominant." This situation changed only during the so called "Military Revolution" of the fifteenth century.

11. David Kaufmann Collection, Hungarian Academy of Science, Budapest, document #22, a, 11.29–31, b, 11.3–5; Taylor-Schecter collection, University

Library, Cambridge, England, document 10 J 12, f. 26, a, 11.18–20; Michael 1965, 2:85.

12. E.g., De Roover 1965; De Roover 1948, 13; and Dollinger 1970.

13. Krueger 1933, 379–80; Krueger 1932, 81–82.

14. Abulafia 1985, 226.

15. Dollinger 1970, 41.

16. De Roover 1948, 13.

17. Gross 1890; Rorig 1967; and Rashdall 1936, 150–53. For a general discussion of the concept of corporation in medieval English law, see Pollock and Maitland 1968, 1:486 ff.

18. An exception is the case of the Maghribi traders. That case, however, seems to reflect the situation in the Muslim world rather than in Europe. See Greif 1992c.

19. Guild members were required to travel together, to live and store their goods throughout their stay in quarters that belonged to the guild, to examine the quality of each other's goods, and to witness each other's sales. See, for example, Moore 1985, 63 ff. As De Roover (1948, 20) noted, the "main purpose of the consular organization [of the Italians in Bruges] was . . . to facilitate the exchange of information. . . ."

20. Lopez 1943, 181–84.

21. Lopez 1943, 181–83.

22. Moore 1985, 301.

23. Moore 1985, 301.

24. Dollinger 1970, 49. See also his description of the embargo on Novgorod (48). Anyone who broke the embargo was to suffer the death penalty and the confiscation of his goods.

25. Dollinger 1970, 65–66.

26. See Gross 1890, 19–20, 38 ff. 65; De Roover 1948, 18–19. Exclusive commercial rights for the guild should not be confused with monopoly rights. Entry into the guild was permitted during the period under consideration. The German *Kontore* were established by the merchants who actually traveled abroad to trade. In England, for example, even individuals who did not live in a specific town could join its merchant guild, and each member had to pay an entry fee. See, for example, Dollinger 1970 and Gross 1890. Note that by creating barriers and consequent rents, such a system also motivates each merchant to adhere to the guild rules, including honoring guild-sponsored embargoes. As shown in the text, this in turn permits a higher volume of trade than would be possible without the entry restrictions.

27. This is not to claim that this was the chief role of these rents. Our analysis examines the role of the merchant guild in the expansion of trade between political units and not within political units.

28. Moore 1985, 298.

29. Clearly, we do not claim that the efficiency attributes of the Hansa that we discuss were sufficient for its emergence. For a general discussion of the relationships between social and political institutions, gains from trade, and the emergence of institutions that facilitate trade, see Greif 1992a, 1992b.

30. For the imperfect monitoring approach, see the pioneering work by Green and Porter (1984). For refinements of this approach, see Abreu, Pearce, and Stacchetti 1986 and Abreu, Milgrom, and Pearce 1991.

31. Weiner 1932, 218.

32. De Roover 1965, 114; Dollinger 1970, 86.

33. Urkundenbuch der Stadt Lubeck, vol. 1, no. 156, 371, translated by Dollinger 1970, 383.

34. Dollinger 1970, 48–51.

35. Dollinger 1970, 49; Weiner 1932, 219.

36. Dollinger 1970, 51.

37. Dollinger 1970, 63.

38. Dollinger 1970, 66. For further details of this embargo, see Dollinger 1970, 63–66 and Weiner 1932, 220.

39. For the relative size of Italian and German cities, see Bairoch, Batou, and Chevre 1988. Some intercity cooperation was also practiced among the Italians, where smaller cities "affiliated" themselves with larger ones. See the discussion in the text.

40. Note that this formulation captures the gains to the ruler from either abusing rights directly or from neglecting to provide merchants with costly protection.

41. This result is not an artifact of our specification of costs. For example, if we had specified that the costs borne by the city included some fixed costs per trader (possibly in addition to the proportional costs), the city would have an even stronger incentive to reduce the number of traders, because it bears only a fraction (τ) of the resulting loss of value but saves all of the service costs. Making costs proportional to value minimizes the distortion in the city's incentives, but still leaves it tempted to seek short-term gains by cutting services at the expense of individual traders when only the bilateral reputation mechanism is at work.

42. Kandori 1992.

43. This is a Nash equilibrium of the game with the properties that (1) the players's strategies at any date depend only on whether a boycott has been announced and (2) each player's strategy at each date maximizes his payoff from that date onward, given the equilibrium strategies of the other players.

44. In addition to the evidence mentioned in the text, see Carus-Wilson 1967, xviii and EHD 1975, 515–16. The role of the guild in securing rights rather than in achieving privileges in Bruges is suggested by the city policy of providing all nations with the same rights. See De Roover 1948, 15.

45. For the relations between the Hansa and England during this later period, see Colvin 1971; Postan 1973.

46. See previous discussion of the Hansa embargoes during the late fourteenth century. Regarding the English traders, see Lloyd 1991; Dollinger 1970. For a general discussion, see Greif 1992b.

47. For details, see Bien 1989; Hoffman 1989; and Root 1989.

48. This argument is developed at length in Weingast 1992.

Rational Actors, Equilibrium, and Social Institutions

Randall L. Calvert

1. Introduction

In their broadest, sociological definition, institutions include "all the beliefs and modes of conduct instituted by the collectivity" (Durkheim 1938 [1895]),[1] that is, beliefs and conduct not depending solely on the judgment, will, or habits of individuals considered in isolation. So defined, institutions range from the simplest informal norms to the most complex formal organizations. For Durkheim, the matter of definition ended there: the collectivity served as the basic unit of explanation, and institutions as the primitives for explaining other social phenomena. This approach, however, begs two compelling questions. First, why does a given institution succeed in constraining individual behavior in some circumstances, but not in others? Second, is there any limit to the combinations of beliefs and conduct that can persist as institutions?

   The rational-actor, or rational-choice, approach to understanding social behavior is nicely suited to addressing these questions, and to studying the behavior of individuals in institutions. It focuses on the conflict between individual motives and social prescriptions; without this conflict there would be no problem of institutional effectiveness or persistence. The purpose of this chapter is to examine how the rational-choice approach can be most effectively applied to address such questions, and to illustrate how both informal and formal institutions can exist as equilibria in the context of repeated cooperation games. Along the way, it will be possible to suggest a more precise definition of "institutions" using the rational-choice model to distinguish the systems of behavior we normally think of as institutions from systems that normally would not receive that title.

Rational-Choice Approaches to Institutions

Within the rational-choice approach to studying institutions, three general methods can be discerned in the recent literature. One approach views institutions as features of individual preferences: the actor's utility function includes arguments for altruism, cooperation, or observance of social norms, and optimal behavior under such a utility function is worked out. Examples include the work of Margolis 1982 and the essays in Koford and Miller 1991. Until an explanation is given for why preferences take these forms, however, this approach is really closer to the Durkheimian one than to rational-actor methods, in that it takes the needs of the social group as the basis for individual behavior. In principle, an explanation for such prosocial preferences in terms of basic psychological mechanisms could bring this approach back to the level of individual action, but a coherent psychological theory of this type has yet to emerge.[2] For the present study, I ignore this approach in favor of more fundamentally rational-choice ones.

The other two approaches adhere more closely to the rational-actor idea. One is to treat institutions as constraints on behavior, or "rules of the game," and to examine rational behavior within the constraints imposed by institutional rules. Examples can be found in North 1981, 1990; Shepsle 1979; and Shepsle and Weingast 1987. In this literature, the rules themselves are either taken as given, or else treated as alternative sets of constraints to be imposed by the creators of constitutions or of basic procedural rules, guided by the results those rules will yield once rational behavior takes place under them.

The third approach, originally suggested by Schotter (1981), regards an institution as an equilibrium of behavior in an underlying game. The aim is to describe institutions in a way that both explains the observed behavior and identifies conditions under which the institution can be effective. The present essay employs this institution-as-equilibrium approach, and uses it to examine the differences between formal and informal institutions, the circumstances under which they can exist, and their effects on the welfare of participants.

The institutions-as-constraints approach is useful for understanding behavior under stable institutions, but it falls short as a tool for understanding institutions themselves. Its failure lies in the fact that it takes as given the institution's effectiveness in channeling behavior. "Rules of the game" are either (a) impossible to violate, due to the specification of the game or the guaranteed actions of other players; or (b) backed up by some form of external sanction.[3] Either form of rule simply pushes the problem of institutional effectiveness and persistence back to another level. How is the choice of actions constrained? Why do others behave in the way that they do? How is the appropriate application of sanctions assured? A full rational-choice explanation of institutions requires that the behavior of each actor, including those applying the sanctions, be consistent with that

institutional
effectiveness

actor's self-interest. Moreover, any discussion of institutional choice or institutional change in the "institutions-as-constraints" model must necessarily be ad hoc.

In the institutions-as-equilibria approach, however, the game is just a description of underlying physical realities: if people behave in a certain combination of ways, nature responds with certain goods or conditions. Any additional structure "instituted by the collectivity" must be described as the behavior patterns of individuals and their expectations about the behavior of others. These patterns of behavior and expectations must be consistent with utility maximization by each individual.[4] In short, an institution is an equilibrium in the underlying game, and different institutional structures correspond to different equilibria, while the rules of the game remain constant. In particular, if the underlying game (that is, nature) does not set apart any individual players as having special opportunities or powers, then such role differentiation can be maintained only as part of an equilibrium.

Not every equilibrium behavior pattern is an institution, however. A game may have atomistic or anomic equilibria in which no player's actions have any bearing on any other's actions, such as unconditional defection by all players in a repeated many-player prisoner's dilemma. Such a pattern of behavior is certainly not what we normally mean by an "institution," although some authors discuss a "norm" of selfish, calculating rationality (e.g., Marsh and Olsen 1989) tantamount to an institution. Even when the behavior of each member of the group depends on that of a few others, the resulting pattern may not really qualify as an institution. For example, consider a situation of repeated random matching of members of a large group, in which each matched pair engages in a two-player prisoner's dilemma, after which the players are randomly matched again, and so on. This game has an equilibrium (shown in section 2 below) in which each pair of players maintains a relationship of reciprocal cooperation, but failure to cooperate is punished by only the partner who was cheated and not by other group members. Such a pattern of behavior is not really an "institution" in the large group, since players' expectations about other players' behavior do not generally have any bearing on that behavior.[5] (Reciprocity would properly be a small-scale institution within each cooperating pair of players, however.) On the other hand, if failure to cooperate with one (previously cooperative) partner were punished by all subsequent partners, an institution of reciprocity would be present in the large group. The institutions-as-equilibria model suggests that we define an institution within a group of individuals as an equilibrium in which individuals' actions are dependent upon the past actions of many others, or upon expectations about the future reactions of many others, to one's present actions. These reactions could include instances of inaction or acquiescence, such as a willingness not to punish a player who imposes an acceptable punishment on a deviating third player.[6]

Within the class of equilibria that qualify as institutions by this criterion, there are institutions with various levels of formality and organizational complexity. A universally sanctioned reciprocity relationship, for example, is an institution in which all members of the group use the same strategy; the institution involves no differentiation of roles. On the other hand, many institutions involve official positions, with rights and responsibilities unique to each office. Members of a group may be sanctioned for failing to act in accord with some official's actions, but failure of the official to act within prescribed limits may incur sanctions as well. At the extreme of such complexity lie those institutions that are referred to as "organizations." In addition, institutions differ as to the formality of their specification by the players. Institutions other than those at the highest levels of organizational complexity may be defined by nothing more than an informal and unvoiced understanding among the group's members, or by a formal written contract or law, or by any level of formality in between. Finally, institutions at all levels of organizational complexity and all levels of formality of specification may be created through a specific process of negotiation and agreement (the U.S. Congress, for example); or they may arise spontaneously by the accretion of practices and precedents over years or centuries (the common law, for example), or by the accidental coordination of like-minded individuals. All institutions, however, must have a common property: it must be rational for nearly every individual to almost always adhere to the behavioral prescriptions of the institution, given that nearly all other individuals are doing so.

[margin note: orgs = complex institutions w/ hierarchy / formal & inf. rules.]

[handwritten: what's the right level of institutional structure?]

Plan of the Chapter

I employ a basic idea of Milgrom, North, and Weingast 1990 to portray various possible institutions in a standard "social dilemma" situation.[7] Section 2 presents a basic model of repeated cooperation built around the two-player prisoner's dilemma (PD). In each iteration of this game, players in a group are paired up at random to play the PD, so (unlike the "Townsend Turnpike" configuration used by Milgrom et al.) cooperation is possible without communication, using only a rule of pairwise reciprocity in which deviation is not punished by the group at large. Conditions are derived for a kind of tit-for-tat strategy to be in equilibrium. This noninstitution equilibrium then provides a point of comparison for the more highly organized equilibria described subsequently.

Section 3 enriches the model to provide opportunities for the players to communicate, but (again unlike the model of Milgrom et al.) such communication is costly. Under demonstrated conditions, I show how cooperation may be possible with such multilateral communication but impossible under the no-communication conditions of section 2. The equilibrium that accomplishes this feat is a true institution, in that the whole group monitors and punishes deviant behavior. Then, in section 4, I construct another equilibrium, this one with "centralized communication," analogous to the "Law Merchant System Strategy" of Milgrom et al. Again, this equilibrium may exist under conditions when the no-communication and multilateral-communication equilibria do not. It represents a formal institution: not only are certain acts of consultation and reporting required of the players, but one player is designated to play a special "official" role.

Finally, section 5 addresses the problem of providing positive incentives for the "official" to eschew corruption, which is rendered possible by the addition of sufficient opportunities for communication and payment. This demonstrates one aspect of how an institution must solve the classical problem of "who watches the watchers"; additional provisions for monitoring and sanctions would likewise have to be incorporated as equilibrium behavior within the original game. Section 6 concludes with remarks on the design or emergence of institutions, and on the application of the equilibrium approach for the study of institutions and of behavior within institutions.

2. Cooperation without an Institution

Consider first the simple setting in which a set of players $\{1, 2, \ldots, N\}$ ($N \geq 2$ and even) engages in indefinitely repeated, pairwise plays of a two-player prisoner's dilemma (PD) game, G, with one another. The game G has the payoffs shown in matrix 1, where $\beta > 0$, $\alpha > 1$, and $\alpha - \beta < 2$.[8] Specifically, in each period $t = 1, 2, \ldots$, players are paired by a random mechanism in which the probability of any player i being paired with a particular other player j is $1/(N - 1)$. Players i and j then play one iteration of G. Players discount payoffs in future periods by some discount factor $\delta < 1$. Each player has complete, perfect information about his or her own past and present interactions, but no information about interactions between pairs of other players. Let $G(\delta)$ denote this entire repeated game with random matching of players.

One equilibrium is of course for players to always defect unconditionally. There are other equilibria in which cooperation occurs. For example, suppose that each player uses a subgame-perfect version of the

		Player 2	
		C	D
Player 1	C	1, 1	-β, α
	D	α, -β	0, 0

Matrix 1. The 2-player PD game, G.

tit-for-tat strategy against each other player, regarding each series of pairwise interactions with the same partner as a separate game from the interactions with other partners. That is, to the usual tit-for-tat strategy we add the prescription that if for any reason a player *does* depart from the strategy and defect, on the next two iterations (here, the next two encounters with the same partner) that player cooperates unconditionally, making "restitution," so to speak, and thereafter resumes conditional cooperative play.[9] I shall refer to this version of the strategy as "TFT." If the discount factor for each pairwise interaction, say γ, is sufficiently large, this would be an equilibrium. In that case, we have what would normally be called a "norm of reciprocity" (Axelrod 1981; Calvert 1989): each player expects his or her opponent to reciprocate cooperation and retaliate against defection in such a way as to make defection not worthwhile. Such reciprocity is a norm in a broad sense, although deviations are of no consequence to the group as a whole, but only to the victim of that defection. By the definition suggested in section 1, this equilibrium does not qualify as an institution.

A necessary and sufficient condition for cooperation to be possible in this setting is that $\alpha \leq 1/(1 - \gamma)$. In that case, the strongest possible punishment, the "grim trigger" strategy of permanent retaliation against a partner who has ever defected, will deter defection even if it is only carried out by the partner against whom the defection occurred. Alternatively, TFT can be implemented provided that γ exceeds a somewhat larger bound; the following results formalize this fact in terms of a condition on the original discount factor, δ.

LEMMA. *In $G(\delta)$, the proper discount factor for interactions with a particular other opponent is given by*

$$\gamma = \frac{\delta}{N - 1 - \delta(N - 2)} .$$

The proof of the lemma, and of all subsequent theorems, is relegated to the appendix. Note that γ is a strictly increasing function of δ. Table 1 indicates some representative values of γ given δ and N. Obviously, increasing group size rapidly washes out the "shadow of the future" (Axelrod 1981) necessary for cooperation.

THEOREM 1. *The strategy profile in which each player plays TFT with each partner individually is a perfect Bayesian equilibrium of $G(\delta)$ provided that δ is sufficiently large. In particular, δ must be greater than both*

$$\frac{(N-1)(\alpha-1)}{(N-2)(\alpha-1)+\beta+1} \quad and \quad \frac{(N-1)\beta}{(N-1)\beta+1}.$$

Table 2 shows the lower bound for δ for several values of α, β, and N.

3. Communication and Cooperation: An Informal Institution

As is apparent from table 2, if N is moderately large a healthy δ may be insufficient to support this cooperative institution in equilibrium. Due to the rarity of repeated meetings between any two players and to the lack of information about one's partner's behavior with other partners, no strategy of reciprocation can be viable under these conditions. Even in large groups, however, it may still be possible to support cooperation in equilibrium if there is more widespread punishment of defectors. This could be done if the players could inform one another about outcomes.

Accordingly, I revise the above model by explicitly allowing for the possibility of communication among the players. Let G^* be the stage game played at each period t; G^* consists of the following substages or phases:

TABLE 1. Representative Values of γ, the Discount Factor for Interactions with a Particular Player, as a Function of the Overall Discount Factor δ and the Number of Players, N

	$\delta = .999$	$\delta = .99$	$\delta = .95$	$\delta = .90$	$\delta = .75$	$\delta = .50$
$N = 5$	.996	.96	.83	.69	.43	.20
$N = 10$	.991	.92	.68	.50	.25	.10
$N = 30$	.972	.77	.40	.24	.09	.03
$N = 100$	.910	.50	.16	.08	.03	.01

1. Players are paired at random; each player knows only the pairing that she herself is in.
2. Players may communicate with one another. Any player i may send a message to any other player j, and messages may be sent to as many other players as desired. For each player j whom she contacts in this manner, player i bears a communication cost c. All of these communications take place simultaneously. The messages must be chosen from some message set or "language" L.
3. Any player who received a message in phase 2 may deliver an immediate, costless response also drawn from L.
4. The paired players play one iteration of G; again, one knows only the outcome in one's own pair.
5. The players may again communicate as in phase 2, simultaneously sending messages chosen from L to as many other players as desired, bearing a cost c for each contact. A player *cannot* verify to her opponent in the current phase what messages were sent to other players.

Let $G^*(\delta)$ denote the repeated game thus defined. As will become apparent, this temporal ordering of communication and play is chosen in order to enable study of the particular equilibria here and in section 4 (in fact, phases 2 and 3 won't be used until section 4). Notice that a strategy consisting of the pairwise tit-for-tat of theorem 1, plus a prescription that the player never communicate and ignore all communication from others, is a subgame perfect equilibrium in $G^*(\delta)$. Likewise the presence of additional communication phases will not affect theorems 2 and 3 below, since any equilibrium in the game as specified here can be extended to specify no sending of messages in the added phases, and ignoring of any messages that are sent in violation of this prescription. Also, the "language" could contain a large and arbitrary set of possible messages without affecting whether a particular strategy profile is in equilibrium; the equilibrium could be extended to specify that any message not from the restricted language used for the equilibrium is ignored.

TABLE 2.   Examples of Bound for Theorem 1

alpha		1.1	1.1	1.1	2	2	2	2	4	4
beta		0.1	0.5	3	1.1	1.5	3	5	2.1	3
N	2	0.091	0.333	0.750	0.524	0.600	0.750	0.833	0.968	0.750
	5	0.286	0.667	0.923	0.815	0.857	0.923	0.952	0.992	0.923
	10	0.474	0.818	0.964	0.908	0.931	0.964	0.978	0.996	0.964
	30	0.744	0.935	0.989	0.970	0.978	0.989	0.993	0.999	0.989
	100	0.908	0.980	0.997	0.991	0.993	0.997	0.998	1.000	0.997

For present purposes, assume that the language L includes all possible pairs (n,a) where $n \in N$ and $a \in \{C,D\}$; for this equilibrium, the message (n,a) may be taken to mean, "My partner in this stage was n; she played a." Now define the strategy of "tit-for-tat with multilateral communication," TFT/MC, in which a player behaves as follows in the phases of each stage:

2. Send no messages before play.
3. Make no replies.
4. If in cooperation status (defined below), play C if partner is reported to be in cooperation status and D if partner is reported to be in punishment status (also defined below); if in punishment status, play C.
5. If in cooperation status, truthfully report partner's identity n and action a to each of the $N - 2$ other players, incurring cost $(N - 2)c$; if in punishment status, do not communicate.

Any communication in phases 2 or 3 and any communication other than [no more] the prescribed reports in phase 5 are ignored. A player begins $G^*(\delta)$ in "cooperation status." A player enters (or remains in) "punishment status" if she fails to play as prescribed in phase 4, or if she fails to report when prescribed in phase 5. A player in punishment status returns to cooperation status immediately upon playing C in phase 4. Note that a player may deviate from this strategy by falsely reporting her partner's status in phase 5; if that happens, then a player in cooperation status [cost of disvowing] may be treated by other players as though she were in punishment status. As the note on the proof of theorem 2 (see appendix) indicates, such lying does not occur in equilibrium.

Just as in theorem 1, it is possible to specify a condition on δ so that this strategy is in equilibrium.

THEOREM 2. *The strategy profile in which all players use the strategy TFT/MC is a perfect Bayesian equilibrium of $G^*(\delta)$ for sufficiently large δ provided that c is less than each of the following values:*

$$\frac{1}{N - 2}, \quad \frac{2 - \alpha + \beta}{N - 2}, \quad \text{and} \quad \frac{\delta}{N - 1}(1 + \beta).$$

The exact lower bound for δ to support this equilibrium is the max of

$$\frac{(\alpha - 1) + (N - 2)c}{\beta + 1} \quad \text{and} \quad \frac{\beta + (N - 2)c}{\beta + 1}.$$

This combination of multilateral communication, cooperation, and retaliation is properly an institution because failure to cooperate and failure to report are punished by every partner encountered until "restitution" is made. That is, any player's actions today affect every player's actions tomorrow. This institution has minimal organizational complexity, however, since every player has exactly the same role in communicating and in punishing deviation. Nevertheless, notice how the "rules of the game" for these players are much more complex than in the pairwise TFT equilibrium of theorem 1: beyond simply interacting with each partner, a player is expected by the whole group to act in a certain way and to communicate certain information at certain times to certain other people. Any failure to act or communicate as expected incurs punishment. However, these rules are not part of the structure of the underlying game; rather, they are features of the equilibrium strategy profile. If discounting is too heavy or communication cost too high, such a system of rules is impossible to maintain.

Notice moreover that the bound on δ is generally much lower using TFT/MC than it was in the more anomic system of TFT. Table 3 shows the bound for the same values of α, β, and N as in table 2, for various values of c: a minimal .001 in the first part, pushing c's upper bound for $N = 100$ in the second part, and even higher, pushing the bound for $N = 30$ in the third part. Especially for low values of α or high values of β, even fairly costly communication makes it much easier to achieve cooperation than it was using TFT.

4. Cooperation Using a Formal Institution

Since communication is costly, its use in the equilibrium just described reduces the resulting gains from cooperation. Each individual must bear a communication cost of $(N - 2)c$ on each iteration, so the communication cost in a large or far-flung group may outweigh even large cooperation gains. In such a group, cooperation would require a more efficient exchange of information. As we will see, such an efficiency gain can be had, but only by achieving a greater degree of organizational complexity.

In place of the multilateral communication used in TFT/MC, I consider next a scheme of centralized communication.[10] Arbitrarily designate player 1 as the "director," who will serve as a central clearinghouse of information. Assume now that the language L includes at least the elements (n,a) as before, plus the messages Q_j for each $j \in N$, which for purposes of this equilibrium may be interpreted as the query, "My opponent is j; what is his status?"[11] Each player i in $\{2, 3, \ldots, N\}$ follows a strategy of "tit-for-tat with centralized communication" (TFT/CC), described as follows. When paired with player 1, always defect and never send any messages (the idea being that, for simplicity, the director refrains from actual play of the PD game). When paired with any other player j in $\{2, \ldots, N\}$, player i observes the following prescription for the respective phases of each stage in the game:

2. In stage $t = 1$, do nothing. In stages $t > 1$, if in punishment status (defined below), do nothing; if in cooperation status (defined below), then pay c to send message Q_j to the director, where j is i's current partner.
3. Do nothing.
4. In stage $t = 1$, play C. In stages $t > 1$, when in cooperation status and told (by the director's reply in phase 3) that i is in cooperation status, play C. Otherwise play D. When in punishment status, play C (make "restitution").

TABLE 3. Examples of Bound for Theorem 2

		Small c ($c = .001$)								
alpha		1.1	1.1	1.1	2	2	2	2	4	4
beta		0.1	0.5	3	1.1	1.5	3	5	2.1	3
N	5	0.094	0.335	0.751	0.525	0.601	0.751	0.834	0.969	0.751
	10	0.098	0.339	0.752	0.528	0.603	0.752	0.835	0.970	0.752
	30	0.116	0.352	0.757	0.537	0.611	0.757	0.838	0.977	0.757
	100	0.180	0.399	0.775	0.570	0.639	0.775	0.850	0.999	0.775

		c at .0001 below bound for $N = 100$								
alpha		1.1	1.1	1.1	2	2	2	2	4	4
beta		0.1	0.5	3	1.1	1.5	3	5	2.1	3
c		0.010	0.010	0.010	0.010	0.010	0.010	0.010	0.001	0.010
N	5	0.119	0.354	0.758	0.538	0.612	0.758	0.838	0.969	0.758
	10	0.165	0.388	0.770	0.563	0.633	0.770	0.847	0.970	0.770
	30	0.351	0.524	0.821	0.660	0.714	0.821	0.881	0.977	0.821
	100	1.000	1.000	1.000	1.000	1.000	1.000	1.000	1.000	1.000

		c at .0001 below bound for $N = 30$								
alpha		1.1	1.1	1.1	2	2	2	2	4	4
beta		0.1	0.5	3	1.1	1.5	3	5	2.1	3
c		0.036	0.036	0.036	0.036	0.036	0.036	0.036	0.004	0.036
N	5	0.188	0.405	0.777	0.575	0.643	0.777	0.851	0.971	0.777
	10	0.351	0.524	0.821	0.660	0.714	0.821	0.881	0.977	0.821
	30	1.000	1.000	1.000	1.000	1.000	1.000	1.000	1.000	1.000
	100	x	x	x	x	x	x	x	x	x

Note: x denotes that c exceeds its upper bound for these parameter values.

5. If in cooperation status, pay c to report j's action (j,a), to the director. If in punishment status (i.e., just played D inappropriately in phase 4) then do nothing.

Player 1, the director, obeys strategy A, described as follows. For all t, in phase 2, make no statement; in phase 4, always defect. In phase 5, make no communication. Otherwise:

3. In stage $t = 1$, say nothing. In stage $t > 1$, if message Q_j was received from player i in phase 2, truthfully report the status of that player's reported opponent — (j,C) if cooperation, (j,D) if punishment — and otherwise communicate nothing;

The cooperation and punishment statuses are defined as follows. At stage $t = 1$, every player is in cooperation status. A player i in cooperation status enters punishment status if any of the following occur: in phase 2, she fails to query as required; in phase 4, she unilaterally fails to cooperate with a partner reported by the director to be in cooperation status; or if she fails to report as prescribed in phase 5. If a player in punishment status cooperates in phase 4, she reenters cooperation status beginning with phase 5.

The following theorem derives the conditions under which the profile TFT/CC can be used by all players (except the director) in equilibrium:

THEOREM 3. *The strategy profile in which player 1 uses A and players 2 through N use TFT/CC is a perfect Bayesian equilibrium of $G^*(\delta)$ for sufficiently large δ provided that $c < \frac{1}{2}$ and $c < 1 - (\alpha - \beta)/2$. The lower bound on δ is the maximum of*

$$\frac{\beta + c}{\beta + c + (1 - 2c)\dfrac{N - 2}{N - 1}} \quad and \quad \frac{(N - 1)(\alpha - 1 + c)}{(N - 3)(\beta - c + 1) + \alpha + \beta}$$

Table 4 gives representative values of this lower bound for the same values of α, β, and N as in tables 2 and 3. Part 1 uses the same values of c as in table 3, Part 2; the second part uses a larger value for the communication cost. Comparing Part 1 with table 3 shows that, in cases where N and c are large, the formal institution using centralized communication makes cooperation possible under conditions in which the informal norm using decentralized communication could not be maintained. Centralized communication is much more efficient, but requires that different players play different roles. As the second part of table 4 demonstrates, even if the communication cost is so high that it burns up 50 percent of the gains from cooperation, the institution with centralized communication compares favorably with TFT in its ability to support cooperation in large groups. Note that table 4 shows larger group size to be an advantage. This happens because higher numbers mean that a player is paired with the director (and thus gets a zero payoff) less often. Of course, if larger group sizes put more strain on the director's ability to cope with her duties, this advantage might disappear.

In the TFT/CC equilibrium, we have an institution that is actually recognizable as an organization. Despite the fact that the underlying game is the same as those used above to illustrate TFT and TFT/MC, this institution defines a special role for one player, forcing the other players to report only to the director and to base their actions on only the director's replies. Moreover, the institution creates unique "actions" that the director can take, namely the accepting of queries and the sending of messages concerning the status of players. This apparent addition of new strategies to the game, however, is akin to the apparent introduction of new rules discussed after theorem 2: the underlying game really remains constant, and only the equilibrium has new features. A player could have departed from TFT/MC and reported other players' statuses all she wanted under the equilibrium of theorem 2, assuming that those messages were in the language; but such reports would not, in that equilibrium, have affected the

TABLE 4. Examples of Bound for Theorem 3

— *c* at .01 below Theorem 2's bound for $N = 100$									
alpha		1.1	1.1	1.1	2	2	2	2	4	4
beta		0.1	0.5	3	1.1	1.5	3	5	2.1	3
c		0.010	0.010	0.010	0.010	0.010	0.010	0.010	0.001	0.010
N	5	0.130	0.410	0.804	0.602	0.673	0.804	0.872	0.976	0.804
	10	0.112	0.369	0.776	0.560	0.634	0.776	0.852	0.972	0.776
	30	0.104	0.350	0.761	0.540	0.615	0.761	0.841	0.969	0.761
	100	0.102	0.345	0.756	0.534	0.609	0.756	0.838	0.969	0.756

— Very large *c* ($c = .25$)									
alpha		1.1	1.1	1.1	2	2	2	2	4	4
beta		0.1	0.5	3	1.1	1.5	3	5	2.1	3
N	5	0.483	0.667	0.897	0.783	0.824	0.897	0.933	x	0.897
	10	0.441	0.628	0.880	0.752	0.797	0.880	0.922	x	0.880
	30	0.420	0.608	0.871	0.737	0.784	0.871	0.916	x	0.871
	100	0.414	0.602	0.868	0.732	0.780	0.868	0.914	x	0.868

note: "x" denotes that *c* exceeds its upper limits for these parameter values.

actions of other players. Likewise, players other than the director could make such statements by departing from TFT/CC, but other players will react only to the director. The TFT/CC institution presents the players with rules that they must, out of their own self-interest, follow; but a change in the game's parameters, such as a lowering of the discount factor, could render those rules ineffective and unenforceable.

One could view the director as a third-party enforcer in this model, since the director in effect pronounces a sentence on the deviant player, a sentence that will then be carried out by rational players. In a more complex model, one could create even more explicit equilibrium punishment schemes, in which a player is designated as "enforcer" and whose instructions to punish are obeyed by a set of deputies. This kind of internal enforcement differs critically from the "third-party" enforcement often used to explain cooperation in collective-action models, however. The designation of, actions of, and obedience to the enforcer must be made in the players' interest for such a system to be in equilibrium. The simple model of TFT/CC in $G^*(\delta)$ illustrates exactly how such a system can be specified. Likewise it should be possible to identify equilibria in more complex models in which a designated "leader" gives "orders" that are "obeyed" by the players, and whose disobedience is punished. Again, all of the required actions and sanctions must be made compatible with rational behavior by all players, including the director, who must be willing to order the actions when appropriate, and willing to forbear punishment except when appropriate, an issue to which I turn in the next section. This, I argue, is how real-life institutions work.

The reader may have noticed that I have said nothing about how such institutions may come to exist. This is a nontrivial question since there are many possible institutions even for such a simple model as $G^*(\delta)$, particularly when communication is allowed, and even if the players all expected to use TFT/CC they would still have to agree on who was to be the director. I return to this issue in the concluding section.

5. Closing the Model: Who Directs the Director?

The model so far omits two important possibilities: that the director might not be willing to serve, or that the director might engage in corruption. To bring closure to the model of institutions as equilibria, it is necessary to provide the necessary inducements and deterrence within the game itself. Suppose that the director collects a fee ϕ each time any player communicates with the director in phases 2 or 5. Then the total cost to a player of communicating with the director becomes $d = c + \phi$ (where c is the inherent cost of communication, as in the model of sections 3 and 4), and each transaction between players in cooperation status using the equilibrium strategy yields the director a payoff of 4ϕ. To make players indifferent between serving as director and being active players, set ϕ so that the total payoff from serving as director equals that from being a player: in terms of per-period payoffs, $4\phi(N - 2)/2 = (1 - 2d)(N - 2)/(N - 1)$, that is,

$$\phi = \frac{1 - 2c}{2N}.$$

Naturally, for TFT/CC to be an equilibrium, all the conditions in theorem 3 must hold for d and not just for c; but with a large group, the difference ϕ will be small.

This leaves the issue of corruption. If the game were to incorporate opportunities for additional communication and for transfers of wealth among players, it would become possible for the director to extort money from a player under the threat that, if the player did not pay the extortion money, the director would falsely report him as being in punishment status. Or, a player in punishment status could bribe the director to falsely report that he was in cooperation status. Several methods may be used to prevent such corruption. First, the players could monitor the director and apply some form of punishment to a director discovered to be corrupt. This approach would impose monitoring costs, and would require additional institutional structure (i.e., a more detailed specification of equilibrium behavior in an appropriately modified version of the game) to carry out the monitoring and punishment. Second, the availability of several directors among whom players could choose by mutual consent could suppress corruption through competition. Third, the refusal of players to continue to cooperate when a director committed extortion would threaten a corrupt director with the loss of the fee from successful transactions.

In the remainder of this section, the latter approach, resembling that used by Milgrom, North, and Weingast to achieve a similar goal, is used in a modified version of the model to demonstrate how to discourage corruption. More elaborate means would be necessary to minimize all forms of corruption, and the costs of these means would add further conditions on the possibility of cooperation. This simple model, however, will serve to demonstrate all of the important building blocks of institutions among rational actors.

To make it possible for the director to extort the players, add a second communication phase 3a, which immediately follows phase 3.

We now assume that it is possible for the director, in response in phase 3 to a player's query, to extort the player rather than answer the question: only in return for an immediate extra payment B in phase 3a (for which there is no additional communication cost) will the director report the player to be in cooperation status. If the payment is refused, the director will falsely report the player to be in punishment status. I assume that this threat is credible, and demonstrate how it can nevertheless be deterred in an equilibrium that in all other respects is subgame perfect.

In the new phase, 3a, the extorted player may either pay the director the amount B demanded, or else pay a communication cost c to warn his partner that the director has acted corruptly. Another extra stage, 3b, is added so that the director may reply to the queries, truthfully or otherwise. Players are assumed to be unable to distinguish, simply from the timing of replies, between corrupt and honest behavior by the director.

To identify an equilibrium that supports cooperation while preventing extortion, suppose that the director now follows strategy $A*$:

3. If a querying player has ever before acquiesced to an extortion attempt and is paired with a partner other than one cheated in the immediately preceding iteration, demand a payment $\alpha - d - \phi/(N - 3)$, unless a larger payment has ever been demanded of a player who had acquiesced at some earlier time; in the latter case, demand a payment of α. Otherwise, take no action;

3b. If a player has refused an extortion attempt, and his partner has queried, report the player as being in punishment status; otherwise, if a player defected or failed to report on the previous iteration due to an attempt to extort one or both players, then report that player to be in cooperation status; otherwise, report honestly as in strategy A;

and otherwise follow A. Suppose further that players 2 through N follow the "antiextortion strategy" (AES). This strategy modifies TFT/CC by stipulating that any player who fails to pay the director's ϕ enters punishment status, and by adding the following instructions:

2. A player who has entered permanent punishment status (see instructions for phase 5 below) does not report; otherwise, report;

3a. A player who is extorted and who has made any extortion payment in the past pays any amount demanded up to and including α, unless in permanent punishment status (but if a higher payment is demanded, or if in permanent punishment status, pays nothing); a player who is extorted, and has never acquiesced to extortion previously, refuses any payment and communicates to her partner (at cost c) that extortion has been attempted;

4. If an extortion attempt has been reported by either player, then D; if no extortion attempt was made and none has ever been paid, follow TFT/CC. If an extortion payment was demanded, or no payment was demanded but extortion has been paid previously, then D;   *punish those who comply*

5. If an extortion attempt was reported by either player in (3a) and both players played D as a result in phase 4, then do not report; if no extortion attempt was made and none has ever been paid, follow TFT/CC. A player who has ever made an extortion payment does not report. If an extortion demand of more than $\alpha - d - \phi/(N - 3)$ was made in (3a), enter permanent punishment status (never report or cooperate in any future iteration).

Under this strategy, no extortion should ever take place, and if it does no payment should ever be made. The final result, then, is:

THEOREM 4. *The strategy profile in which player 1 uses A^* and players 2 through N use AES is a perfect Bayesian equilibrium (even assuming that the director can commit to his extortion threat) for sufficiently large δ, provided that the other conditions of theorem 3 are met with d in place of c.*

Obviously the conditions of theorem 4 are slightly more stringent than those of theorem 3: besides supporting the increased communication cost d, it must also now be rational for the extorted player to resist.[12]

This is the kind of closure required to really explain an institution. Notice that the equilibrium defines an organizational form, puts an individual in a position of authority, mandates and carries out enforcement (in this case decentralized), and thus "constrains the behavior" of the individuals involved. The institution thus defined requires no outside enforcement, nor does it depend on any irrational commitment to observe or enforce the equilibrium. Rather, the institution is no more than a regular behavior pattern sustained by mutual expectations about the actions that others will take when anyone violates the rules — whether the violation be defection, lying, nonpayment of fees, extortion, or malfeasance in office. The institution is just an equilibrium.

6. Conclusions

Using a modified version of the repeated two-player PD game, I have demonstrated various kinds of equilibria and the conditions under which they can support cooperation. These range from a collection of unconnected two-person reciprocity arrangements that, taken together, would not qualify as an institution, to a complex combination of expectations, required communication, and formal roles that serve to provide monitoring and sanctions and to ensure against malfeasance. For large groups or groups with significant costs of communication, the formal institution makes cooperation possible while the series of informal understandings does not.

Another way to restate the point of this whole exercise is that there is, strictly speaking, no separate animal that we can identify as an institution. There is only rational behavior, conditioned on expectations about the behavior and reactions of others. When these expectations about others' behavior take on a particularly clear and concrete form across individuals, when they apply to situations that recur over a long period of time, and especially when they involve highly variegated and specific expectations about the different roles of different actors in determining what actions others should take, we often collect these expectations and strategies under the heading of *institution*. This is not to say that institutions do not exist. Rather, it is to say that there are no institutional "constraints" or "preferences" aside from those arising out of the mutual expectations of individuals and their intentions to react in specific ways to the actions of others, all in an attempt to maximize utility in a setting of interdependency. *Institution* is just a name we give to certain parts of certain kinds of equilibria.

The idea of institutions as equilibria can be fruitfully applied to analyze the stability and effects of institutions in various areas of social life. Such an analysis would begin by portraying the game that underlies a given institution: the production of value, the opportunity for gains from trade, cooperation, coordination, or whatever. Along with this basic interaction, most institutions depend upon information transfer, and so opportunities for communication must be built into the game. The institutions and behavior observed in real life should constitute an equilibrium to the game so constructed. An examination of how the model's equilibrium behavior varies with variations in the game's parameters (payoffs, number of players, discount factors, etc.) then provides predictions about how marginal changes in the real-world environment will influence real-world behavior. It may be possible to identify parameter changes under which the observed institutional features will cease to be in equilibrium (as happens in the hypothetical institutions modeled in the previous section if the discount factor drops below a certain value). Further, interrogation of the model yields results concerning Pareto improvements that might be available under alternative equilibria, or strategic opportunities for coalitions. Empirical analysis of such a model would consist of tests of those comparative statics results, along with the detection of infrequent behavioral patterns predicted by the model but not previously noticed in the real-world case at hand.

Looking at institutions as equilibria, it is possible to understand institutions themselves in terms similar to those in which we understand rational action within them. One can describe institutions that are stable at one time but change or fall apart at another, without appealing in one's analysis to exogenous forces other than the revelation of information in the course of play or some exogenous parameter shift. Such an analysis generates predictions for the stability and instability of the institution in the form of theoretical responses of player behavior to the parameters of the game. In short, this approach is a useful tool to guide empirical study of institutions. It can clarify the nature and workings of real-life institutions either through formal game-theoretic modeling or through informal application of the principles.

In the two sections that follow I illustrate this approach, first with a new informal application to an existing controversy, and then with interpretations of several analyses already in the literature. The section following that discusses the problems of institutional formation, and of their functionality or dysfunctionality for the welfare of their participants.

Congressional Committees and the *ex Post Veto*

The exchange between Shepsle and Weingast (1987) and Krehbiel (Krehbiel, Shepsle, and Weingast 1987) concerning the foundation of committee power and the control of interchamber conferences to resolve bills in the U.S. Congress provides a nice illustration of how an informal application of the institutions-as-equilibria approach can clarify our thinking about a specific political institution. Shepsle and Weingast, using a pure institutions-as-constraints analysis, conclude that committees' control of the introduction of bills together with their ability to kill a bill at the conference stage if it is amended beyond their liking, the *ex post veto* power, enables them to extensively control legislation within their respective jurisdictional areas. In particular, Shepsle and Weingast discount norm-based theories of "deference to committees" to account for apparent committee power, arguing that there are insufficient means to protect such informal reciprocal agreements from the ubiquitous opportunities for "reneging and opportunistic behavior."[13] Instead, committee power must be accounted for by more formal means of enforcement, and the *ex post veto* is key among them. According to Shepsle and Weingast, this *ex post veto* power derives from committees' nearly automatic ability to supply members for conference committees, and from standard floor procedures that effectively constrain the House and Senate, when voting on conference committee reports, to a simple up-or-down vote.

Krehbiel criticizes this view, arguing that committees hold no such power because a majority in either chamber (he concentrates on the House, as do Shepsle and Weingast) can easily override any committee attempt to exercise a conference-stage veto by using other procedures at their disposal, such as instructing their delegates to the conference committee, bargaining directly with the other chamber without going to conference, or discharging the conferees and reclaiming the bill. Shepsle and Weingast respond, in part, by pointing out that on major bills the process nearly always operates as they have described, and that there are occasional instances (at least during the strong committee era preceding the 1970s) of conference committees killing bills in a manner consistent with the *ex post veto* story. This indicates, say Shepsle and Weingast, that committees effectively have the *ex post veto* power even though methods of circumvention are available. Presumably, they conclude, the *cost* of circumventing the conference committee on a major issue is usually prohibitive. However, they leave vague the nature of these costs, which are unobservable and, as they and Krehbiel all point out, can only be inferred after the fact, when we can observe the use or disuse of the methods of circumvention.

The institutions-as-equilibrium approach provides a clearer view of the nature of such process-based power, giving a solid theoretical basis to the "cost" that holds conference procedures in place, and forcing a modification of Shepsle and Weingast's view of the inefficacy of informally enforced agreements.[14] Consider the problem that conference procedures are created to address. When the two chambers pass bills that differ in many respects, and that elicit a whole spectrum of opinion on each point of disagreement in each chamber, the problem of negotiating a compromise bill is a messy one. If not managed correctly, the negotiation promises to be time- and effort-consuming and has a large probability of failing; meanwhile, other goals of the legislators involved in the negotiation go unaddressed. In any such bargaining process, efficiency requires that an acceptable offer be generated as quickly as possible; even though that offer may be better for some members of a majority than for others, its quick acceptance would then clear the way for all of them to consider other matters and address other goals, including those of members whose needs were not completely met by this bill. In short, this is a garden-variety problem of coordination with "mixed motives" (Schelling 1960).

Congress has developed several methods for conducting this bargaining that correspond to Krehbiel's list of circumvention methods

(Krehbiel, Shepsle, and Weingast 1987, 930–31). One chamber can simply accept the bill passed by the other chamber, a useful device when there is little disagreement between some pair of majorities. When there is moderate disagreement, the chambers can "message" a bill back and forth, each either insisting on its own provisions or concurring in the other's. This is a more ponderous method, since each acceptance or counteroffer must be agreed on through a parliamentary process involving the whole chamber. The conference process offers a more streamlined way to generate a compromise that majorities in both chambers can live with: negotiation is conducted by a small group of conferees, and the proposal typically gets only an up-or-down vote in the two chambers. If either (1) the conferees represent a wide range of opinions from each chamber, or (2) members of each chamber are willing (in the expectation of similar future considerations) to allow their conferees wide latitude, then the conference process can generate an acceptable proposal much more easily and quickly than could messaging between the two chambers.

In order for a chamber majority to "roll," or amend the report of, a conference committee, it is necessary to put together the necessary voting coalition in one's own chamber to agree on an alternative also acceptable to some majority within the other chamber. This is another complicated bargaining problem, and if the original conference report is not too bad, attempting to amend it may just not be worth the trouble; aside from the costly effort involved, there is again usually a high probability of failure. As a result, the members of the conference committee, since they have some leeway to propose various compromise bills, can propose ones to their own liking. If the original conference committee fails to reach an agreement (even if "on purpose," as the Shepsle-Weingast *ex post veto* threatens), it may likewise not be worth the trouble to put together an alternative conference committee or to use more cumbersome means to produce a compromise bill.

Notice that the appointment of conferees is itself a bargaining or coordination problem in the chamber, given that the conference procedure itself is in place. In the absence of some standardized, generally accepted method (such as the Speaker appointing members of the committee and subcommittee of original jurisdiction), identifying a group of conferees acceptable to a majority may again cost more than it is worth in terms of time and effort forgone for other purposes. The result is that the people who get to select the point of coordination (here, the conferees) have a measure of real power relative to other participants.[15]

In short, if for present purposes we take other legislative rules and procedures as fixed, the "institution" of the committee-dominated conference process is an equilibrium (and a welfare-enhancing one, at least if you are often in the majority) in the underlying coordination game of reaching agreement between the chambers. This view of the process identifies the cost of overriding the conference committee as a function of the difficulty of the coordination problem that members must face if they pursue an override. More extensive disagreement between and within chambers makes an override more costly. For example, the presence of organizational alternatives to the conference committee, such as a preexisting, informal "caucus" with many members and similar goals on the bill, makes it easier and therefore less costly to roll the conference committee. When the value of opportunities forgone due to the override attempt is high, such as late in a Congress in which many important bills remain to be considered, the override is more costly. Overall, the trick for conference committee members is to moderate the extent to which they change (or eliminate) the content of bills so as to stay within the limits that define whether rolling the committee is worthwhile. True to Krehbiel's argument, there are clearly limits on the *ex post veto* power. True to that of Shepsle and Weingast, however, standing committees would be weaker if they did not have this opportunity to modify the bill after it leaves the floor, and did not benefit from the chamber majority's inclination to accept the conference report as a coordination solution.

A more formal model would have to include a more elaborate specification of the game underlying the legislative process, and would address a wide array of procedural rules than just the conference provisions, since ramifications of flouting the conference committee could spill over into other areas of legislative politics. The maintenance of an effective conference procedure is a collective good for most members of Congress; members may therefore design a system in which respect for the conference process can be enforced partly by sanctions outside that process, such as by a committee in the consideration of a later bill, or by party leaders in the awarding of valued perquisites (in which case a stronger legislative party organization ought to cause stronger conference committees). The institutions-as-equilibrium approach views all such legislative rules, norms, and prerogatives as being enforced within the context of equilibrium in the underlying game. Formal rules and unwritten norms alike must ultimately be enforced through the expectations and rational behavior of members. This view calls into question, then, the broad argument of Shepsle and Weingast that informal agreements are unsustainable due to the nature of legislative interactions. I would argue instead that *all* rule enforcement is endogenous, and that, just as the maintenance of informal agreements is always problematic, so is the enforcement of formal rules. Perhaps Shepsle and Weingast's claim should be modified to say that it is harder to enforce particular agreements about legislative specifics than to enforce broad agreements about legislative procedure. Such a claim, however, would require much more empirical or theoretical support than it has accumulated in the literature thus far.

Finally, the institutions-as-equilibrium model increases the analyst's ability to conduct "comparative statics" analysis of institutions, a function that Shepsle and Weingast identify as a key useful feature of their analysis. Their suggestion is that new procedures introduced beginning in the early 1970s weakened the *ex post veto* consistent with Krehbiel's general thrust, and that the effect on legislative outcomes of such rule changes should be predictable using the *ex post veto* model as a starting point.[16] The institutions-as-equilibria model can go much further, however, by providing a direct model of the underpinnings of the institution to subject to comparative statics analysis. Such analysis could treat institutional change in a much less ad hoc fashion than is possible with the Shepsle-Weingast model. In particular, the present model offers predictions on the relationship between the strength of the *ex post veto* and various prior, observable correlates of override costs.

Some Existing Studies of Real Institutions as Equilibria

Actually, a few analyses of this general type have already appeared in the literature, although they have probably not been recognized by most readers as a genre. The brief examples used by Schotter (1981, chaps. 1–2) to introduce his "economic" theory of institutions are the first of which I am aware. The first extended analysis is that of Milgrom, North, and Weingast (1990), who study the Law Merchant, an institution for long-distance trading in eleventh-century Europe. Milgrom et al. construct a stylized model of trading in which numerous merchants deal exactly once with each partner, so that deterrence of cheating requires some method for enforcing sanctions across interactions. The TFT/CC and AES institutions above are close relatives of the Law Merchant system that Milgrom et al. derive. The analyses by Greif, Milgrom, and Weingast (1990) of merchant guild organizations, and by Greif (1991) of Genoese and Maghribi traders' use of trade agents, take similar approaches.

In her study of the changing institutional structure of the U.S. Senate, Sinclair (1989) analyzes norms by treating them as cooperative equilibria in a repeated PD, and informally examines the properties of those equilibria as external conditions change, exactly as the institutions-as-equilibria approach suggests. In a series of more formal analyses of the impact of parliamentary procedure in the legislature, Baron and Ferejohn (1989) and Baron (1989, 1991) stylize the process of recognition, proposal, and voting on the floor as a specialized type of bargaining game. Important features of formal and informal legislative practices such as conditions governing the breadth of distribution of benefits among the members; conditions under which amendments will or will not be proposed under an open rule; and conditions under which members prefer closed or open rules appear as equilibrium behavior in this game. In other words, there is an underlying game of recognition, proposal, and majority-rule voting (whose rules are assumed) that members of a legislature must play; within that, they may adopt various recognition rules, amendment rules, and strategies, governed by equilibria that depend on the parameters of the game. Similarly to my PD illustration and to Sinclair's (1989) analysis of Senatorial norms, then, certain institutional features may persist as equilibrium behavior patterns in the underlying game, depending on conditions.[17]

The Emergence and Initiation of Institutions

The institutions-as-equilibria approach as presented in this chapter says nothing directly about the emergence of institutions. Indeed, the traditional equilibrium approach explicitly ignores such questions, assuming in effect that the players arrive unanimously at identical equilibrium expectations through a priori reasoning. However, this leaves several important matters to be resolved: how likely is a given institution (equilibrium) to arise in real life? Can it rise spontaneously or does it require explicit specification and agreement by members of the group? If it is formed by explicit agreement, what considerations govern the group's choice among possible institutions?

The spontaneous emergence of an institution is fundamentally a problem of coordination. In the model examined in this paper, several different institutions are derived, and many more are possible; even within the TFT/CC definition, there is the question of which player comes to be agreed upon as the "director." The problem for the players is to arrive together at one such equilibrium. Still, the institutions in this chapter are not all that complex, and over an extended period of play it is reasonable to expect that similar institutions could arise by trial and error with a minimum of purposeful planning. A good example of the partly spontaneous emergence of an institution of similar complexity might be the gradual formation of stock exchanges such as the London Exchange in the early eighteenth century (Hirst 1948) and the American Exchange in the late nineteenth (Sobel 1970) as central locations for the facilitation of trade in bonds and corporate shares. Only after the initial, decentralized emergence of securities trading in a central location did the rules of the Exchange become matters of authoritative, centralized decision making.

Recently, new game-theoretic techniques have been suggested to explicitly address the emergence of equilibria in games. In the "evolutionary" or "learning" approach, for example, the mix of strategies used by the set of players evolves through a process of imitative learning or natural selection to a stable equilibrium state (see, for example, Maynard Smith 1982 and Selten 1983); the set of such equilibrium states is closely related to the set of Nash equilibria, and the well-behaved members of either set generally tend to belong to both.[18] Another approach, due to Crawford and Haller (1990), models the process of learning to coordinate through trial and error in a game of pure coordination. Such models, building on a foundation of game-theoretic equilibrium analysis, hold out the hope of more explicit models of the spontaneous emergence of institutions. In all of them, Nash equilibria are, generally speaking, the ultimate outcomes; but the choice among equilibria depends on initial conditions, on the assumptions about the dynamic process, and on the realizations of random variables such as when mixed strategies are played out or when moves by "nature" take place.

Hechter (1990a) contrasts the latter approaches, which he labels "invisible-hand" theories of institutional formation, with more purposeful design of institutions through "social contract." Should players explicitly agree on a particular equilibrium of the underlying game as an institution, and then in some sense end their communication about institutional design, they will have the proper incentives to adhere to the agreement since it is an equilibrium. We might thus portray the process of creating an institution as a bargaining problem, in which participants anticipate the effects on them as individuals of each possible (equilibrium) institutional arrangement. Any agreement reached is then automatically enforced (since it is self-enforcing), as required for a bargaining problem. All of the potential problems of bargaining, such as incomplete information about other players' preferences, could then intervene to forestall the reaching of any agreement. Alternatively and equivalently, a prominent and acceptable suggestion of an equilibrium institution by a leader, in the absence of coherent multilateral communication among players, can provide a "focal point" (Schelling 1960) that all players find advantageous to follow. Obviously combinations of these two processes are possible as well — consider the U.S. constitutional convention of 1787, in which a small group of prominent men thrashed out an agreement that a wider group of citizens then agreed to support.

Hechter argues that interesting real-world institutions more often emerge through contract than via the invisible hand. While this may be true (I remain agnostic, and in any event it depends on the universe of institutions being examined), in real-world negotiations it is generally impossible to specify all contingencies in such a contract. Much is either left up to customary interpretations (that often have emerged spontaneously) or determined along the way through a trial-and-error working out of the contract's unspecified details. The development of the U.S. Constitution is a perfect example of such a process. It is the quintessential social contract, but many hugely important details of that institution have been worked out on the fly through presidential interpretations, court decisions, and public opinion. Thus, in contemplating the development of institutions as equilibria, it pays to consider the nature of spontaneous emergence.

The cooperative equilibria derived in this chapter could be imagined either to have evolved through trial and error or to have resulted from some initial communication phase in which the players made suggestions about how to proceed. However, the literature still lacks an explicit model of the evolution of equilibria in repeated games, where the space of possible strategies is much more complicated than in a simple normal-form game. A demonstration of the evolution of equilibria in that context would make it more plausible that institutions as equilibria could actually emerge in the real world.

It is important to keep in mind that institutions, whether designed or spontaneous, can be dysfunctional as well as functional. A small coalition might agree to cooperate in such a way that they can suppress by violence the efforts of other players to obtain higher payoffs, creating an institution that makes the vast majority worse off than they would be without any organization at all. Or, an evolutionary process can result in a Pareto-inferior equilibrium, such as in the example of parents choosing the sex or height of their children (Schelling 1978, chap. 6), where the pressure to be just slightly different leads to an extreme outcome making all people worse off than if they had sought no advantage. Presumably, when groups design institutions they attempt to make at least some members of the group better off; and evolutionary processes among groups of strategic and communicative players may be relatively easy to steer away from dysfunctional results. However, the theory of institutions as equilibria says nothing in general about the functionality of institutions, consistent with the variety of welfare effects seen to flow from real-life institutions.

Conclusion

Schotter's (1981) "economic" treatment of social institutions underlies the general idea presented here, that institutions are equilibria. This chapter has developed and specialized Schotter's idea, applying it to "underlying games" involving problems of cooperation and opportunities for communication. The generality and parsimony of this approach, along with its ready applicability to specialized empirical analysis as demonstrated by Milgrom et al., Baron, and others, should make it a primary method for analysts of all kinds of institutions, from the most particular matters of legislative procedure to the broadest aspects of social order. Viewing institutions as equilibria in some underlying, unalterable game makes it possible for the first time to examine under a single model both behavior within institutions and change of institutions.

APPENDIX: PROOFS OF LEMMA AND THEOREMS

Proof of Lemma: The proof uses induction to calculate the expected discounted present value (DPV) of interactions with a given partner, ignoring the current period; it is shown that this is equal to the sum over $t = 1$ to infinity of $\gamma^t y$, where y is the payoff in each period and γ is as defined in the lemma. Thus γ is the effective discount factor as required. For notational convenience, let $q = 1/(N - 1)$, the probability of meeting a given partner on a given turn.

First, calculate the expected DPV of the payoff from the next single interaction with the given player. This will be the sum from periods 1 through infinity following the present period of the probability of having the next interaction with the partner in that period, times the discounted payoff if that happens:

$$\sum_{t=1}^{\infty} (1 - q)^{t-1} q \delta^t y = y \frac{\delta q}{1 - \delta(1 - q)} = \gamma y,$$

where γ is as defined in the statement of the lemma.

Now, consider the expected DPV of the payoff from the $(T + 1)$-th encounter with this partner after the current period, assuming that the payoff from the T-th encounter is $\gamma^T y$. The probability of the first encounter taking place t periods after the present is $(1 - q)^{t-1} q$; once that happens in period t, the expected DPV (discounting from the present period, $t = 0$) of the T-th encounter thereafter is $\delta^t \gamma^T y$. Summing over t gives the expected DPV of the $(T + 1)$-th encounter from the present:

$$\sum_{t=1}^{\infty} (1 - q)^{t-1} q \delta^t \gamma^T y = \gamma^T y \delta q \sum_{t=1}^{\infty} (1 - q)^{t-1} \delta^{t-1}$$

$$= \gamma^T y \frac{\delta q}{1 - \delta(1 - q)} = \gamma^{T+1} y.$$

Thus the expected DPV of all future interaction with the given partner is

$$\sum_{t=1}^{\infty} \gamma^t y = \sum_{t=1}^{\infty} \left[\frac{\delta q}{1 - \delta(1 - q)} \right]^t y,$$

and substituting $1/(N - 1)$ for q gives the desired result.   □

Method for proofs of theorems. All the proofs below proceed by demonstrating that there is no profitable one-period deviation from the equilibrium strategy; this includes deviations made *after* leaving the equilibrium path, since the equilibrium strategy specifies what is to be done in those situations as well. To see why this is sufficient, consider the following argument. When examining the incentives of a given player, the strategies assumed for all of the other players, along with the structure of the game, specify a dynamic programming problem for the given player. This is an infinite-horizon problem with discounting, so if there were some infinitely long sequence of departures from the specified strategy that made the player better off, there would also be a *finite* sequence of departures that improved payoff (since beyond some distant future point all further gains are minuscule once discounted back to the present). Suppose there is no single-period departure that alone makes the given player better off, however; then no longer-duration, finite-length sequence of departures will do so either, for in the next-to-last period of the sequence of departures, to depart for one more period cannot be profitable. Thus, in order to show that there can be no profitable departure of any duration from the specified strategy by a single player, it suffices to show that there is no profitable one-period departure.[19] Again, however, note that it is important to show that even if a player has departed from the strategy, it must then be optimal to carry out the appropriate off-equilibrium behavior specified by the strategy.

Proof of Theorem 1: Theorem 1 follows directly from the lemma, along with standard results of the repeated prisoner's dilemma;[20] it is proved here for completeness, as well as to give a simple illustration of the general technique of proof to be used subsequently. The standard proof is given in terms of γ, and the final result is obtained by application of the lemma.

Suppose that both players cooperated on the previous iteration (or that the game is in iteration 1). In such a situation, the DPV of all present and future payoffs to a player from adhering to TFT by cooperating on the current iteration, and then playing according to TFT thereafter (for a payoff of 1 in every period), can be written as $1 + \gamma + \gamma^2/(1 - \gamma)$. The payoff from the one-period deviation of defecting now and adhering to TFT in the future (including the consequent "restitution") is $\alpha - \gamma\beta + \gamma^2/(1 - \gamma)$. For cooperation to be the equilibrium move, then, requires $1 + \gamma \geq \alpha - \gamma\beta$, or, $\gamma \geq (\alpha - 1)/(\beta + 1)$. Using the lemma to substitute for γ gives the first bound stated in theorem 1.

Suppose that one player conformed to the equilibrium strategy on the previous iteration, but that the other deviated. TFT then calls for the conforming player to play D on the current iteration, which for any γ obviously gives a higher payoff than playing C since that D will not be punished subsequently. Consider the decision of the deviant. To return to the equilibrium path by playing C yields a payoff of $-\beta + \gamma + \gamma^2/(1 - \gamma)$. The one-time deviation of playing D now and then returning to TFT (that is, beginning "restitution" on the next iteration instead of the present one) pays $0 - \gamma\beta + \gamma^2/(1 - \gamma)$. Thus for TFT to be in equilibrium requires $-\beta + \gamma \geq -\gamma\beta$, or $\gamma \geq \beta/(1 + \beta)$. Applying the lemma gives the second bound stated in theorem 1.

These cases represent all of the possible situations in which a player could consider a one-period deviation from TFT; in each case, the one-period deviation would be unprofitable. Therefore the strategy profile in which both players use TFT is an equilibrium. $\Box$

Proof of Theorem 2: Phases 2 and 3 require only that the players not engage in costly communication that will in any case be ignored by other players using the assigned strategy. It remains only to show that there are no profitable one-period deviations beginning in phases 4 or 5.

In phase 4, if player i is in punishment status, playing C as prescribed by TFT/MC yields an expected payoff (in discounted present value from that point on) of

$$[-\beta - (N - 2)c] + \delta[1 - (N - 2)c] + \frac{\delta^2}{1 - \delta}[1 - (N - 2)c],$$

while playing D and then returning to TFT/MC would yield a payoff of

$$0 + \delta[-\beta - (N - 2)c] + \frac{\delta^2}{1 - \delta}[1 - (N - 2)c].$$

Thus, in order for TFT/MC to be in equilibrium we must have the latter no larger than the former, or

$$-\beta - (N - 2)c + \delta[1 - (N - 2)c] \geq \delta[-\beta - (N - 2)c].$$

By the second bound on δ given in the theorem, this condition is satisfied. Note that such a δ always exists since we assumed $c < 1/(N - 2)$.

Consider next a player in cooperation status in phase 4. If the player's partner is reported to be in punishment status, then obviously it is optimal for the player to defect as prescribed. If the partner is reported in cooperation status, playing C gives a payoff of $[1 - (N - 2)c]/(1 - \delta)$, which can be written as $[1 - (N - 2)c] + \delta[1 - (N - 2)c] + \delta^2/(1 - \delta)[1 - (N - 2)c]$, while deviating to D gives

$$\alpha - \delta[\beta + (N - 2)c] + \frac{\delta^2}{1 - \delta}[1 - (N - 2)c].$$

The resulting necessary condition for equilibrium is then

$$[1 - (N - 2)c](1 + \delta) \geq \alpha - \delta[\beta + (N - 2)c],$$

which reduces to

$$\delta \geq \frac{\alpha - 1 + (N - 2)c}{\beta + 1}.$$

Since we assumed $c < (2 - \alpha + \beta)/(N - 2)$, this can be satisfied by sufficiently large $\delta < 1$.

Finally, turn to phase 5. Obviously a player in punishment status will be content not to report, as prescribed. For a player in cooperation status, reporting yields a payoff of

$$-(N - 2)c + \frac{\delta}{1 - \delta}[1 - (N - 2)c] + \frac{\delta^2}{1 - \delta}[1 - (N - 2)c],$$

while failing to report at all puts the player into punishment status and yields a payoff of

$$0 + \delta[-\beta - (N - 2)c] + \frac{\delta^2}{1 - \delta}[1 - (N - 2)c].$$

The resulting equilibrium condition is

$$-\delta\beta - \delta(N - 2)c \leq -(N - 2)c + \delta[1 - (N - 2)c],$$

which reduces to

$$\delta \geq \frac{(N-2)c}{1+\beta}.$$

Thus again, sufficiently large $\delta < 1$ satisfies the condition. Notice that this right-hand side is smaller than that derived for cooperation status in phase 4, so the previous condition subsumes this one.

It remains to show that it is optimal in phase 5 to report to all of the remaining $N - 2$ players, rather than to just report to some of them. Let K be the number of players to whom player i reports in phase 5, $0 \leq K \leq N - 2$. Let $V_{ab}(K)$ represent the value of optimal continuation when player i's status is $a \in \{C,D\}$, i's current partner's status is $b \in \{C,D\}$, i reports to K other players in phase 5 of the current iteration and to $N - 2$ others thereafter, and all other players always report to all $N - 2$ other players in phase 5. Then in the next iteration, the probability that player i will meet one of the players to whom she reported is $(K + 1)/(N - 1)$ (the K to whom she reported plus her current partner), while her probability of meeting a player to whom she did not report, thus having to make restitution, is $(N - K - 2)/(N - 1)$. We can then write player i's total expected payoff beginning with phase 5 in the current iteration as

$$V_{ab}(K) = -Kc - \delta\left[\frac{K+1}{N-1}V_{cc}(N-2) + \frac{N-K-2}{N-1}V_{DC}(N-2)\right].$$

The derivative of $V_{ab}(K)$ with respect to K is

$$-c + \frac{\delta}{N-1}[V_{cc}(N-2) - V_{DC}(N-2)].$$

Clearly, $V_{CC}(K) \geq V_{DC}(K)$ for all K since in the former i's partner begins by cooperating, while in the latter the partner begins by defecting. Hence, as long as c is sufficiently small, the optimal K is as large as possible, that is, $K = N - 2$. The bracketed term in the derivative reduces to $1 + \beta$, giving the third bound on c in the statement of the theorem.   □

Note on the Proof of Theorem 2. There is no temptation for player i to falsely report that i's partner has played D in phase 5 since, because the partner will not know that i lied, the partner will assume that she is in cooperation status in the future and will not make restitution. If a player's report could be made known to that player's partner, a temptation to lie would be present—subgame perfection would require a player falsely reported in punishment status to behave as though really in punishment status, so lying would pay off if the liar met the same partner on the very next iteration. Thus, if the report were assumed to be known to the player's partner, the equilibrium behavior of theorem 2 could not be maintained without a modification of the equilibrium strategy to deter lying. This modification could be accomplished by the addition of a kind of tit-for-tat in truthful reporting, that is, a separate punishment scheme in which a player whose partner lies retaliates by lying on the next meeting between the same two players in which both are in cooperation status. This would add a second condition on the discount factor, but the new condition would be less stringent than that presently given in theorem 1 since, although the retaliation is heavily discounted, the reward from lying is itself discounted, accruing as it does only with probability $1/(N - 1)$. Details of this proof are available from the author on request. A similar modification would apply to theorem 3.

Proof of Theorem 3: The director has no incentive to violate any of the strategy's prescriptions, so consider the incentives of players 2 through N. In phase 2, obviously no such player in punishment status will wish to query. For a player in cooperation status, querying gives a payoff of

$$1 - 2c + \frac{\delta}{1 - \delta} (1 - 2c) \frac{N - 2}{N - 1},$$

while failing to query yields

$$-\beta - c - \frac{\delta}{1 - \delta} (1 - 2c) \frac{N - 2}{N - 1}.$$

The resulting condition for equilibrium is simply $1 - 2c \geq -\beta - c$, which is true since $0 < c < \frac{1}{2}$ and $\beta > 0$.

In phase 4 when the player is in punishment status, cooperating as prescribed gives a payoff of

$$-\beta - c + \frac{\delta}{1 - \delta} (1 - 2c) \frac{N - 2}{N - 1},$$

while defecting yields 0 in the present period and a payoff of X beginning with the next period, where

$$X = \frac{N-2}{N-1}\left[-\beta - c + \frac{\delta}{1-\delta}(1-2c)\frac{N-2}{N-1}\right] + \frac{1}{N-1}\delta X,$$

for a total payoff of δX for defecting. (The complicated structure here is due to the fact that a deviant cannot make "restitution" until she is paired with a player other than the director; this occurs in any given stage with probability $(N-2)/(N-1)$.) Solving for X,

$$X = \frac{N-2}{N-1-\delta}\left[-\beta - c + \frac{\delta}{1-\delta}(1-2c)\frac{N-2}{N-1}\right],$$

so the relevant equilibrium condition is

$$-\beta - c + \frac{\delta}{1-\delta}(1-2c)\frac{N-2}{N-1} \geq \delta\frac{N-2}{N-1-\delta}\left[-\beta - c + \frac{\delta}{1-\delta}(1-2c)\frac{N-2}{N-1}\right],$$

which is true if and only if

$$-\beta - c + \frac{\delta}{1-\delta}(1-2c)\frac{N-2}{N-1} \geq 0;$$

that is,

$$\delta \geq \frac{\beta+c}{\beta + c + (1-2c)\dfrac{N-2}{N-1}}.$$

The latter is always possible for sufficiently large $\delta < 1$ since $c < \frac{1}{2}$.

If a player is in cooperation status in phase 4 and his partner is in punishment status, obviously there is no reason not to play D as prescribed. If both the player and the partner are in cooperation status, the payoff to playing C is

$$1 - c + \frac{\delta}{1-\delta}(1-2c)\frac{N-2}{N-1},$$

while the payoff from defecting is $\alpha + \delta X$, where X is as defined above. Moving α to the left-hand side, the condition for equilibrium in cooperation status in phase 4 becomes

$$-\alpha - c + 1 + \frac{\delta}{1-\delta}(1-2c)\frac{N-2}{N-1} \geq \frac{\delta(N-2)}{N-1-\delta}\left[-\beta - c + \frac{\delta}{1-\delta}(1-2c)\frac{N-2}{N-1}\right].$$

The resulting condition on δ is thus

$$\delta \geq \frac{(N-1)(\alpha - 1 + c)}{(N-3)(\beta - c + 1) + \alpha + \beta}$$

This is true for sufficiently large $\delta < 1$, provided that the right-hand side is less than 1, which it is provided $c < 1 - (\alpha - \beta)/2$.

In phase 5, a player in punishment status obviously will not wish to report. A player in cooperation status gains $-c + (1 - 2c)\delta(N - 2)/[(1 - \delta)(N - 1)]$ by reporting, and $0 + \delta X$ by failing to report, where X is as defined above. The resulting equilibrium condition is the same as that derived above for punishment status in phase 4, except that $-\beta$ is removed from the left-hand side. Thus the condition above is sufficient to make the cooperation-status player report in phase 5 as well. Finally, an argument similar to that explained in the note on the proof of theorem 2 shows that a player has no incentive to report falsely in phase 5.   □

Proof of Theorem 4: To begin with, it is necessary to calculate the optimal extortion payments for the director to demand when, off the equilibrium path, a player is acquiescing to extortion. Once a player acquiesces, he is forever extorted and forever acquiesces. On each iteration, he pays the demand, is reported (falsely) to be in cooperation status, plays D and does not report in phase 5. The only exception is when he is paired with the director (probability $1/(N - 1)$), or with the same partner as was cheated on the previous turn, and who would recognize the director's false report. The optimal payment to demand, then, is one that leaves the victim just indifferent between continuing this pattern and switching to permanent defection status, for a payment of 0 in perpetuity. A payment of $\alpha - d - \phi/(N - 3)$ accomplishes this exactly: the extorted player's present value payoff for the remainder of the game is

$$V_p = \frac{N-3}{N-1}\frac{\phi}{N-3} + \frac{-\phi}{N-1} + \delta V_p$$

and solving yields simply $V_p = 0$. This extortion strategy yields the director a present value payoff of

$$V_d = \frac{N-3}{N-1}(\alpha - c) + \frac{1}{N-1}0 + \frac{1}{N-1}\phi + \delta V_d$$

or simply $V_d = (N - 3)(\alpha - c)/[(N - 1)(1 - \delta)]$. Finally, this must be compared to an alternative extortion startegy available to the director: demand the largest possible payment that the player, having already paid the phase 2 reporting fee, will be willing to pay even if that results in the player subsequently entering permanent punishment phase. The corresponding payment would be just α, the amount the player can get from playing D on this iteration. For the director to eschew this larger demand requires $\alpha \leq V_d$; solving this inequality for δ yields the condition $\delta \geq 1 - [(N - 3)/(N - 1)][(\alpha - c)/\alpha]$. Thus for sufficiently large δ, the strategy of ongoing extortion is superior for the corrupt director.

For the director, in phase 3, if a player has never before paid extortion, then not extorting yields 2ϕ for the remainder of this period and 2ϕ per period in future interactions with the player in question. An extortion attempt yields 0 for the remainder of this turn and 2ϕ in the future, so honesty is the best policy. If a player has paid extortion before, not extorting yields 0 now and $\alpha - c - \phi/(N - 3)$ (that is, the $\alpha - d - \phi/(N - 3)$ extortion payment plus the ϕ in fees) per period thereafter in periods when the player is not matched with the same partner cheated on the previous turn (since according to this strategy the director will subsequently resume extortion), while extorting yields $\alpha - d$ now and $\alpha - c - \phi/(N - 3)$ per period in the future. Thus continued extortion would be rational for the director. Finally, notice that to report a nonpaying, cooperation-status player who refuses extortion as being in punishment status would result in a loss of the phase 5 payments; hence the director "forgives" a player who refuses to submit to extortion. (This is why it was necessary to assume at the outset that the director would carry out his one-period threat—even that would be irrational.)

Next consider the position of a player who has never paid extortion and is now extorted for a payment $B > 0$. Submitting to the demand would result in a future of constant, maximal extortion demands, so the payoff to submitting would be $\alpha - B$ for the remainder of this period and zero in every period thereafter. Refusing the demand and proceeding according to AES would result in a payment of c to warn the partner and no other payoff in the present period, and a resumption of cooperation in the next period. The relevant equilibrium condition is then

$$-c + \frac{\delta}{1 - \delta}(1 - 2d)\frac{N - 2}{N - 1} \geq \alpha - B.$$

This must hold for any $B > 0$; hence the condition for deterring an extortion attempt can be written by setting $B = 0$ and solving for δ, which gives

$$\delta \geq \frac{1 - 2d}{1 - 2d + (\alpha - c)\dfrac{N - 1}{N - 2}}.$$

To show that it will be rational for such a player to bear the cost of warning his partner, note that not warning results in the player entering punishment status due to the corrupt director's report. To restore cooperation (rational under TFT/CC given δ sufficiently large), the extorted player who does not warn will unilaterally play C, then report as always in phase 5; cooperation is restored in the next iteration. Thus the condition for warning one's partner is simply $-c \geq -\beta - d$, which always holds since $\beta + \phi > 0$.

Finally, suppose a player has paid extortion before, and now $\alpha - d - \phi/(N - 3)$ or less is demanded. Then not paying results in a payoff of 0 this turn, paying results in 0 or more, and all future periods will yield 0 in either case. If more than $\alpha - d - \phi/(N - 3)$ is demanded the player expects future demands of α. Obviously it is at least as good to be in punishment status forever (payoff 0) as to continue this extortion pattern. If the demand is no more than α, the player will pay it, play D, and then enter permanent punishment status. Larger demands will result in immediate refusal and permanent punishment status.   □

NOTES

Earlier versions of this chapter were presented at the Public Choice Society annual meetings, New Orleans, 20–22 March 1992, and at the Workshop on New Institutional Theory at Cornell University, 8–10 November 1991. The author is grateful to Victor Nee, Andy Rutten, and other participants in the workshop, as well as Jeffrey Banks, Jack Knight, Peter Stone, and David Weimer, for encouragement, comments, and helpful conversations. Research for this project was funded by the National Science Foundation through grants SES-8908226 and BNS-9700864, the latter through the Center for Advanced Study in the Behavioral Sciences, which generously supported the author as a fellow during 1990–91.

1. As quoted by Hechter, Opp, and Wippler 1990, 1.

2. A possible exception, close perhaps in spirit to rational-actor theories, is the approach of Robert Frank (1985, 1988), who attempts in several instances to derive unselfish preferences from selfish ones via evolutionary arguments. The origin of this idea lies in the explanation of "kinship altruism" given by Trivers (1974).

3. Alternatively, one might argue, along with March and Olsen (1989) and Johnson (1990), that institutions represent the limits of individuals' abilities to imagine alternative strategies, in effect specifying the strategy sets of the players in a game. I balk at this explanation of institutions' ability to constrain behavior

because it assumes away the creativity that people often bring to bear in attempting to gain advantage under social constraints. My own game-theoretic approach is already weak enough in this respect.

4. As a halfway measure, one might assume that certain stable background institutions define the underlying game, and then conduct an institutions-as-equilibria analysis to study the formation of additional institutions. Schotter's example of the institution of the week takes this form: trading institutions (e.g., the geographical location of a marketplace) are taken for granted, and the week evolves as an equilibrium solution to a coordination problem concerning the length of time between market days (Schotter 1981, 31–35)

5. This would rule out the often-cited legislative norm of reciprocity as an institution if the reciprocity were solely a matter between pairs of legislators. However, if a refusal to reciprocate with one partner were looked on by others as an indication of lack of trustworthiness, then the reciprocity would in effect be enforced by the whole group, and would be a real institution.

6. Normally, too, we consider a certain behavior pattern to be an institution only if it persists over a long period of time. For present purposes, the requirement that an institution be an equilibrium pattern of behavior captures this requirement. In a richer model than the one presented in this chapter, an equilibrium should be considered an institution only if it persists despite the occurrence of normal changes over time in the underlying game, such as when old players depart and new players enter the game.

7. "Social dilemma" is a term coined by Dawes, van de Kragt, and Orbell (1990) to describe situations in which some form of group coordination or cooperation can improve the welfare of all members of the group, but in which such coordination or cooperation runs somehow counter to the short-run incentives or abilities of the group's members. It includes prisoner's dilemma situations as well as a multitude of other public good, externality, provision, and participation problems.

8. The notation for G is identical to that used by Milgrom, North, and Weingast (1990) in order to facilitate comparisons.

9. This version of tit-for-tat was, to my knowledge, first suggested by Sugden (1986).

10. The equilibrium constructed in this section resembles the "Law Merchant System Strategy" (LMSS) central to Milgrom, North, and Weingast (1990), in its use of the pretrade (pre-PD) query and the central communicator. In the LMSS, a player whose partner deviates from cooperative play registers a complaint with the "judge," who assesses a fine against the deviant and reports the deviant to be a noncooperator until the fine is paid. The present model dispenses with such fines, instead simply making the director the reporter of whether a player is supposed to be punished, TFT style, in the play of the PD. Further, the present analysis considers the cost of communication, while that of Milgrom, North, and Weingast does not. My main point, however, is to make a direct comparison between this relatively highly structured equilibrium and the less structured ones presented in sections 2 and 3.

11. The reason for including the queries is so that the director can learn who is playing whom (and thereby identify anyone who fails to report in phase 5) without expending any search costs.

12. The reporting of extortion, it turns out, is possible under the same condition already required in theorem 5 in the text, using d.

13. The quote is from Krehbiel, Shepsle, and Weingast 1987, 936; see also Shepsle and Weingast 1987, 85–86.

14. The argument that informal agreements in a legislature are likely to fall prey to opportunism is first given in Weingast and Marshall 1988.

15. This effect, that the player selecting the coordination point has genuine "power," plays an important general role in the nature of political leadership. See Hardin 1990 and Calvert 1991.

16. Implicit in their theory is also the idea that changes in committee preferences can be used to predict changes in legislative outcomes, in a manner such as that described by Weingast (1981).

17. Note that in both Sinclair and in the Baron-Ferejohn work, some institutional features (e.g., basic parliamentary procedures) are taken as fixed so that others (e.g., reciprocity norms or party arrangements) may be studied. Such a "partial equilibrium" approach is likely to be the most useful in studying real-life institutional features.

18. See, for example, the study by Samuelson (1991), which derives a correspondence between "limit evolutionarily stable strategies," on the one hand, and pure-strategy Nash equilibria among strategies not weakly dominated and satisfying a property called "role-equivalence," on the other.

19. This is the strategy of proof adopted by Milgrom, North, and Weingast, which they describe as an appeal to the optimality principle of dynamic programming (1990, 8).

20. Such as Taylor 1976 or Axelrod 1981.

Models, Interpretations, and Theories: Constructing Explanations of Institutional Emergence and Change

Jack Knight

Rational-choice theories of institutional emergence and change take many forms. They all share an initial premise that social actors pursue some set of preferences in a rational way. This means that social actors seek to achieve their most-preferred outcome in the least costly manner. From this initial assumption, however, rational-choice theorists develop quite different explanations of how social institutions emerge and change. The main differences in the explanations of change lie in (1) the different ways in which the theorists conceive and model the basic social interactions that produce institutions and (2) the different features of the social context that they invoke in order to resolve the strategic problems inherent in these interactions (where the institutions are the product of repeated efforts to resolve these problems).

The significance of these differences for explanations of institutional change calls attention to the importance of some basic issues related to the use of rational-choice models in the construction of social-scientific explanations. Theory building involves more than the development of a model or the solving of a game. Explanations of social life require the demonstration of the interrelationship between models and the actual phenomenon to be explained. This requires that we give close attention to the fact that models require interpretation. In the process of interpretation, we assess the results derived from a model in light of several factors, the most important of which for purposes of explanation are (1) the initial assumptions used to develop the model, (2) the mechanisms invoked to solve the model, and (3) the more general theoretical framework of which the model and the resulting explanation are a part. Furthermore, this process of interpretation involves a reconsideration of both the assumptions and the mechanisms in light of the actual phenomenon to be explained.

Consider the relevance of this process of interpretation for rational-choice accounts of institutional change. As I will discuss in detail below, most rational-choice accounts of institutional emergence and change employ some model involving a game with multiple equilibria. Related to each equilibrium is an institution (a rule of action) that would, if selected, resolve the strategic problem inherent in a situation in which there are a number of ways of doing something and the task is to establish a common way of doing it. To solve these games, we must invoke a mechanism (either a refinement of the assumption of rational decision making or some feature of the social context) to explain why the actors arrive at one of these equilibria and thus institutionalize a particular rule of action.

The main focus of the interpretive analysis is on the relationship between the analytical results derived from the rational-choice model and the substantive conclusions about institutional emergence and change. The explanatory force of this relationship rests in large part on issues of consistency (both internal to the model and external, between the model and the general theoretical framework) and relevance or correspondence (to the actual social context and to the social institution to be explained.) Let me suggest three questions crucial to this relationship. First, what is the relationship between the initial assumptions of the model and the mechanisms invoked to solve the strategic problems in the game? Here the main concern is one of consistency. In the process of interpreting these models, we need to ask whether the mechanism invoked is consistent with the initial assumption of individual rationality and the other assumptions about the context of the interaction.

Second, what is the relationship between the mechanisms invoked to resolve the multiple-equilibria problem in the game and the actual social context in which the social institution to be explained exists? Here the main concern is one of the relevance of the analytical results for the explanation of institutional change. We need to ask if the analytical mechanism can be identified as part of (or, in a weaker version, related by analogy to some feature of) the actual context in which social actors seek to resolve issues of institutional development and change.

Third, what is the relationship between initial assumptions (of both the general theoretical framework and the specific rational-choice model) and the substantive conclusions about institutional change drawn from the model? Here the concerns are both consistency and relevance. We need to ask if the characteristics of a social institution, initially highlighted by the analytical model and subsequently invoked in conclusion as the primary explanation of its emergence and change, are consistent with the assumptions about individual rationality and social context on which the model is based. In addition, we should also ask if the resulting story of institutional change based on these characteristics corresponds in some persuasive way to our existing historical understanding. This last point is especially relevant in those cases where we assess the relative merits of competing explanations.

All of these questions are a necessary part of the process of developing a social-scientific explanation: from model to interpretation to explanation and theory. While some of this may seem trivially true when stated in this form, close attention to the various stages of this process is often lacking in rational-choice theories of social phenomena.[1] This is manifest in the analyses of both proponents and critics of such theories. The problem with the proponents of rational-choice accounts is that they are often insufficiently careful in their interpretations of the models that they produce; that is, the move from the rational-choice model to the social theory of institutional change is often underelaborated or, even worse, inconsistent with the model's underlying premises. The problem with the critics of the approach is that they fail to acknowledge the diversity in the nature and content of the explanations offered by analyses grounded in the rationality of social action. This failure causes such critics to underestimate the potential explanatory power of the approach.

In this chapter I focus on a comparison of different theories of evolutionary institutional change. The common goal of these theories is an explanation of the decentralized emergence of various social institutions, especially the informal conventions and norms that form the basis of social life. Through this comparison I will illustrate the relevance of issues of model interpretation for an assessment of the relative merits of different explanations of institutional change. In addition, this comparison allows me to exemplify the range and diversity of the explanations that can be developed from an initial assumption of rational decision making.

Overview

In this chapter I will assess three distinct accounts of the decentralized emergence of social institutions: a theory of the evolutionary emergence of social conventions, a market-based theory of exchange and selection through competition, and a bargaining theory that explains the emergence of institutions in terms of the asymmetries of power in a society. Each builds its explanation from the microlevel, arguing that social institutions emerge from repeated interactions among small numbers of social actors. On each of these accounts social institutions resolve the strategic problems inherent in social interactions characterized by multiple equilibria: each of the equilibria could serve as the resolution of the social interaction, but the actors need to identify a common equilibrium to pursue.

Each theory must provide answers to the two main questions inherent in a theory of decentralized, or spontaneous, emergence: (1) how does a particular institutional rule get established as the solution to a single microlevel interaction? and (2) how does this rule become generalized as the solution for the society as a whole? It is in the answers to these two questions that the three approaches differ. The differences are a product of four main factors: the different conceptions of the basic social interaction, the different emphasis given to institutional effects, the different mechanisms invoked to resolve the single microlevel interaction, and the different aspects of the social context invoked to explain how a rule is generalized for the society as a whole.

My analysis proceeds as follows. In this section, I present a simple game-theoretic model that is representative of the types of models used by the different theories. Using this model I identify the main conceptual differences among the three approaches. In the next section, I present a brief discussion of the three theories in order to show how each approach constructs an explanation of institutional emergence and change from its initial model. In the final section, I assess the strengths and weaknesses of the different explanations in terms of the interpretive questions developed in the introduction. Here the main thrust of the analysis focuses on the relationship between the substantive conclusions of the different explanations and the initial assumptions about individual rationality and social context that drive the analytical models. One of the goals of this final analysis is to establish under what conditions each of the three approaches might best explain the decentralized emergence of social institutions.

Let me begin by positing a simple two-person game that is intended to model the basic social interaction out of which social institutions emerge. The model starts from the following premise about the role of institutions in social life: institutions are rules that structure social interactions in ways that allow social actors to gain the benefits of joint activity. In any social situation there are usually a number of ways that rules could structure these interactions. The process of institutional development culminates in the establishment of one of these rules as the common institutional form in a community.

Thus, the requirements of the model are straightforward. Each of the social actors must have at least two choices of action in his feasible set. At least two of the outcomes produced by the interdependent

		Player 2	
		X	Y
Player 1	X	a_1, a_2	b_1, b_2
	Y	b_1, b_2	a_1, a_2

Fig. 1. A game-theoretic model

choices of the actors must be characterized by payoffs that incorporate the benefits of joint activity. In each of the theories that I consider here, these outcomes take the form of Nash equilibria; that is, there are at least two strategy combinations that would produce an outcome that the actors would accept as the resolution of the game. The task for the actors in the interaction is to find a way to produce one of the equilibrium outcomes. In this model a social institution is a rule of action that identifies and induces compliance with one of these equilibrium-strategy combinations.

These requirements are met by the game in figure 1. Although it abstracts from much of the complexity of many social interactions, it allows us to concentrate on the central elements of the process by which informal rules emerge. The two actors, players 1 and 2, have two choices of action, X and Y. This produces four possible outcomes in the game, and the outcomes can be characterized by their strategy combinations $(X,X; X,Y; Y,X; Y,Y)$. The payoffs are characterized by the variables a and b. If $a_{1,2} > b_{1,2}$, then there are two Nash equilibria in the game, (X,X) and (Y,Y). The strategic problem for the players rests in the fact that, without more information about the social context in which the interaction takes place, they do not know on which equilibrium to focus their strategic choice. In this situation, two possible institutional rules could emerge: either one that recommends a strategy choice of X or one that recommends a strategy choice of Y.

With this simple model I can illustrate which features of the social interaction the different approaches choose to give primary emphasis. As a shorthand, I will refer to the approaches in terms of the mechanism that underlies the different explanations: convention (for the theory of social conventions), contract (for the exchange-and-selection-through-competition approach), and bargain (for the bargaining approach.) First, each of the three approaches relies on the assumption that $a > b$.

In the convention and bargain approaches this is straightforward; they conceive of the basic social interaction as a multiple equilibria game. In the contract approach this assumption requires brief explanation. In the latter conception, social institutions are often conceived of as rules that resolve social interactions that take the form of prisoner's dilemmas. In a one-shot prisoner's-dilemma situation, the relationship $a > b$ does not hold and thus the promises contained in the contract are not self-enforcing. On the other hand, if the theory is based on the assumption that exchange relationships are characterized by ongoing and repeated interactions, then the theory of collective action demonstrates that there are many circumstances in which the contracts can be self-enforcing (Kreps 1990, 505–15). Given the fact that the assumption of ongoing and repeated interactions is an important part of the contract approach to institutional emergence and change, it is reasonable to transform the prisoner's dilemma into a multiple equilibria game and to adopt the assumption that $a > b$.

Second, from this initial assumption the bargain approach differs from both the convention and contract approaches in terms of the additional features of the social interaction it emphasizes. Both the convention and contract approaches emphasize the following relationship: $a_1 + a_2 > b_1 + b_2$. This relationship emphasizes the following feature of the outcomes induced by the social institution: the aggregate benefits produced by the rule exceed the aggregate benefits of failing to produce a rule. The comparison is between social outcomes induced by a social institution and social outcomes without social institutions. As I will show in the next section, this emphasis on the collective gains produced by social institutions is found in explanations that emphasize characteristics such as social efficiency, Pareto-superiority, the minimization of transaction costs, and so on.

The bargaining approach, on the other hand, incorporates additional assumptions about the social context in which the social interaction takes place directly into the payoffs. This approach, then, emphasizes the following relationship: the two equilibria are distinguished by the fact that $a_1 > a_2$ in one equilibrium and $a_2 > a_1$ in the other. This relationship emphasizes the following feature of the outcomes induced by social institutions: the institutions have distinctive distributional consequences (that is, the institutions affect the distribution of benefits of joint activity). The bargaining approach shifts the focus from aggregate effects to the effects on the benefits of the individual social actors. Here the comparison is between the outcomes induced by the different social institutions.

Thus, in seeking to explain how the institutional rule emerges to direct the choices of the actors to either the (X,X) or the (Y,Y) equilibrium, the three approaches model the basic social interaction somewhat differently. The convention and contract approaches differ mainly in the differing weights they give to their two primary relationships: the convention approach weighs the $a > b$ relationship more heavily, while the contract approach gives greater weight to the $a_1 + a_2 > b_1 + b_2$ relationship. The bargaining approach gives primary emphasis to the relationship that characterizes the differences in the values of a_1 and a_2 for the different equilibria. In doing so, they give primary explanatory emphasis to different features of the social situation out of which social institutions emerge. These features are reflective of the different effects of institutions on social life.

The significance of this emphasis should not be underestimated. The choice of emphasis is an important part of the process of interpreting a rational-choice model. The choice represents a substantive claim about what the proponents think are the primary factors relevant to explaining the emergence of social institutions. This emphasis is central to subsequent claims about the importance of social context, about the mechanisms for resolving the strategic problem of multiple equilibria, and about the content of the substantive explanation and theory. For it is upon this primary emphasis in the analytical model that the different approaches must build their explanations of institutional emergence and change.

Theories of Institutional Development

From the different relationships highlighted in the analytical model, proponents of the different theories must develop an argument about a mechanism that will cause the actors to identify a common equilibrium strategy combination. Then they must explain by what process this identified combination comes to be generalized as a rule to govern the society as a whole. In this section I describe how the three approaches answer these questions, as they progress from model to interpretation to explanation and theory. The task here is to look at how the different approaches draw on assumptions about individual rationality and on aspects of the social context in which these basic social interactions occur to give content to, and thus to justify the emphasis on, the basic analytical relationships.

The Theory of Social Conventions

The logic of social conventions has been the source of numerous explanations of the development of social institutions. It was the basis of one of the earliest efforts to employ formal game-theoretic models to develop a general theory of decentralized emergence and change (Schotter 1981). It has long been the foundation for efforts to explain the emergence of specific social institutions (from language [Lewis 1969] to norms [Ullman-Margalit 1977] to property rights and morality [Sugden 1986]). It is the philosophical justification for the recent explosion of work in evolutionary game theory seeking to explain the general evolution of society.[2]

The approach builds on the $a > b$ relationship to emphasize that any rule that guarantees both actors a payoff of a can be the culmination of a process of institutional emergence. From this point it builds a theory of institutional emergence based on a characterization of institutional rules as social conventions, as the unintended consequences of repeated social interactions in which the actors can mutually benefit from coordinated behavior. The logic of the theory proceeds as follows. Each of the actors would prefer to coordinate (either implicitly or by explicit agreement) on one of the beneficial conventions, as opposed to arriving at an outcome that involves a failure to coordinate. Each of the actors also knows that the other actors share this preference. The rules of the convention provide the information about the future actions of others necessary to achieve that coordination. In formal terms, the convention induces an equilibrium outcome for the actors in the game: compliance with the convention is their best reply to the strategic choices of the other actors. Hence, if they can successfully coordinate on a particular role, the rule will be self-enforcing.

The substantive explanations of institutional development rest on an account of how the convention is recognized and coordination is achieved. This brings us to the two basic questions that any theory of decentralized emergence must answer. The main answer to these questions builds on Schelling's (1960) conception of salience. According to Schelling's account, since each of the individual actors would prefer coordination at one of the cooperative outcomes as opposed to the non-coordination alternatives, they will readily use whatever salient information they have at their disposal as a way of achieving that coordination. The mechanism central to the conventional account of institutional emergence is the existence of focal points that coordinate social expectations. The salience of a particular cooperative outcome is established by some feature of the social context in which the relevant interaction occurs.

Coordination on one of the beneficial outcomes is achieved as the actors come to recognize, through repeated interactions, similar salient characteristics of that outcome and formulate their expectations accordingly. The focal point may identify something in the relationship between a certain type of actor and the social outcome in question or something in the nature of the relationship between the actors. Since all of the actors prefer to be at one of the stable equilibria, as opposed to being at one of the points of no cooperation, some of them will eventually focus on a particular outcome and the others will in time follow suit, establishing a convention as to how to resolve the interaction.

By the conventional explanation of institutional emergence, the mechanism of selection is coordination through the salience of focal points, and the process of generalization is the adaptation and learning motivated by the benefits of cooperation in repeated social interactions. Beyond the emphasis on the $a > b$ relationship, the only feature of the social interaction that the conventional approach emphasizes is the $a_1 + a_2 > b_1 + b_2$ relationship. This has several implications for the substantive conclusions drawn about institutional emergence and change. First, the rule evolves *arbitrarily*. The evolutionary process is unconsciously driven by whatever salient factor focuses the attention of the actors. The interests of any particular actor or group of actors do not determine the nature of the final institutional arrangement: that is, the distributional differences produced by different rules will not be invoked in the explanation. The information that keys the coordination on a particular rule may come from anywhere: environmental characteristics in the community, the nature of the activity, or some visible characteristic of the actors involved, for example. The selection of information is arbitrary: social actors will use whatever information resources they have in order to achieve a coordination of their activity. This description by Schotter captures the underlying nature of the evolutionary process:

> The important point to be made, and the one that makes this approach unique, is that the social institution that is actually created . . . is a stochastic event, and that if history could be repeated, a totally different convention could be established for the identical situation. The point is that the set of institutions existing at any point in time is really an accident of history and that what exists today could have evolved in a very different manner. (1981, 79)

A second implication is that the resultant rule produces an outcome that is Pareto-*superior* to uncoordinated exchange. Here the emphasis on the $a_1 + a_2 > b_1 + b_2$ relationship is crucial, because the comparison is between the aggregate benefits produced by different social outcomes. Any evolutionary theory must detail the mechanism that guarantees Pareto-superiority. These theories satisfy this part of their explanation by arguing that while the actors do not intentionally produce the rule, they would not rationally adapt to a rule that was not Pareto-superior to uncoordinated activity and, more importantly, that they would adopt any rule that was. Many evolutionary theories acknowledge that the process will not necessarily lead to Pareto-*optimal* institutional arrangements. Various reasons are offered for this failure. What is crucial to note here, however, is that such theories do predict that changes in existing rules will involve Pareto-*improvements* over the status quo. This restriction is justified with the reasoning that rational actors will not respond to a movement toward a Pareto-inferior alternative. Only Pareto-superior alternatives will be sought.

The Theory of Exchange and Competitive Selection

The logic of contracting has been the source of many explanations of institutional development and change (see, e.g., Brennan and Buchanan 1985; Heckathorn and Maser 1987; Williamson 1975, 1985; North 1990; Ostrom 1990). I focus here exclusively on explanations of evolutionary development and change: a process that synthesizes aspects of intentional decision making with a decentralized selection mechanism based on marketlike competition among contractual forms. The underlying thrust of this approach is captured by Eggertsson (1990):

> changes in contractual forms may often be a long process, particularly when there is a lack of experience with arrangements that would be best suited to a new situation. Once a successful experiment has been made, the forces of competition establish new *equilibrium contracts*. It is also reasonable to expect that a community that has a very long experience with stable technology and a stable range of relative prices has settled on contractual forms that minimize costs for each branch of production, given the state of knowledge about contractual arrangements and the basic structure of property rights. (55; emphasis in original)

In order to identify the relationship between the analytical model and the mechanisms of institutional selection invoked in the process of interpretation and explanation, it is helpful to focus separately on the two main components of the contracting explanation: the individual exchange and the competition over alternatives.

Consider first the contracts produced by individual exchanges. The logic of the exchange relationship is one of mutual benefit. The motivation for the development of the contract is quite simple. When any two social actors perceive that they can achieve benefit from mutual exchange, they must agree on the terms of that exchange. Among these terms are the rules governing the actions of the parties during the course of the exchange relationship.

In the context of the general theory, these contracts constitute the social institutions produced by social actors to facilitate the achievement of socially beneficial outcomes. The main mechanism that explains the selection among possible contracts is *voluntary agreement*. Social actors create these institutional rules because they can achieve benefits that they would not enjoy without them. Hence the importance of the $a > b$ relationship. The contracts produced by voluntary agreement can take many forms, however. The mechanism of voluntary agreement is therefore constrained by an assumption about the kinds of contracts social actors will try to produce. The dominant answer builds on Coase's (1960) insights into the effects of transaction costs. That social actors would be concerned about transaction costs is understandable given the fact that these are the costs incurred in establishing and enforcing institutional rules. The greater the transaction costs involved in an exchange, the lower the level of aggregate benefits enjoyed by the social actors. Consider, for example, North's (1990) explanation of the development of property rights in a society. Say that two actors share an interest in a common piece of property. Their task is to determine the best way to structure their use of that property. There are a range of possible choices, from some form of shared or common property rights to various divisions into private property shares. North (1990, 37–43) argues that these actors will contract for rights which minimize the transaction costs involved in the ongoing exchange, subject to a set of constraints on their ability to identify the most efficient contract (e.g., ideology, lack of knowledge, lack of capacity). They minimize transaction costs in order to maximize the benefits gained from the property. The contracting problem is one of structuring incentives in such a way that the person who has the greatest incentive to maximize the benefits from a piece of the property has the rights to that parcel. The emphasis on cost minimization and/or benefit maximization highlights the central importance of the $a_1 + a_2 > b_1 + b_2$ relationship.

In this contract approach, once the actors have established the property rights according to the minimization standard, they will maintain them as long as the relevant external circumstances remain stable. However, there is always the possibility that some factors external to the exchange relationship will change in such a way as to affect the enjoyment of the benefits of the property. North (1990, 109) lists several changes in relative prices that will affect benefits: in the ratio of factor prices, in the costs of information, and in technology. If any of these

Δ is a result of Δ in exogenous costs / benefits

changes are substantial, then they will affect the relative value of the different ways of institutionalizing property rights. If the result of these changes is that a new property-rights scheme would produce greater aggregate benefits than the existing system, the contracting parties will consider the following cost-benefit calculation: do these additional benefits exceed the costs involved in changing the present contract? If the answer is yes, then the actors will enter into a new contract institutionalizing new rights (North 1990, 67). Here we see the third element of the contract mechanism invoked by the transaction cost theory: institutional change will only occur if the resulting outcome is Pareto-superior to the previous institutional arrangement.

Note that at this point this is merely a discussion of the motivations of the actors in an individual exchange. As Eggertsson (1990) clearly points out, the more sophisticated versions of the transaction-cost approach invoke more than the intentions of the actors in an individual exchange to explain the emergence of social institutions. Individual exchanges merely produce the variety of possible institutional forms; the second selection mechanism invoked by the contract approach is competition. This brings us to the question of how individualized contractual forms come to be generalized in the society as a whole. Many explanations of institutional development and change situate the decision to establish social institutions in the context of a market or a marketlike environment. The main influence of the market on the choice of institutional form rests in the competitive pressure it supposedly exerts on the institutionalization process.[3]

Competition can serve as a dynamic selection mechanism that determines the survival of various institutional forms on grounds of reproductive fitness. This is the logic behind the Alchian (1950) model of evolutionary competition employed by most economic analyses of institutional emergence. The existence of a large number of firms seeking profits from a common pool of consumers produces pressure for survival. Over time those firms who employ less efficient techniques will lose profits to those who are more efficient. Losing profits eventually translates into extinction. As the competitive process continues, only those firms employing efficient techniques will survive.

The logic of this dynamic effect forms the basis of the theory of exchange and competition. On this account, competition selects the institutional form that maximizes $a_1 + a_2$. The invocation of competition as a selection mechanism draws on a particular conception of the social context in which these social interactions take place. It is important to remember that competition is not an either/or phenomenon; there are degrees of competition and therefore degrees of competitive effect. The extent to which competitive pressure will serve as a selection mechanism for efficient institutions depends on the degree to which the social context manifests the requisite empirical conditions under which competition will emerge.

Lists of necessary conditions for marketlike competition are numerous. Drawing on the analysis of competition developed by Scitovsky (1971), the following conditions are necessary for competition in social institutions to exist: (1) a large number of competitors in pursuit of a common pool of resources, (2) a set of institutional alternatives differentiated only by their distributional consequences, (3) full information about the availability of alternatives, and (4) low transaction costs. If an explanation of institutional change is to invoke competition as a relevant factor, then these conditions of social context must be empirically satisfied.

The Theory of Bargaining and Distribution

The logic of bargaining has been used as the basis of a number of recent efforts to explain the intentional creation of political and economic institutions (see, e.g., Heckathorn and Maser 1987; Bates 1989; Ensminger 1992; Miller 1992). In Knight (1992), I proposed a bargaining-based explanation for the decentralized emergence of social institutions. Here I want to set out the basic logic of that explanation.

A bargaining approach to institutional emergence and change seeks to explain the emergence of social institutions primarily in terms of the characteristics that distinguish different institutional forms. Rather than seeking an explanation of institutional selection in a comparison of the differences between social outcomes induced by institutional rules and those outcomes that lack an institutional basis (the logic of the convention and contract approaches on the issue of institutional emergence), this approach places primary emphasis on a comparison of the different outcomes induced by the possible institutional alternatives. Given the reliance on an assumption of rational self-interest as the basis of the theory, the main focus of the analysis of institutional differences is the distributional effect of the alternatives. The theory builds its explanation on the distributional relationship highlighted in the basic analytical model: the two equilibria are distinguished by the fact that $a_1 > a_2$ in one equilibrium and $a_2 > a_1$ in the other.

On this bargaining account, social institutions are a by-product of strategic conflict over substantive social outcomes. By this I mean that social actors produce social institutions in the process of seeking distributional advantage in the conflict over substantive benefits. In some cases they will create institutional rules consciously; in other cases the rules will emerge as unintended consequences of the pursuit of strategic

but decision to term to inst.
. is exogenous

advantage. In each case the main focus is on the substantive outcome; the development of institutional rules is merely a means to that substantive end.

The mechanism of selection among the possible institutional alternatives is bargaining competition among the actors over the various alternatives. Institutional development is a contest among actors to establish rules that structure outcomes to those equilibria most favorable for them. As in any bargaining situation, there are some factors that distinguish the actors and thus influence the bargaining outcome in favor of one of the parties. These factors are what we usually refer to when we speak of bargaining power (Bachrach and Lawler 1981; Raiffa 1982). The task of a theory of decentralized emergence is to identify those factors that are most likely to explain (1) how bargaining is resolved in a single interaction and (2) how a particular outcome becomes generalized for the community as a whole.

In Knight (1992) I developed a theory that identified the asymmetries of resource ownership in a society as the main factor explaining the resolution of bargaining over social institutions. The main thrust of the argument is that asymmetries in resource ownership affect the willingness of rational self-interested actors to accept the bargaining demands of other actors. Here the asymmetries of resource ownership serve as an *ex ante* measure of the bargaining power of the actors in a social interaction.[4] In explaining the establishment of particular social institutions, bargaining demands become claims about commitments to particular rules of behavior. The relevant question becomes: what will cause a social actor to accept the commitment of another actor to a particular course of action and thus a particular social outcome?

Return to the basic analytical model in figure 1. In bargaining interactions the most important resources are those available to the actors in the event that bargaining is either lengthy and costly or ultimately unsuccessful. For any particular bargaining interaction, many factors may determine the availability of these resources. We can think of these as the existing resources that an actor might retain after the effort to achieve a bargain breaks down. Or we might think of them as the other options available to the actors if they are left to achieve a bargain with some other party. In the model in figure 1, these resources determine the values of $b_{1,2}$, values that can be interpreted as a measure of the costs of noncoordination on an equilibrium outcome. If $b_1 = b_2$, then the costs are equal and we can conclude that there are no key resource asymmetries in the game. But if either $b_1 > b_2$ or $b_1 < b_2$, then we have an example of an asymmetry in resources and thus asymmetric bargaining power. Here we see an additional analytical relationship that the bargaining approach emphasizes, but that the other two approaches do not: the possibility that the b values are not equal.

The standard view in bargaining theory is that if A has greater bargaining power than B, A will usually receive a greater share of the benefits of the bargaining outcome (Maynard Smith 1982, 105; Osborne and Rubinstein 1990, 88–89). We can capture the underlying intuition of this view through the effects of differences in the values of b. Here the mechanism by which asymmetries of resource ownership influence social outcomes is in its effect on the credibility of the commitments in the bargaining interaction. To see this, consider a game in which $a_1 > a_2$ in the (X,X) equilibrium, $a_2 > a_1$ in the (Y,Y) equilibrium, and $b_1 > b_2$. Now the costs of noncoordination are greater for player 2 than for player 1. If player 1 is now able to communicate to player 2 that she will choose X regardless of what 2 does, what will 2 do? That is, what will this information do to 2's choice? The answer depends on how credible 2 finds 1's commitment to be. There are important reasons to believe that 2 will accept the credibility of the commitment in this case and respond by choosing X.

The principal idea here involves the relationship between available resources and attitudes toward risk.[5] Resource ownership influences one's attitude toward risky situations. There is a positive relationship between ownership of resources and risk acceptance, a negative relationship between ownership and risk aversion. Considered from the perspective of player 2, this relationship suggests two related reasons why he would find 1's commitment credible and choose X. First, since 1 will suffer fewer costs of failing to coordinate, then she is more likely to accept the risk and attempt the commitment to X. As Maynard Smith puts it in his analysis of asymmetric evolutionary games, "[a] player who has less to lose from a breakdown is more likely to risk one" (1982, 153). If 2 is aware of the asymmetry, then he has good reason to believe that 1 is sincere in the commitment. Second, since 2 will suffer greater costs of noncoordination, then he is more likely to be risk-averse and is, therefore, less likely to challenge 1's commitment. The risk aversion leads to a willingness to accept the commitment and to choose X. The greater the differences in resources between the actors, the stronger the relationship between costs of noncoordination and risk attitudes should be. That is, the greater the differential between b_1 and b_2, then the higher the probability that 2 will choose X.

Through its emphasis on asymmetries in resource ownership, the approach grounds its mechanism of rule selection in an important feature of many social interactions: social actors suffer significant costs for the failure to coordinate on equilibrium outcomes, yet those costs need not be suffered uniformly. When social actors are aware of these differentials, this awareness can influence the credibility of certain strategies. Those who have either fewer alternatives or less beneficial ones will be more inclined to respect the commitments of those who have more or stronger ones. In this way, the existence of resource asymmetries in a society can significantly influence the choice of equilibrium alternatives.

If successful commitments are achievable by strategic actors, then they face the second half of the task of institutionalization: the generalization of these constraints to rules governing the community as a whole. If institutions are going to arise out of bargaining interactions, then we would anticipate the following emergence process. Individual bargaining will be resolved by the commitments of those who enjoy a relative advantage in substantive resources. Through a series of interactions with various members of the group, actors with similar resources will establish a pattern of successful action in a particular type of interaction. As others recognize that they are interacting with one of the actors who possesses these resources, they will adjust their strategies to achieve their best outcome, given the anticipated commitments of others. Over time rational actors will continue to adjust their strategies until an equilibrium is reached. As this becomes recognized as the socially expected combination of equilibrium strategies, a self-enforcing social institution will be established.

In this bargaining account, the implications of the analysis of the bargaining model are related to a significant feature of the social context in which bargaining occurs: the asymmetries of resource ownership in a society. Unlike other sources of bargaining power, asymmetry of resource ownership is a factor common to a wide range of bargainers in a society. This is a desirable feature of any theory of decentralized emergence. Only those factors that are widely shared throughout a society will produce the kind of systematic resolution of repeated bargaining interactions necessary for the decentralized emergence of social institutions.

A Comparative View

The three approaches to institutional emergence and change start from the same initial premise: Institutions are the product of a process of repeated social interactions among rational self-interested actors. From this premise they develop explanations of this process that account for both the resolution of the multiple-equilibria problem at the microlevel social interaction and the generalization of this solution as a rule of behavior for the society as a whole. In this last section I assess how well each of the three approaches integrates the basic features of its account into substantive conclusions about decentralized emergence. The basic features to be considered are: the assumption of individual rationality, the choice of emphasis on certain primary relationships in the analytical model, the mechanism of selection that resolves the multiple-equilibria problem, and the incorporation of social context.

My goal here is to show that the different approaches are grounded in quite different claims about the actual empirical conditions under which social institutions emerge and change. The joint criteria of consistency and relevance constrain the ways in which the different approaches can integrate the various features of their accounts. The initial assumptions that the proponents make in the positing of the basic analytical model commit them to certain interpretive positions when they begin to elaborate the mechanisms of selection and to incorporate social context into the substantive explanations. If we give close attention to how these differences are manifest in the move from model through interpretation to explanation, we can gain a better understanding of the relative merits of the three approaches by establishing the actual conditions under which an approach best explains the emergence of social institutions.

Fundamental to this analysis is an assessment of the implications of the assumption of individual rationality. Each of the approaches constructs its explanation of decentralized emergence on this basic assumption, along with an additional assumption about the nature of the preferences of the actors. The actors are assumed to be motivated by self-interest. From this it follows that the social actors are motivated by a preference for social institutions that best serve their individual interests.[6] Therefore, on all three accounts the explanation of institutional emergence and change must be reconciled with the underlying premise that social institutions are the product of the interdependent choices of rational, self-interested actors.

This reconciliation requires us to ask several questions of the different approaches. Institutions have a number of effects on social life. An important part of the process of model interpretation is the task of identifying the effects of social institutions and clarifying the role that these effects play in the explanation of emergence and change. Each of the three approaches identifies a different effect as the primary source of its explanation. Which of these effects is most consistent with the assumption of individual rationality? The mechanisms of selection invoked by the approaches are closely related to these identified effects. To what extent are these mechanisms of selection a plausible explanation of how rational, self-interested actors would resolve the multiple-equilibria problem? The social context in which the repeated social interactions take place establishes the conditions for selection and generalization. Given the assumption of rational self-interested behavior, what are the conditions under which the different proposed mechanisms seem most relevant and thus most plausible as an explanation of emergence and change?

Conventions

The convention approach emphasizes the $a > b$ and, to a lesser extent, the $a_1 + a_2 > b_1 + b_2$ relationships in the basic model. From this it develops an explanation of institutional emergence that identifies the coordination effects of social institutions. It emphasizes the Pareto-superiority of outcomes induced by social institutions over outcomes characterized by the lack of institutional coordination.

The mechanism of selection involves the recognition of focal points that enhance the salience of a particular equilibrium outcome. The focal points must be identified in the social context in which the interactions occur; in this way context enters the explanation as a coordinating device. From the perspective of individual self-interest, the focal point is an arbitrary solution. The social actors are indifferent as to which outcome is established. They merely prefer any outcome that a focal point will make salient over a noncoordination outcome.

Given the assumption of rational, self-interested behavior, the coordination approach will best explain institutional emergence when the actual empirical conditions are such that $a_1 = a_2$. This is a case of pure coordination, a case where there are no distributional effects of the institutions. However, in nonpure coordination cases the distributional effects are relevant considerations. In those cases the actors will have conflicting preferences among the institutional alternatives and the arbitrary resolution developed by the convention approach will seem less plausible in comparison with the other approaches.

Here it is important to note a challenge to this last claim offered by Sugden (1986). He argues against the relevance of many distributional effects on the grounds that most social institutions that evolve in these types of cases are "cross-cutting." He distinguishes the adverse effects of a single interaction from the cumulative effects of repeated interactions. If the relevant actors are not, in the long run, adversely affected by such rules, then they will have no reason to seriously favor one asymmetry over another. He emphasizes that even though actors may prefer one stable equilibrium over another in a particular game, they will have no similar preference in repeated plays of the game, so long as the asymmetry upon which the convention is based is "cross-cutting." An asymmetry is cross-cutting if "each individual will sometimes find himself on one

side of the asymmetry and sometimes on the other" (1986, 157–59).
With such a convention, the disproportionate distributional effects will
even out over repeated interactions. Thus, the persuasiveness of the
social-convention theory depends, in part, on the empirical question of
whether social institutions are truly cross-cutting.

The plausibility of Sugden's argument rests on an empirical question about actual social conditions. If most social institutions that have
distributional effects are cross-cutting, then the conventions approach
can be preserved as an explanation for a broader category of cases. If,
rather, there is, as I have argued elsewhere (Knight 1992), a dearth of
truly cross-cutting social institutions, then the plausibility of the convention approach is quite limited.

Contracts

The contract approach emphasizes the $a_1 + a_2 > b_1 + b_2$ and the $a > b$
relationships in the basic model. From this it develops an explanation of
institutional emergence that identifies the efficiency effects of social
institutions. The conceptualization of these effects takes many forms
(the minimization of transaction costs, wealth maximization, social efficiency), but they share the basic idea that institutions enhance the aggregate benefits $(a_1 + a_2)$ of joint activity. This approach emphasizes the
greater efficiency of outcomes induced by social institutions over outcomes that are produced without institutional assistance.

There are two components of the mechanism of selection in the
contract approach: (1) the voluntary contract and (2) the pressure of
competition. The initial selection among the possible contracts occurs at
the microlevel interaction through the voluntary agreement of the parties. For example, according to the transaction-costs approach, the parties will agree to the contract that minimizes costs, subject to the constraints on their knowledge and capacities. From the perspective of
individual self-interest, the plausibility of the voluntary selection by contract mechanism is open to question in those situations where the institutions affect the distribution of benefits. In those cases rational, self-interested actors will prefer a contract that maximizes their individual
benefits over a contract that maximizes aggregate benefits. Only in the
cases where one contract satisfies both criteria will the contract mechanism provide a satisfactory explanation of selection. Thus, the argument
at the level of voluntary contract is most likely to explain the emergence
of social institutions under the condition $a_1 = a_2$.

When there are distributional effects, the second mechanism, competitive selection, serves as the primary source of explanation. The argument here rests on claims about the nature of the social context in which contracts are made. If conditions of competition exist in a society, then those conditions will have two important, and related, effects on the selection of institutions. The first is the pressure for survival: competition selects out those joint activities that fail to maximize $a_1 + a_2$ in the long run. The second is the effect on the bargaining power of the actors: competition diminishes the differences in resource ownership among social actors. When conditions of competition exist, asymmetries in the levels of resources and opportunities available to the actors in case an agreeable contract cannot be reached diminish. In such cases the bargaining power necessary for an actor to achieve a distributionally favorable contract is absent. Then bargaining over distributional consequences does not adequately explain the selection of institutions and the contract approach becomes a more plausible explanation of the emergence of social institutions.

Therefore, given the assumption of rational self-interested behavior, the contract approach will best explain institutional emergence when the actual empirical conditions are such that $b_1 = b_2$. Here the nature of the social context becomes central to both the interpretation of the model and the development of the substantive explanation. In order to assess the level of competitive pressure in the social context we must ask a set of questions about the actual social phenomenon to be explained.[7] These questions relate to the nature of (1) the joint activity from which an institution emerges, (2) the social actors involved in the activity, and (3) the institution that structures the activity. Each of these factors affects the level of competitive pressure.

The importance of the nature of the joint activity can be seen by considering exactly what gets selected by competition. Competition exists among actors who are involved in common social interactions. These joint activities are structured and facilitated by institutions. It is the institutional rule that gets selected in the competitive process, the rule that does the best job of facilitating survival and reproduction. Thus, the relevant units of analysis for institutional selection are the *sets of actors* involved in the joint activity and not the isolated individuals. The relevant criterion for selection is the aggregate level of benefits produced in the interaction, not the level of benefits provided to any particular individual.

Here understanding the nature of the joint activity is essential to answering one of the main questions related to the competitive selection mechanism: how intense is the pressure for survival? This is a function of the number of competitive groups, their capacity to consume resources, and the speed at which the competitive process takes place. For competition to induce a pressure for survival, there must be a demand for resources greater than the available supply. For this condition to be satisfied, the joint activity must be such that there is a greater overall demand for the benefits of that activity than there are the resources to satisfy it.

The importance of the nature of the actors involved in the joint activity is primarily related to the effect of competitive pressure on the bargaining power of the actors. The competition that produces the effects on power asymmetries is competition among individual actors over the other individuals with whom they will interact. The different possible rules can be seen as the offers used in this competition. The relevant units of analysis are *individual social actors;* the relevant criteria are the individual benefits that actors receive from different institutional forms. Competition diminishes the importance of power asymmetries to the extent to which actors have other alternatives that are more preferable than accepting the offer of any particular actor.

In addition to the question of intensity, there are two questions about the nature of the social actors that directly affect competitive pressure on bargaining power. First, how are the actors distributed for the different roles in a particular joint activity? Competition requires that the actors who will fill the various roles be approximately equal in distribution. If there is a scarcity on one side of the relationship, then it diminishes the effects of competition and enhances the power of the actors in the scarce group. Second, how interchangeable are the different actors? The interchangeability of the alternatives in any social interaction is central to the leveling of resource asymmetries, at least to the extent that these asymmetries are a function of the other opportunities available to the actors. The greater the interchangeability of the actors with whom we might engage in a joint activity, the more equal are the opportunities available to the different social actors. If individual actors are not interchangeable, then competition for social collaborators will be diminished.

Finally, much of the contract account of institutional emergence rests on empirical claims about the nature of the set of alternative rules from which an institution can be selected. The contract approach assumes that the range of institutional possibilities is broad enough that a socially efficient alternative will be selected. The relevant question is: how numerous and diverse is the set of institutional possibilities? The empirical accuracy of this assumption affects the plausibility of the contract-based explanation.

The quantity and diversity of the set of alternatives affect the likelihood that competitive pressure will select the alternative that maximizes aggregate benefits. This follows from the fact that selection will only occur among those rules that strategic actors find it in their self-interest to introduce. The contract approach rests on the notion that if the range of alternatives is broad enough, there will be a correspondence between the rules that maximize aggregate benefits and the rules that give the distributional advantage to the more powerful groups in a society. If such a correspondence holds, there will exist within the set rules that both maximize aggregate benefits and produce distributional advantage for those who have the resources to establish a rule. Then the tension created by the distributional effects of the different rules will not constrain the selection of an efficient rule.

But there are three characteristics of social institutions that may affect the empirical accuracy of the assumption and thus the plausibility of the substantive claim. First, since institutions are rules that structure social interactions, they relate to people in ways that substantive goods do not. We create rules to govern classes of activities in which we ourselves are involved. As long as we remain part of the interaction, then we remain governed by the rule. Unlike a good that you can produce without any intention of consuming it, a rule cannot be alienated in the same way; generally when we produce a rule, then we also figuratively consume it. Besides the enhanced concern for the ongoing consequences of institutional rules that it produces in social actors, this relationship constrains the number of actors in a community who might be producers of any particular institution. This limits the number of potential competitors. An entrepreneur can in principle produce any kind of private good for which there is a demand in a community; social actors will generally produce only those institutions for which they have a personal demand.

Second, institutional rules are often related to activities in which the actors are not interchangeable. Our level of benefits from social interactions may be contingent on a specific group of individuals; the interaction would not be the same if it involved other groups. This can manifest itself in interactions as small as a marriage or other personal relationship or in an attachment to groups as large as a particular ethnic group or nationality. One of the requirements of competition is that the nature of the interaction must be such that the actors can treat each other interchangeably. That is, an actor's choice of rules must be based on the distributional consequences and not on the identity of the other actors involved. If their identity is crucial to the interaction, then those who make an institutional choice are limited in their range of feasible alternatives.

Third, the set of possible rules from which most social institutions are developed is finite. This suggests that there are only a limited number of ways of acting in most contexts, and only so many different rules to structure most social interactions. To the extent that this is true, the range of alternatives may be such that there is not sufficient correspondence between efficiency and distributional advantage to offset the effects of individual self-interest on the selection of a particular rule. The only pure exceptions to the implications of a finite set can be found in those institutions, like certain property rights schemes, that translate benefits into a continuous metric, like money. In such cases the distributional benefits of some types of rules can be compensated for by side payments, producing a situation in which the maximization of aggregate benefits is consistent with individual self-interest. In other cases the finite nature of the set of institutional alternatives will affect the effects of competition on institutional emergence.

Bargains

The bargaining approach emphasizes the relationship in the basic model in which the two equilibria are distinguished by the fact that $a_1 > a_2$ in one equilibrium and $a_2 > a_1$ in the other. From this it develops an explanation of institutional emergence that identifies the distributional effects of social institutions. It emphasizes the fact that social institutions determine the ways in which the benefits of joint activity are distributed and can thus be distinguished by their distributional consequences.

The mechanism of selection involves bargaining over the alternative distributional arrangements. The bargaining is resolved by the asymmetries of resource ownership in a society. Here the social context enters the analysis in the form of the asymmetries of resources that exist in a society in which social actors are involved in repeated interactions. Context is captured in the model by varying the values of b_1 and b_2 so that they reflect the idea that some actors will have more resources than others. From the perspective of individual self-interest, rational actors will be most concerned about the individual benefits that they derive from social institutions. If the institutions have distributional consequences, they will seek those institutions that provide them the highest value of a. The argument in support of the bargaining approach suggests that those actors with the higher b values will be able to cause the selection of more favorable social institutions.

As long as the institution is such that $a > b$ for those actors with the lowest b values (an assumption that all three approaches share), the bargaining approach provides a plausible mechanism for institutional selection. Given the assumption of rational, self-interested behavior, the bargaining approach will best explain institutional emergence when the actual empirical conditions are such that $a_1 \neq a_2$ and $b_1 \neq b_2$. The greater the differences in these values, the more likely it is that the bargaining approach will provide the best explanation of institutional emergence and change.

The key empirical conditions necessary for the bargaining explanation to pertain are systematic differences in both the distributional consequences of informal rules and the ownership of resources in a society. The implications for the type of social context in which these systematic differences will be found can be drawn from the previous discussion of the other two approaches. The conditions necessary to support the convention and contract explanations are just those conditions in which the bargaining approach is least likely to provide a plausible explanation. The greater the degree to which the social context fails to correspond to the conditions of either pure coordination or competition, the more the conditions necessary to support the bargaining approach are met.

Summary

What this analysis reinforces in the end is the fundamental importance of the idea that models must be interpreted in light of actual empirical conditions in the process of constructing social explanations. These conditions establish the terms under which we assess the relationship between the analytical assumptions about individual rationality and mechanisms of selection and the substantive conclusions we draw about institutional emergence and change. Each of the three approaches offers an explanation consistent with the basic assumption of individual rationality for a certain set of social conditions. What is distinctive about the bargaining approach is that it accommodates the assumption of rational, self-interested behavior for a broader and less restrictive range of conditions. For this reason, the convention ($a_1 = a_2$) and contract ($b_1 = b_2$) approaches might be considered special cases of a more general social-conflict theory of institutional emergence and change.

NOTES

1. Of course, this is often true of the other approaches in the social sciences, but my critical concern here is with rational-choice accounts.

2. See the articles in the special issue of *Games and Economic Behavior* (1991) for examples of the range of recent work in evolutionary game theory related to these issues.

3. In the next section I consider a second potential effect of competition on institutional emergence: the implications of competition for the effects of bargaining power on the emergence of institutions.

4. The introduction of bargaining power as an explanatory concept has been the subject of great debate in the social sciences. I want to stress that the bargaining model that I propose here does not fall prey to the standard objection that power is introduced as an *ex post* explanation of a social phenomenon and thus produces merely a tautological description of that phenomenon. My explanation requires an *ex ante* identification of the relevant asymmetries in resource ownership. This allows for a subsequent assessment of whether the asymmetry does serve to resolve the bargaining conflict and lead to the selection of a particular institutional rule.

5. There is a related argument in Knight (1992) that emphasizes the relationship between available resources and time preferences. Drawing on Rubinstein's analysis (1982) of the effects of time preferences on bargaining, I argue that the implications of differentials in time preferences for the resolution of a bargaining conflict over institutions are substantially the same as that of differentials in risk aversion.

6. Clearly this is a restrictive assumption about the possible preferences that social actors might have in the process of developing social institutions. Other motivations (such as concerns for collective welfare, justice, equality, or fairness) might enter into the decision to construct institutions. The point here is merely that the restrictive assumption of self-interest is fundamental to all of the existing explanations of the decentralized emergence of such institutions. If a proponent of one of these approaches wanted to invoke a mechanism of selection that was grounded in one of these other motivations, she would have to rethink the initial assumption upon which her analysis was based.

7. What I want to do here is to limit the analysis of the nature of competitive pressure to those issues that are unique to the question of competition over social institutions. In doing so I ignore certain general requirements of the competitive model that are seldom satisfied. One main example is the problem of incomplete information. To the extent that the actors lack information about the different institutional alternatives, the effects of competition are diminished.

The Experience of Creating Institutions:
The Framing of the United States Constitution

William H. Riker

One good way to understand the development of institutions is to analyze crucial turning points when people consciously try to change the way the institutions work. This perspective gives the analyst a chance to look at earlier and initial interpretations, at the motives and goals of reformers, and at available equilibria at the time of reform. A particularly good example of a crucial turning point is the framing of a new constitution for a polity, when, necessarily, participants are consciously trying to rearrange political structures so as to redirect incentives for future political actors. Many constitutions have been written in the past two centuries and a careful examination of the framing of any one of them would doubtless be instructive about institutional development. However, since scholars have studied the framing of the United States Constitution systematically and in great detail, I will use that event as a step toward the study of institutional development generally.

Before undertaking this case study, however, I wish to emphasize two general propositions that guide my analysis. The first is that no institution is created de novo. Consequently, in any new institution one should expect to see hangovers from the past. Also, there is no reason to expect these hangovers to be internally consistent or to fit perfectly with the goals of reformers. My second general proposition is that there is no reason to expect internal consistency from reforms carried out by a group. Individuals can, with effort, impose consistency on their goals and instruments, but groups seldom can. As the combined result of these two features, every institution is a collage of disparate parts. By chance the collage may fit together symmetrically and artistically, but it is much more likely that the collage will be poorly blended and quite ugly. Usually, in fact, the collage is acceptable, not because it was cleverly and appropriately designed, but only because over time its users have revised it on a daily basis until it works in a satisfactory way, or at least in a way satisfactory enough to forestall another major reform. Nevertheless, it is sometimes possible to start out with a substantially consistent institution, provided that a single person frames it or greatly influences the framing.

With these two general principles in mind, I turn now to an interpretation of the framing of the United States Constitution, looking first at the predecessor institutions and then at the group activity of framing.

Predecessor Institutions

At any point in institutional development, humans start with some pre-existing customs that influence new departures. Indeed, even nonhuman creatures have institutions, some perhaps genetic, but others certainly cultural. Mammalian brains have large structures devoted to recognizing other creatures and places. (Even in humans this structure is large, much larger, for example, than the structure devoted to words and talking.) While the main use of visual memory is probably to identify food, food sites, and friends and foes, this memory still allows for cultural development by enabling creatures to recognize signals and cultural arrangements like social hierarchies, kinship, and territorial boundaries. According to Goodall (1986), chimpanzees have a biologically fixed repertory of auditory, facial, and body signals, but these signals can mean different things in different chimpanzee groups. This is clearly a cultural or institutional modification of the fundamental biology of communication.

When we look at contemporary primitive societies, which, possibly, are stuck in about the same cultural situation as stone-age man, we find a large array of political institutions: customary law guarded and interpreted by shamans and elders; patterns of kinship and inheritance; hierarchies of influence from, for example, elders and shamans to other adult males, to adult females, and to children; rituals for the settlement of disputes; and so on. Indeed, most of the institutions observable in civilized life are also observable in contemporary primitives, though of course in rudimentary form. Presumably these rudimentary institutions existed in primitive societies of ancient times. At least in the earliest excavated remains of human construction we can see clear evidence of hierarchy, territoriality, ritual, and markets.

It seems pretty clear, therefore, that hominids (at least chimpanzees and humans) have always had cultural institutions. If this is true, then every new institution must be a composite of features of the old and inventions for reform. Consequently, I begin my analysis of the framing of the United States Constitution with some comments on its predecessor institutions.

These predecessor institutions vary in temporal contiguity to the Constitution. The closest are the Articles of Confederation (1781–89) and the national government of the Continental Congress (1774–89) that the Articles had regularized. Simultaneously with that national government stand the thirteen state governments (beginning variously in 1775 and 1776, and lasting until today, though all of them went through constitutional revisions after 1789). Earlier are the colonial governments, both those in North America and, more importantly, the government in London with colonial administrators, the privy council, the cabinet, and the king. Of wider significance is the whole government of the motherland as a political model. Finally, standing behind all of these is the historical knowledge of earlier federal governments: the Dutch Republic (from 1570 and still existing in 1787, though fallen from its seventeenth-century glory), the Swiss Confederation (from the late fourteenth century and still existing in 1787), the dual monarchy in Britain (from the accession of James I, 1603, to the Act of Union, 1707), the ancient Greek leagues, and so on.

I think the last group of conceivable influences, that is, the institutions that no one alive in 1787 had experienced personally, were wholly insignificant for the framing. Theoretically, there must be some terminus to the backward search for influence. This is for two reasons, one psychological, one social: psychologically, it is well established that humans can call into active cognitive consciousness only a limited number of considerations, such as earlier events and institutions. For each of us, presumably, the more remote an institution, temporally or spatially, the less likely it is that we will choose to consider it in place of a recent and nearby one that we have participated in or observed. Socially—and this is probably the more important reason—an earlier institution can be significant for a later one only if the great bulk of the participating framers comprehend its relevance. If only a few so comprehend, they really cannot communicate with the uninstructed others unless they instruct them. It is undoubtedly easier, however, to immediately discuss some mutually well-understood institution than to teach about unknown institutions so that they can then be discussed.

There are therefore good theoretical reasons, rooted in the nature of the human psyche and group structure, for only recent institutions to influence developing institutions significantly. At best a remote institution may influence its immediate successor, which in turn influences its immediate successor, and so on until the present, but it is hard to ascribe causal influence to a remote institution at the beginning of such a chain, when the influential structure has been modified repeatedly. Certainly when a remote influence is transmitted through some immediate predecessor, the latter deserves the credit. Beyond this, however, there is also good historical evidence in the case of the drafting of the American Constitution that remote institutions did not count (Riker 1957, 1987). Quite a large number of earlier federations were mentioned during the drafting and ratification of the Constitution.[1] By far the most frequently mentioned was the Dutch Republic, which was discussed thirty-seven times in the Philadelphia Convention and the state ratifying conventions. It is very difficult, however, to show that Dutch institutions influenced the American framers. In the first place, Americans knew little about the Netherlands. Apparently no framer could read Dutch. In American libraries, there were very few English or French books about Dutch politics. In the second place, almost all of the available sources repeated the misleading half-truth that the Union of Utrecht imposed a rule of provincial unanimity on the legislature. Consequently, Americans knew very little about the way the Dutch Constitution really worked, about the quasi-majoritarian loopholes, about the role of the House of Nassau, about the insignificance of five of the seven provinces, and so on.

For these two reasons, the actual Dutch example could not have a direct influence on framers. Since they all knew about the unanimity rule, however, they could use a reference to Dutch experience as a metaphor for their own unanimity rule that they understood very well. According to whether a speaker or writer disapproved or approved of that provision of the Articles of Confederation, he interpreted Dutch institutions as either a bad or good example. That is the entire influence of the Dutch example on the American Constitution: a convenient, though inappropriate, metaphor in debate. Though I lack evidence about other remote institutions, I am confident that careful study would reveal that they are equally irrelevant.

The temporally and spatially closest institutions to the American framers were the thirteen state governments in 1787 and the national government under the Articles of Confederation. The framers understood these institutions very well. The fifty-five delegates to the convention in Philadelphia were all active politicians—they had all been elected by state legislatures to that office. All but one had also been elected to other offices, often many offices and often many times. Forty of the fifty-five had been delegates to the Continental Congress at some time in the previous thirteen years. Consequently, the framers had among them substantial knowledge of the current political institutions. It seems worthwhile, therefore, to look at these immediate predecessors in order to find influences on the Constitution.

Most of the state governments in 1787 were versions of the British three-branch system with legislative, executive, and judicial parts. The states developed this system from the colonial governments, who in turn had inherited it from seventeenth-century Britain. The framers continued the three-branch system in the Constitution, so there is a direct line of descent from seventeenth-century Britain to the contemporary United States. All of these governments are quite unlike the main alternative, namely the continental systems of either the seventeenth century or today.

The structure of the states' three-branch system included a lower house for which the eligible electors were the bulk of the adult, white males—a much wider suffrage than for the House of Commons at that time. Most of the states had an upper house; but, since there was no aristocracy to form a House of Lords, either the lower house or eligible voters chose the members of the upper house. (In some cases the upper house was a governor's council, rather more like the privy council than the House of Lords.) Then there was in all cases an executive—in eleven states a single person, just as in Britain. Again, however, since there was no hereditary monarch, either the legislators or the voters elected the executive. Finally, the judicial system copied the English common-law courts and the British enforcement officers (sheriffs).

There does not seem to have been much dissatisfaction with this basic three-branch structure, as indicated by the fact that the framers copied it more or less directly. In two states, however, the framers of the state constitution had developed a quite different system: Pennsylvania, copied by Georgia, had a single house and a plural executive. Pennsylvania divided sharply on the merits of this constitution, which was, in fact, closer in spirit to the Articles of Confederation than to the other state governments. In the 1780s, Pennsylvania alone of all the states had two named political parties, and the nominal point of division was this constitution. Those who supported it, mostly agrarian radicals, were "Constitutionalists," while those who opposed it, mostly rural moderates and commercial interests, were "Republicans."

Of the eight Pennsylvania delegates to the Constitutional Convention, seven were Republicans. Two of these, James Wilson and Gouverneur Morris, were extremely outspoken in denouncing proposed structural features reminiscent of the Pennsylvania constitution. The only Constitutionalist was Benjamin Franklin and he was, at this point in his life, above party politics; on structural issues he shared the views of Wilson and Morris. Naturally, delegates from other states received a highly unfavorable account of the Pennsylvania constitution. In the end, therefore, the Federal Convention rejected all structural features reminiscent of the Pennsylvania system of a one-house legislature and an executive committee. Instead, they adopted the conventional three-branch system, just like the rest of the country.

In one respect, however, the framers reached back to colonial institutions. They were convinced that the government of the Articles was a failure. This government consisted of a poorly organized, unicameral legislature in which states were represented equally. This legislature had relatively little authority and most of the governmental initiative resided in the state governments. There was also a small bureaucracy, inadequately supervised by constantly changing committees of the legislature. The framers were especially distressed by the lack of sufficient authority for the central government and by the lack of a strong, independent executive. To remedy the decentralization, they strengthened the national legislature with additional authority over subjects formerly governed exclusively by the states. At the same time, to forestall abuse by the central authority, they divided the legislature into three houses (i.e., two legislative houses and the executive with a conditional veto). To remedy the lack of an executive, they created a single-person executive, whom they strengthened by a conditional veto on legislation and by an electoral procedure that (partially) bypassed the legislature. The net result was that the new form of the national government recaptured the centralization formerly lodged in the government in London (i.e., in the cabinet and privy council). At the same time, a three-branch system (with separated powers to prevent abuse) replaced the unrestrained, though ineffective, legislature of the Articles.

There is no question that most of the framers thought the government of the Articles was inadequate. Of the fifty-five delegates to the Federal Convention, forty-nine ended up preferring the Constitution to the Articles. Suppose we could arrange the framers on a scale (as in fig. 1) of "consolidation" (i.e., centralization) from the left end of decentralization to the right end of centralization. The Articles would be at point A on the left and the Constitution at point C on the right. The midpoint between them is M and, if the framers had Euclidian preferences on this subject, those to the left of M would oppose the Constitution and those to the right of M would favor it. As shown in figure 1, there are six framers left of M and forty-nine to its right. But not all of those left of M were fully satisfied with the Articles. Probably Luther Martin (MD), who was the most articulate and persistent opponent at Philadelphia, was close to and perhaps even left of A. So also were John Mercer (MD), who was present for only a couple of weeks, and John Lansing (NY) and Robert Yates (NY), both of whom went home after about a month (out of three and one-half months). However, two others of the six opponents, Elbridge Gerry (MA) and George Mason (VA), were

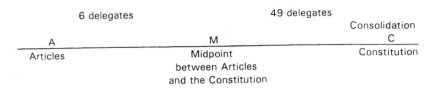

Fig. 1.   Range of opinion on consolidation at the Federal Convention

active reformers through most of the convention. They revealed their opposition only toward the end. Presumably, therefore, they were not located at A, but were somewhere between A and M, not satisfied with the Articles but in the end preferring the Articles to the Constitution. So by this calculation, only four of the fifty-five were truly satisfied with the Articles.

Why? What was so wrong with the Articles? After all, when it came to a popular vote, probably 45 percent of the voters for delegates to ratifying conventions were somewhere to the left of M on the scale of figure 1. Yet only 11 percent of the delegates to the Federal Convention lay in that range. Clearly the framers were much more disillusioned with the Articles than was the general populace. What did the framers know and believe that made them so hostile to the Articles?

At the simplest level, they knew that the Articles didn't work. Forty of them had been congressmen and so understood the Congress of the Articles. (Incidentally, only Elbridge Gerry of those who ended up left of M had been a congressman and Gerry lay somewhere to the right of A. The other five lacked experience with Congress and perhaps did not realize how truly inadequate it was.) However, even those framers who had not been congressmen had a pretty clear picture of the state of Congress in 1787. Consider this remark of Caleb Strong (MA), who had not himself been in Congress. Apropos of his decision to support the motion for equal representation of the states in the Senate, which would, of course, work to the disadvantage of Massachusetts, Strong said: "It is agreed on all hands that Congress are nearly at an end. If no Accomodation [between the large and small states on Senatorial representation] takes place, the Union itself must soon be dissolved" (Farrand 1966, 1:7, 14 July 1787). Elbridge Gerry (MA) also supported the motion for this reason. Thus, two large-state delegates—one from each side of M in figure 1—chose to support the small-state position because they recognized that the Articles had simply ceased to work. Incidentally, these two were certainly the marginal voters who carried the motion and, in my opinion, the motion was itself essential for the adoption of the Constitution. Thus, the imminent collapse of the government of the Articles was the apparent spur that led these two delegates to act, against the myopic interests of their state, to supersede the Articles.

Strong, Gerry, and many others were undoubtedly correct in thinking that the Congress was collapsing. There is good objective evidence on this point. Not enough states sent delegates to Congress to do business. Effective attendance at the Continental Congress had declined ever since the Articles had required two delegates in order to cast a state's vote. By the summer of 1787, during the months (May to August) that the convention was in progress, the nine states requisite to pass substantive motions were present on only 8 percent of the working days (Riker 1987). When Caleb Strong said "Congress are at an end" he was simply reflecting this statistical fact.

Beneath this obvious decay were a myriad other defects. For example, Congress itself was poorly organized: term limits forced the retirement of experienced legislators; a system of ad hoc committees prevented members from becoming informed specialists; and an organization without leadership (i.e., no party caucuses and a weak presiding officer) discouraged and delayed decision. Even worse than these structural defects was the absence of the ability to take action: Congress had no regular source of funds. It requisitioned funds from the states and the states paid or not as they chose. Twice Congress had sought an impost (i.e., a 5 percent tariff) and, owing to the rule of unanimity for revisions of the Articles, had failed each time by a one-state veto. Even if Congress had had more resources, however, it still lacked authority to take action on national problems, such as the regulation of interstate commerce.

In short, there were many constitutional defects in the Articles and the framers correctly saw the need for reform. So did most of the state legislatures. All but one of them had observed and predicted the decline of the Articles from the defects I have already listed. That is indeed why twelve of them sent delegates to the Constitutional Convention. It is true that, subsequently, the ratification was closely contested. That does not mean the opponents thought the Articles were adequate, however. Rather, it means that they thought the framers had gone too far toward consolidation. Their judgment was against the Constitution, not in favor of the Articles.

While the Articles were thus generally disapproved, the framers did not initially agree on the essential features of the defects. Early in the convention when the New Jersey Plan, which retained the main structure of the Articles, was put against the Virginia Plan, which provided for a consolidated national government with the three-branch system, the vote was 7 to 3 with one state divided in favor of the Virginia Plan. By this decision and repeated subsequent emphasis, however, the majority persuaded the minority to a position that is perhaps best described by James Madison's paper, written in April 1787, "The Vices of the Political System of the United States" (Rutland 1975, 345–58).

Madison listed twelve vices that can be summarized in two categories: (*a*) the inability of the national government to control the excesses of the states and (*b*) the tendency of the states to commit irresponsible actions. Madison's evidence for the first kind of vice included Congress' inability to undertake actions in the common interest, to coerce states or people to obey national laws, to collect requisitions, to punish states' refusal to abide by the peach treaty with Britain, or to resist state encroachments on national authority or the rights of other states. While Madison presented less evidence for the second kind of vice, he mentioned the multiplicity, mutability, injustice, and impotence of state laws. He seems mainly to have had in mind the rapidly spreading movement for paper money inflation. Certainly he believed a strong national government would not tolerate paper money for, as he said in a letter to George Washington, even the weak Congress would never "give assent to paper money" (Rutland 1975, 384, 16 April 1787).

Taking Madison's description of the vices as the defects that most framers sought to repair, one sees immediately how they arrived at their new structure for the national government. Madison also devised their working model. In a series of letters in the spring of 1787 to Thomas Jefferson, Edmund Randolph, and George Washington, Madison outlined appropriate provisions (Riker 1987; Rutland 1975, 317–22, 368–71, 382–87, 19 March, 8 April, and 16 April 1787). The Virginia delegates, who arrived on time (14 May 1787) for the Philadelphia convention utilized their waiting time until other delegates showed up (May 25) with revising and adopting the provisions in Madison's letters as a formal proposal for the convention, to be called the Virginia Plan. The Constitution is a clear-cut descendant of the Virginia Plan (and of Madison's letters).

The essential features of this plan were that the states had almost no role in it and that it embodied the three-branch system of the states and the British government. Had the Virginia Plan been adopted exactly as initially presented, the Constitution would have established a fully consolidated national government, with the states reduced to something like today's cities and counties. It provided for a lower house elected directly by the people (without intervention by states), for an upper house elected by the lower from nominees proposed by state legislatures (which was the only concession to states in the entire plan), for an executive and judiciary selected by the national legislature, for plenary national power over all matters of national concern (including taxes), and, most astonishingly, for a national veto on state laws. This last provision was Madison's favorite and when it was excised (because other framers thought the judiciary would indirectly carry out this function), he was convinced the final system was deeply flawed. After the convention he wrote to Thomas Jefferson in France to explain his disappointment. Saying the veto was needed "to prevent encroachment on the general authority" and "to prevent instability and injustice in the legislation of the States"—the characteristic defects of federations—and contrasting parliamentary authority in Britain, he then wrote: "If the supremacy of the British Parliament is not necessary, as has been contended, for the harmony of that Empire; it is evident that without the royal negative or some equivalent control, the unity of the system would be destroyed" (Rutland 1975, 109–10, 23 October 1787).

As this discussion of the proposed veto reveals, Madison saw it as recapturing the prerevolutionary centralizing structure of the privy council (i.e., the royal negative). In adopting a system into which this veto fit neatly, Madison, the Virginians, and ultimately the whole convention were reestablishing the sovereign authority of the tried and true three-branch system. They rejected the unicameralism attempted in Pennsylvania and in Congress, because a sovereign unicameral body could be tyrannical and an alliance-type unicameral body was demonstrably anarchic. So back they went to something like the prewar Constitution of the British Empire.

Internal Consistency

Having outlined the predecessor institutions, I now turn to an interpretation of the internal consistency of the Constitution. By internal consistency I mean that the details of the institutions are all aimed at achieving goals in an ordered way. Thus, if framers prefer goal a to goal b, then they do not adopt an instrument to achieve b that interferes with the achievement of goal a. The only way to guarantee such internal consistency is to order the group's goals transitively. An ordering is an arrangement such that, for three goals, a, b, and c, the group prefers a to b and c, and b to c. This transitive arrangement means that some goal, here a, is unequivocally best. If the arrangement of goals is intransitive (e.g., the group prefers a to b, b to c, and c to a), however, then it is impossible to say what goal is socially best.

To see the consequence of uncertainty about what is best, consider a group with transitive goals, a, b, and c, and alternative institutional details, j and k. Let j be highly effective for satisfying a and in lesser degree b, but harmful for c. Let k be effective in the same degree for satisfying b and highly effective for satisfying c, but harmful for a. In this case, there is no problem of choice: j is clearly better. Now assume the same group has intransitive goals, a preferred to b, b preferred to c, and c preferred to a. It is now completely unclear whether j or k is better. Whether the group chooses j or k is not determined by what the group as a whole wants to achieve, but rather by the luck and parliamentary skill of the subgroups that prefer a to b or c to a. In any event, since the groups overlap, some majority is bound to be disappointed and to believe that it lost unfairly.

The only way to guarantee the internal consistency of institutions is to have a transitive social ordering of goals. Yet this is extremely difficult in large social groups with many goals. In the case of forty or fifty decision makers and a large number of goals, the a priori expectation of a transitive ordering is zero (Niemi and Weisberg 1968). If there are several dimensions of judgment (as in the case of the Constitution, where there were clearly at least two: consolidation and liberty), then, generically, the expectation of an ordering is also zero (McKelvey 1979). Within a well-organized polity the structure of decision helps people to reduce the number of dimensions to one and to reduce the several interest groups to a small number. Hence, it is often possible to arrive at an ordering of goals and thus to fit the details of an institution neatly together. In making a constitution for a polity, however, which activity, by definition, takes place prior to the time the polity is properly organized, the chance of ordering goals is close to zero. That is why internal consistency is so difficult to achieve in the typical situation of framing a constitution.

There is one situation, however, in which it is possible for a group to achieve internal consistency: one person can always, with greater or lesser intellectual effort, achieve consistency. Therefore, a group that is dominated by one man may, if he is conscientious and thoughtful, impose consistency on the group product.

Rousseau, a traditional writer who lacked the apparatus of social-choice theory and the notion of ordered goals, nevertheless reached something of this conclusion. In perhaps a rather mystical way, he recognized that some leaders could imprint a moral code on a whole society. In this case, then, citizens would think very much alike, would recognize and work to achieve the general interest of society, and would adjust institutions to fit this moral code. Rousseau called such leaders "Great Legislators" and his examples were Solon, Moses, Mohammed, and Calvin. That three of these legislators were primarily religious, not secular, leaders merely confirms the central role that the moral code plays in inducing popular agreement on the general interest.

Ignoring the mythic elements in Rousseau's assertion about charismatic legislators, I restate it in modern terms: Single-person framers write internally consistent constitutions. (Of course, this formulation does not entirely eliminate the charismatic feature. It is hard to understand how a single person might be allowed to frame a constitution unless in some way the framer appeared charismatic.) One can even, perhaps, reverse the sentence: Internally consistent constitutions come from single-person framers. So stated, single-person framers are a necessary and sufficient condition for internal consistency.

This claim, which is unproven although it has a lot of theoretical support, is useful for my case study. Tentatively accepting the condition, I ask: To what degree did a single framer produce the Constitution?

On the face of it this question seems foolish, because there were fifty-five people in Philadelphia and most of them played an active part in the framing. Nevertheless, one person, James Madison, played a very important, indeed dominating, part, perhaps approaching a single-person authorship. Of course, Madison lacked the personal authority to dominate on his own, no matter how thoughtful and clever he was. However, George Washington, who had the requisite personal authority, did endorse Madison's work, so that indirectly there was something closer to a single framer than might otherwise have been the case. In any event, the special roles of Madison and Washington suggest that the question is worthy of further examination.

There is no doubt Madison provided the outline of the Constitution. As I noted previously, the Virginia delegates waited in Philadelphia for ten days until the other delegations showed up. Virginians utilized the time to draw up a plan or agenda for the convention. Edmund Randolph, as governor, presented the so-called Virginia Plan as the first substantive business of the convention, but the plan was clearly Madison's. In table 1 I have listed the provisions of the plan in the left-hand column. In the three right-hand columns, I have listed the details of the plan that appeared in Madison's letters to Jefferson, Randolph, and Washington. It is apparent from this table that (a) Madison's thinking about the work of the convention grew more precise as the spring progressed and (b) by the time of the letter to Washington, Madison had worked out nearly everything in the Virginia Plan. Doubtless he presented his ideas to the Virginia delegates during their wait and persuaded them to adopt his plan almost as it was. Most of their changes were technical and their biggest change was so consonant with Madison's plan that I think it was likely that he himself suggested it. He had waffled about the election of the houses of the national legislature, whether to be by the people or by the state legislatures. In the Virginia Plan there is no waffling: the people elect the lower house and it in turn elects the upper house from nominees selected by state legislatures. Since Madison wanted to exclude state

TABLE 1. History of the Principal Features of the Resolutions of the Virginia Plan

Resolution No.		Included in Madison's Letters to		
		Jefferson 19 March 1787	Randolph 8 April 1787	Washington 16 April 1787
1	Correction and enlargement of Articles	x	x	x
2	Proportional representation of states	x	x	x
3	Two-branch legislature	—	x	x
4	First branch	—	x	x
	POPULARLY ELECTED	—	x[a]	x[a]
	term	—	x	x
	age, stipends, ineligibility, *recall*	—	—	—
5	Second branch	—	x	x
	ELECTED BY FIRST	—	—	—
	term	—	x	x
	age, stipends, ineligibility	—	—	—
6	Legislative authority	x	x	x
	as vested in Congress	—	x	x
	when states incompetent or harmony interrupted	—	x	x
	negative on unconstitutional state legislation	x[b]	x[b]	x[b]
	military power	—	x	x
7	Executive (separated powers)	x	x	x
	chosen by national method	—	—	x
	specifically, the national legislature	—	—	—
	authority	—	undecided	undecided
8	Council	—	x	x
	executive officers	—	—	x
	national judiciary	—	—	—
	conditional veto	—	—	—
9	Judiciary	—	x	x
	supreme and inferior tribunals	—	—	x
	chosen by national method	—	—	x
	specifically, the national legislature	—	—	—
	admiralty jurisdiction	—	x	x
	interstate and foreign jurisdiction	—	x	x
	taxes, impeachment	—	—	—
	national peace and harmony	—	x[c]	x[c]
10	Admission of new states, nonunanimous	—	—	—
11	Guarantee of republican government	—	x	x

TABLE 1—Continued

		Included in Madison's Letters to		
Resolution No.		Jefferson 19 March 1787	Randolph 8 April 1787	Washington 16 April 1787
12	Continuance of Congress until adoption	—	—	—
13	Amendment of new Articles by states only	—	—	—
14	Binding state officers by articles	—	—	x^d
15	Ratification by state conventions	x	x	x

Source: Riker. 1987, 26–27.

Note: Items in upper case: resolution more nationalistic than Madison; in italic: resolution less nationalistic than Madison.

[a]Madison offered the alternative of election by state legislatures.

[b]Madison emphasized *all* state legislation.

[c]Madison inferentially stated.

[d]Madison mentioned only state judges.

governments from national decisions, this change is certainly one he would have welcomed. In only one instance did the Virginia delegation significantly depart from the spirit of Madison's plans. It added state recall of national legislators. During the convention, however, this dropped out quietly.

The true author of the Virginia Plan was thus Madison, and his plan then served as the agenda for the convention. Randolph presented it (29 May 1787) and the convention immediately referred it to the Committee of the Whole. This committee revised it and reported (June 13 and 19). The convention then revised the committee report, in several ways substantially, and referred it to the Committee on Detail (July 26). This Committee fleshed out the propositions and reported back (August 6). The convention then revised the committee report and referred it to the Committee on Style (September 10), which reported back to the convention (September 12). The convention then adopted the Constitution (September 17). From this recital of its history it is clear that Madison's plan, as frequently revised, became the basic terms of the Constitution.

Several other plans were briefly discussed, but they got nowhere. Charles Pinckney (SC) presented a plan on May 29 but it was never discussed and has not survived. Alexander Hamilton devoted all of June 18 to the presentation of a three-branch plan, similar to the Virginia Plan except that the senators and president were to be life officers. The framers paid no attention to this quasi-monarchical proposal. The only alternative plan considered at all seriously was the so-called New Jersey Plan, which amounted to a revision of the Articles while providing for slightly more regulatory and fiscal authority for the Congress. The New Jersey delegation, supported by Delaware and part of Maryland, proposed this plan in order to preserve the equal representation of the states in the national government. The majority of the New York delegation, which opposed a change from the Articles, also supported it. After four days of discussion, however, the convention decided by a vote of 7 to 3, with one state divided, to stick with the Virginia Plan as its agenda (Farrand 1966, 1:322, and, for the political alignment, 1:242).

Assuming, then, that Madison provided the agenda and the outline of the ultimate Constitution, it is reasonable to inquire as to what he sought to accomplish. The answer lies in the themes of his paper on the "Vices of the Political System," where he emphasized the tendency of states to make bad laws and the inability of the national government to control state excesses. The Virginia Plan was therefore aimed at remedying these defects. In the first place, the states had no way to control the national government. Except for the fact that state legislatures were to nominate members of the upper house, no national officers were dependent on state governments for election. The people were to elect the lower house. The lower house was to elect the upper house. The two houses together were to select the executive and the judiciary. There was simply no role for the states. Furthermore, the national government was to have full legislative authority (implicitly including taxation because the plan did not mention requisitions from the states, but did require many national expenditures). In short, the plan created a new sovereign in which states had no role. At the same time, the legislature of this sovereign was to have the authority "to negative all laws passed by the several States, contravening in the opinion of the National Legislature the articles of Union," which, of course, would allow the national government to veto paper-money laws and other "bad" legislation.

Such is the intellectual coherence of the Virginia Plan, mostly, for certain, the work of one man, James Madison. The institutional details are all neatly worked out to satisfy the goals set forth in the "Vices. . . ." Had the Virginia Plan been adopted as written, it would have been as coherent as any constitution ever written, certainly as coherent as those praised by Rousseau. But, of course, the Virginia Plan was just an agenda for a set of constitution writers, and they modified it considerably because they had goals of their own, goals not necessarily consonant with

Madison's goals. I turn now, therefore, to an analysis of these modifications with the inquiry of whether or not the initial coherence of the Virginia Plan survived into the Constitution.

In the discussion of the convention it became apparent that other delegations had orderings of goals quite different from the Virginians. Delegates from the small middle-Atlantic states, while fully as nationalistic as Madison, were nevertheless determined that their states not lose the equality of representation they had in the Congress of the Articles. Often they appeared to be arguing for the decentralization of the Articles. The New Jersey Plan, devised to bring New York into alliance with New Jersey and Delaware, did guarantee equal representation by means of keeping most of the system of the Articles. However, the division between New York and the others appeared when the New Jersey Plan failed. The New Yorkers went home, while the middle-Atlantic delegates stayed until they obtained equal representation in the Senate. Then they were satisfied with an otherwise highly nationalistic plan. Indeed, when it came time to ratify the Constitution, with equal representation assured, the New Jersey and Delaware conventions ratified unanimously and the Maryland convention by a huge majority (85 percent), while other supposedly more nationalistic states (e.g., Virginia, Massachusetts) ratified by very close margins. Thus, these middle-Atlantic delegations shared Madison's nationalism, but put equality of representation as a superior goal. All of this is nicely summarized in a remark John Dickinson (DE) made to Madison: "You see the consequence of pushing things too far [for Madison had led in the floor debate for representation on the basis of population]. Some of the members from the small States wish for two branches in the General Legislature [i.e., unlike the New Jersey Plan], and we are friends to a good National Government; but we would sooner submit to a foreign power than to be deprived of an equality of suffrage, in both branches of the legislature, and thereby be thrown under the domination of the large states" (Farrand, 1966, 1:242).

Another variation in the ordering of goals is apparent in the whole Connecticut delegation and rather widely among individuals in other delegations. Delegates from Connecticut expressed a belief in the superior efficiency of state governments and small governmental units generally and they were in the forefront of the movement to retain a big role for the states. Roger Sherman expressed their view nicely: "All the states were sensible of the defect of the Powers of Congress. . . . [But] Each State like each individual had its peculiar habits, usages and manners. . . ." (Farrand 1966, 1:341, 343). The Connecticut delegates, of course, proposed the "Connecticut Compromise," which provided the states with representation in proportion to population in the lower house and equality in the upper house. Beyond this, however, Sherman frequently warned against depriving the states of authority (e.g., Farrand 1966, 1:34, against the use of the word "national" and 2:388, on the militia) and Oliver Ellsworth successfully moved to delete the word "national" (Farrand 1966, 1:335; "national" had been inserted by a narrow majority over the objection of the Connecticut delegation on the first day of debate, 1:35). The Connecticut delegates' position on the role of the states thus differed considerably from the position of the middle-Atlantic delegates. As Charles Pinckney (SC) cynically remarked: "Give N. Jersey an equal vote, and she will dismiss her scruples and concur in the Nat'l. system" (Farrand 1966, 1:225). In fact, this turned out to be correct. The Connecticut delegates, however, saw a positive value in state governments and they did not want to lose it even though they saw the need for a more centralized national government. Like the middle-Atlantic delegates, the Connecticut delegates placed equality above nationalism, but they were considerably less enthusiastic nationalists than delegates from New Jersey, Pennsylvania, Virginia, or South Carolina.

Still a third variation in the ordering of goals was apparent in the Pennsylvania delegates. Like Madison and Washington, they were extreme nationalists and they very much wanted to keep states out of the national decisions. However, they were not willing to accept the legislative supremacy embodied in the Virginia Plan. Their main sticking point was the method of election of the executive. In the Virginia Plan, the two legislative houses were to elect the executive who, by his veto, was then to be a conditional third house. However, for Pennsylvanians, this structure reminded them too much of their own populistic state legislature, which they despised. They were appalled that the national government might repeat their state flaws of legislative domination of the executive. Therefore, throughout the convention they fought for some alternative method of selecting the executive, some method that made him as independent of the legislature as was the British king. Their rationale was the ideal of the separation of powers. They emphasized that the executive "will be the mere creature of the Legisl. if appointed and impeachable by that body" (Farrand 1966, 2:29, G. Morris). James Wilson therefore initially proposed popular election, but it was more or less generally rejected because, as George Mason observed, it would be like referring "a trial of colours to a blind man" (Farrand 1966, 2:31). Gouverneur Morris, who was the most consistently determined on this point, eventually secured the passage of (and perhaps invented) the electoral college. To do so, however, he had to create a system that allowed the states a greater role in the selection of the executive than contemplated in the Virginia Plan. In the original Constitutional provision for the electoral college, the electors were chosen as the state legislatures directed. Initially, this meant that the state legislature itself chose them, although by 1828 most of the states had switched over to popular election. More significantly, for the framers, the Constitution provided that, lacking an electoral college majority, the election should be made in the House of Representatives with each state having one vote. Since the House was to choose among the five candidates with the highest electoral votes, this suggested that the college would act as a nominating body and the state delegations in the House as the actual electors. Gouverneur Morris, the manager of the motion and the probable inventor of the college, believed that ordinarily the college would elect (Farrand 1966, 2:512), but many of those who favored legislative election disagreed. Whatever the expectation, it seems clear that the college so constructed brought state legislatures into the electoral process, whether as nominators or electors. Clearly those who fought for this modification of the Virginia Plan were more concerned about effectively institutionalizing the ideal of the separation of powers than they were about subordinating states to the national government.

This disagreement in goals with the Virginia Plan does not, however, generate as much incoherence as might be thought. The author of the plan himself accepted Gouverneur Morris's argument from the ideal of the separation of powers. Indeed, in Madison's *Notes* his own speeches on this subject are even more eloquent than Morris's, even though Morris was unquestionably one of the most articulate and eloquent delegates. To us today, the elevation of the separation ideal above the nationalistic ideal may appear a serious compromise of the goals of the Virginia Plan, but since Madison apparently did not think so, I don't think we can make too much of this disagreement.

A final variation in the ordering of goals appears in the discussion of the Virginia Plan's provision for a national negative on unconstitutional state legislation. Madison, in his April letters, had favored a verbally stronger statement: A negative on "all" state legislation. However, the Virginia caucus had weakened it to "unconstitutional." I imagine that they thought the word "unconstitutional" covered the serious cases. On the floor it turned out that there was considerable opposition and the clause was deleted. The two main speakers against the provision were Roger Sherman (CT), who, as we have already seen, valued state government more positively than many of the nationalists, and Gouverneur Morris, who, as we have also seen, was willing to put ideology above the goal of nationalism (Farrand 1966, 2:28). In this case, however, I suspect

Morris was moved more by instrumental goals than by ideological ones. He feared that the "proposal . . . would disgust all the States" and, since he saw a less offensive alternative ("A law that ought to be negatived will be set aside in the Judiciary . . ."), he was eager to eliminate a provision that might well endanger ratification (Farrand 1966, 2:28). Madison was devastated and, when he reported to Jefferson in October about the convention, he included a long digression on the negative, which he interpreted as a protection against local injustice—an argument that has the flavor of his argument in *Federalist* No. 10 (Rutland 1977, 209ff.). Putting the best face on his defeat, he reported that the provision lost by a "bare majority"—but he misremembered, for the provision was excised by a vote of 3 to 7. In my opinion this difference in goals did not generate incoherence in the final document. In the first place, the disagreement was more about instruments than goals and in the second place, Morris was right: Judicial review was an adequate substitute for the negative.

Altogether these modifications do, however, reveal that the whole group of framers did not entirely share Madison's or the Virginians' goals. So the question is: were these modifications, based as they were on different goals, sufficient to induce incoherence in the finished document?

One way to approach this question is to examine the Constitution in relation both to possible alternatives and to Madison's goals. To do so, I begin by pointing out that the Articles of Confederation and the constitutions of all previous federations can be interpreted as a degree of centralization halfway between an alliance among a set of independent units and a unitary government over these units, as depicted in figure 2. (This figure shows all of the possible degrees of consolidation, from complete independence at the left end to complete unity at the right. Naturally alliance is near the left end.) These previous federations were all highly decentralized in the sense that the locus of authority to make national decisions rested, not in the national government, but in the governments of the participating units. I call such federations "peripheralized" to indicate that the authority to make decisions for the federation resides in the peripheral governments rather than in the center.

Madison sought to move from a peripheralized federation to a unitary government. It is not surprising that he failed to make this audacious leap. What happened instead is that the convention as a whole invented a new kind of government, which I call centralized federalism. This new government has federal features, but it is more like a unitary government than it is like the earlier peripheralized federations. In discussing it in *Federalist* No. 39, Madison analyzed the various parts of the Constitution to assess whether they were federal or national. While he

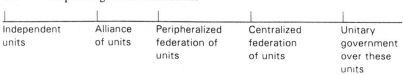

Fig. 2.   Degrees of centralization of a set of political units

was able to say of each part that it was federal, national, or a mixture, he could not define the spirit of the whole Constitution.

Looking back today, however, we can see what this new kind of government was. Madison was really more successful than he knew. While the state governments initially had considerable influence in filling national offices, the spirit of the system—or perhaps the interest of national officers mainly chosen nationally—was so hostile to state influence that the state government influence faded out rather quickly.

So far as I can tell, no one objected from a nationalistic point of view to the state legislative election of the electors. However, just one crisis with the electoral college resulted in popular election of electors and the exclusion of state legislators.

Similarly, the state legislatures soon discovered that they had very little influence over the senators they elected. The legislatures had been accustomed to detailed control of delegates to the Continental Congress. Since the terms were for one year and since even within the one year the legislature could recall its delegates, the legislatures could and did instruct their delegates on how to vote. It was different for the Senate, however. The terms were for six years and there was no recall. Although state legislatures continued to instruct senators right up to 1913 (when popular election replaced state legislative election), senators ignored or obeyed the instructions as they wished. State legislatures had no sanctions. Suppose they gave unpalatable instructions to a senator. If it was early in his term, he could ignore them, knowing that the state legislators would be replaced before he faced them again. If it was late in his term, he knew that the legislature was unfriendly and he would not be reelected, so he could ignore them anyway. State legislatures did try to find some kind of sanction for their instructions, but the best they could do was to try to make obedience a matter of honor, with the understanding that a senator who could not in good conscience obey instructions would be obligated to resign. As can well be imagined, this substitute for recall did not work more than a few times. Therefore, long before the election of senators changed from state legislatures to popular vote, state legislatures lost their role in controlling the senators they elected. In fact, they never had much of a role (Riker 1956, 1987).

Though Madison was extremely disappointed by the loss of the national negative over state laws that he had sponsored as a key element of his plan, the fact is that those like Gouverneur Morris who saw judicial review as a substitute for it were entirely correct. From the very beginning the Supreme Court disciplined states, and the great legal centralization under Chief Justice Marshall (1801–35) really consisted of repeated judicial restrictions on state laws. Even though Madison was by then a political enemy of Marshall, Marshall was still in fact carrying out exactly the program that the Madison of 1787 had advocated.

Madison, other Virginians, the Pennsylvanians, the South Carolinians, and the delegates from Massachusetts were deeply disappointed by their failure to obtain representation in proportion to population in the Senate. However, they recognized that the Connecticut compromise was necessary to obtain ratification by the smaller states. While this feature of the Constitution did not in itself give state governments a voice in the national government, it did overrepresent small state interests. As it turned out, however, the anticipated conflict between large and small states never materialized. As Madison pointed out in the convention, the real political issue in 1787 was between northern and southern states:

> The great danger to our general government is the great southern and northern interests of the continent, being opposed to each other. Look to the votes in congress, and most of them stand divided by the geography of the country, not according to the size of the states. (Farrand 1966, 1:476)

This remained true throughout most of the nineteenth century. By the twentieth there were so many states that large and small made little difference. The overrepresentation of the small states has made almost no political difference. Some might say that today the overrepresentation gives agricultural interests an excessive voice in policy. However, in European countries agricultural interests seem to have the same kind of excessive voice and yet they are not overrepresented. In less-developed countries, agricultural interests are a majority (whether over- or underrepresented), yet typically their voice seems quite small. It is therefore hard to say that small-state overrepresentation has ever had any significant political effect, for exactly the reason Madison adumbrated in 1787. On the basis of that reason he ought to have been indifferent to the overrepresentation so long as the national government was strong. His intense emotion on the subject was probably just part of the enthusiasm generated by political conflict.

In only one respect did a provision of the Constitution, namely, the residency requirement for Congress, permanently and consistently import a state influence into national decision making, and that provision seems to have been put in without much understanding or prescience. It appeared first (apparently from Randolph [VA]) in the report of the Committee on Detail. It was briefly debated and recognized as a federalizing feature out of harmony with the nationalizing tone of the Virginia Plan (Riker 1987). Still, it stayed in the committee report, probably because most of the debate concerned the meaning of words "resident" and "inhabitant," not the requirement itself. Nevertheless this requirement is probably today the most significantly federal feature of the whole Constitution and, without it, the central government might easily dominate the states completely. The requirement states that "No Person shall be a Representative . . . who shall not, when elected, be an Inhabitant of that State in which he shall be chosen" (Art. I, section 2, clause 2). Art. I, section 3, clause 3 imposes the same requirement on senators. The effect of these clauses is that they render nominations local. Unlike almost all unitary governments, the national leaders of political parties cannot impose nominees on states and districts. Congressmen thus owe their offices to local figures. This fact undoubtedly gives rise to a high degree of localism and state influence on national policy. It means that when state or local officials urge a member of Congress to support a particular measure, he or she is likely to comply, lest these officials cause trouble for him/her in the next nomination or election.

To summarize about the degree to which the convention floor deprived the Virginia Plan of the consistency it had from its single-person authorship, my judgment is that not much consistency was lost. The spirit of the Virginia Plan was so thoroughly nationalistic that the federalizing provisions imposed from the floor of the convention did not severely detract from its nationalism. The main federalizing features did indeed allow the states a continued role in governing, but not much role in the national government. Furthermore, the national features were so pervasive that the federal features have been gradually excised. Only the residency requirement remains a significant support for decentralization, but the kind of decentralization it supports is, of course, very little more than the constituency influence one expects in a democratic government. So it is the case that the net effect of the Virginia Plan and its modifications was a highly centralized federation, distinguishable from a unitary government, of course, but in practical operation not much different from one.

The proof of this last assertion about the similarity of the United States Constitution to unitary constitutions is the very popularity of centralized federations ever since the framers invented it in 1787. Prior to that time all federations had been peripheralized, some hardly more than alliances. Consequently, federation had not been a widely used form of government. Presumably the purpose of bringing independent units together in a federation is to obtain the benefits of a larger government. If the larger government is not strong enough to work, however, the benefits are illusory. So only rarely prior to 1787 had constitution makers thought federations worth the trouble of creating them. After 1787, however, federation became a popular form of government, and of course all of these federations were centralized on the United States model. In the two centuries since 1787 the following centralized federal constitutions have been written: in North America, Canada, and Mexico; in South America, Argentina, Brazil, and Venezuela; in Europe, Austria, Germany, and a revised and centralized Swiss constitution; in South Asia, Australia, India, Malaysia, and Pakistan; in Africa, Nigeria. Furthermore, there were a number of federations that ultimately failed: several in Latin America in the nineteenth century, several in Africa since the second World War, and in Europe, the Soviet Union, Yugoslavia, and Czechoslovakia. In short, the framers created a kind of federation not greatly different from the unitary government Madison had in mind.

Consequently, it is reasonable to say that the United States Constitution displays the internal consistency characteristic of single-person authorship, modified only slightly because it went through a process of review by a representative body. Because almost all of the members of that body shared Madison's belief in the desirability of centralization, they did not substantially revise his work, although they did place some federalist goals above Madison's nationalism and hence embodied them in marginal features of the institution.

The net result of their work was a Constitution that was internally consistent, so much so that it encouraged the subsequent users of the institution to revise it generally in terms of its ruling spirit. Doubtless this is what has allowed it to survive for over two centuries.

For the purposes of understanding institution making, we can draw one important lesson from the work of 1787: namely, that one way to ensure the effectiveness of an institution is to arrange its construction by a single individual who is able thereby to work out an internally consistent plan. On the other hand, institutions constructed by a group and containing provisions reflecting diverse goals are likely to be ineffective and unstable. An example is the constitution of the French fourth republic. In that act of framing there was no single party, like the nationalists of 1787, who dominated the process and hence no single framer who might provide a coherent plan. The result was a government with superficial plenary power to govern, but with built-in arrangements for deadlock (e.g., a peculiar kind of proportional representation and multiple parties). The compromise that produced this constitution was a fair one: each party was to have a chance of winning, with the consequence that no party did. A better French constitution was produced under the influence of one man, DeGaulle, in 1959. The moral is: coherence is important. Committees are not good at generating coherence; individuals are. I conclude with a suggestion: Let us look at all modern constitutions. I believe we will find that successful ones are coherent and coherent ones are the product of one individual, or at least one unified party.

NOTES

Grateful acknowledgment is made to Kluwer Academic Publishers for permission to reprint table 1, which originally appeared in *The Development of American Federalism* by William H. Riker (Boston: Kluwer Academic Publishers, 1987), 26–27.

1. For example, Hamilton (as Publius) discussed Greek leagues; in the convention Rufus King discussed the dual monarchy (Farrand 1966, 1:493); Madison collected books on earlier federations and wrote summaries of their defects; and so on.

Equal or Proportional? Arguing and Bargaining over the Senate at the Federal Convention

Jon Elster

Whenever smaller bodies are formed to represent larger ones, a mode of representation has to be chosen. One extreme is to give all of the larger bodies the same number of representatives, regardless of their size. The other extreme is to let representation be strictly proportional to size. In between, there are all sorts of compromise arrangements. This situation arises, among others, in the following cases. In coalition governments, smaller parties always demand, and often get, a more-than-proportional—although rarely an equal—number of ministries. (Exact analysis is rendered difficult by the unequal weighing of ministries: the prime minister, the finance minister, and the foreign minister usually count for more than an ordinary cabinet post.) In the United Nations and other international bodies, representation often follows the principle of "one nation, one vote." In the Security Council, however, a principle more closely approximating the proportionality principle is adopted. In federally organized countries, one chamber in parliament often represents the constituent states. In the Czech and Slovak Federal Republic, the Czech and Slovak lands have equal representation in the upper house, even though the former outnumber the latter two to one. In the German Federal Republic, the representation of the Länder in the Bundesrat falls somewhere between equality and proportionality.[1]

In trying to explain why a given body adopts equality, proportionality, or something in between, a number of considerations may be relevant. First, there is sheer bargaining power. Intuitively, we feel that the larger partners, having more clout, will never accept equal representation. Second, there are considerations of justice. Defenders of both equality and proportionality tend to appeal to notions of fairness and equity in favor of their proposals. Furthermore, efficiency may also be a consideration. Under some circumstances, proportionality may yield an inefficiently large body. Finally, the principle of representation may owe much to the procedures by which it is adopted.

All of these mechanisms were at work in the process that forms the topic of this article: the debate over the representation of the states in the Senate at the Federal Convention in Philadelphia. Although delegates from the larger states argued for proportional representation in both houses of Congress, the upshot was to adopt proportionality for the House of Representatives and equality for the Senate.[2] In one sense, this was a compromise solution. In another and more real sense, it was an out-and-out victory for one side. As nobody at the convention proposed equal representation in the lower house, the adoption of proportional representation for that body cannot be seen as a concession. Although proposals were also made (1:405, 488, 490, 510–11; 2:5)[3] to strike a compromise within the Senate itself, by which the representation of the smaller states would go beyond proportionality but fall short of equality, this idea never came to the forefront. I shall present the issue, therefore, as a confrontation of two extreme proposals.

We are, I believe, presented with a puzzle. Why did the small states get their way? How could they expect to survive outside the Union? Was their threat to leave it credible? I do not claim to provide a full answer to these questions. However, I shall offer some partial answers, or possible answers. The exact weight and relevance of these solutions is a matter I leave to those with the necessary historical competence. My aim is at once more modest and more ambitious. It is more modest in that I have rather weak explanatory pretensions; but also more ambitious in that I believe the mechanisms identified below can also be part of the explanatory story in other cases of a similar sort.

Arguing and Bargaining

Most forms of collective decision making are based on communication among the participants. In theory, however, they could just get together, cast their votes, record the majority outcome, and then disperse, without any communication. This, in fact, was Rousseau's ideal of political decision making. Communication among the voters, he thought, invited rhetorics and demagogy. By contrast, "if the citizens had no communication among themselves, the general will would always emerge from the large number of small differences, assuming that the people was sufficiently well informed."[4] This view is hard to take seriously, because of the implausible premise that the citizens could obtain information without communicating with each other. In practice, we cannot imagine collective decision making without communication.

In such communication we may distinguish between two basic types of speech acts: arguing and bargaining.[5] On the one hand, the participants may engage in rational discussion about factual or normative matters, making assertions with a claim to *validity*. The best analysis of the constraints on such communication is probably that of Jürgen Habermas.[6] On the other hand, they may engage in threat-based bargaining, uttering statements with a claim to *credibility*. On this point, the seminal work is that of Thomas Schelling.[7]

In constituent assemblies such as the Federal Convention, both arguing and bargaining have a central role. Two situations closer to the extremes of pure argument and pure bargaining are, respectively, ordinary legislative debates and collective wage negotiations. Yet even in these cases both types of speech act are observed. In legislatures the government can threaten to resign or to dissolve parliament unless its proposal is adopted. Legislators may use the threat of filibustering and engage in logrolling. (Note, however, that all of these forms of bargaining behavior are based on resources created by the political system itself. Threats to the adversary's life, reputation, or purse are not observed.) Conversely, even adversarial wage bargaining contains a good deal of rational argument. Professions that are prevented by law from striking nevertheless engage in wage negotiations. Even when the repertoire of the parties includes strikes and boycotts, bargaining over wages often includes discussion of purely factual matters, such as the wage increases of other groups, the financial health of the firm, or the expected rate of inflation. One cannot negotiate over such matters any more than one can negotiate over the weather.

Constituent assemblies are privileged, however, in that they often exhibit both arguing and bargaining in their most striking forms. Compared to other assemblies and committees, they differ both in their goal and in their setting. On the one hand, the matters that have to be decided are far removed from petty, self-interested, routine politics. Because the goal is to create a legal framework for the indefinite future, the requirement of impartial argument is very strong. Interest-group pluralism doesn't work when some of the parties are generations as yet unborn. The special setting works in the opposite direction. Constitutions are often written in times of crises that invite extraordinary and dramatic measures. In Philadelphia, many of the states threatened to leave the union unless they got their way on specific issues, such as the maintenance of the slave trade and proportional representation of all states in the Senate. The first threat was successful;[8] the second, as we shall see, was not.

According to Habermas, arguing presupposes commitment to the norms of factual truth, normative rightness, and subjective truthfulness or sincerity. It follows that speakers who want to *appear* to be engaged in arguing rather than bargaining must also appear to be committed to these norms. It is an exceedingly well-known fact of political life that speakers often pay lip service to the public interest, disguising their self-interest behind impartial arguments about the general good. In debates over electoral systems, for instance, the following pattern is found over and over again. Small parties argue for proportional representation on the grounds that it is more respectful of democratic rights (and not because it improves the chances of small parties). Large parties argue for single-member districts, on the grounds that this system enhances governmental efficiency and stability (and not because it improves the chances of large parties). What is less well understood, however, are the causes and the consequences of such behavior. I offer a few comments on this question at the end of the chapter.[9]

As just stated, strategic actors may find it in their interest to substitute an impartial argument for a direct statement of their interest. In addition, they may also find it useful to substitute truth claims for credibility claims. Instead of making a *threat,* whose efficacy depends on its perceived credibility, they may instead utter a *warning* that serves the same purpose and avoids the difficulties associated with threats. The terminology on this point is not settled.[10] I use *warning* to denote utterances about events that are not within the control of the actors and *threat* to denote utterances about those that are. Threats are statements about what the speaker *will do;* warnings are statements about what *will (or may) happen,* independently of any actions taken by the speaker. Thus understood, warnings are factual statements that are subject to the normal rules of truth-oriented communication. Disregarding a warning is more like disbelieving a statement about the past than it is like calling a bluff.

Procedure and Precedence

As briefly mentioned above, one explanation of the choice of a particular arrangement on the continuum from equal to proportional representation may lie in the rules of the decision-making body. Although that body may be free to adopt its own procedures, a natural focal point will often be some preexisting arrangement, which may in turn come to shape the outcome of the proceedings.

This is certainly part of the story of what happened at the convention. A crucial feature was that voting was by majority vote, each state having one vote. Although the Pennsylvanians wanted to refuse the smaller states an equal vote, their proposal was never put on the table (1:10 n.). When a committee was formed to forge a compromise on the upper house, James Wilson "objected to the committee because it would decide according to that very rule of voting that was opposed on one side" (1:515), but to no avail. Yet equality of votes at the convention could not in itself ensure that the outcome would be equal representation in the Senate, as decisions were taken by majority vote among the states, and the small states formed a minority. The large states failed, but not because the rules of voting in the convention made equal representation a foregone conclusion.

On closer inspection, the process of decision making involves three stages. In the first stage we have the convocation of the assembly by Congress. In the second stage we have the adoption of a voting procedure to be used at the convention. In the third stage we have the adoption of a voting procedure for the future Senate. *In all three stages, the principle "one state, one vote" was followed.* It is tempting to read a causal connection into this fact. The convention adopted the principle for its own proceedings because it was used by the institution that had called it into being, and it proposed the principle for the future because the smaller states at the convention benefited from the disproportionate strength that they derived from its use at that stage. As I said, the principle cannot by itself explain the final decision of having equal representation in the Senate, but it may have been a contributing, perhaps even a pivotal, factor.

Consider first the causes of the one-state, one-vote principle. Although, as I said, the convention was free to choose its own procedure, the mode of choosing that procedure could not also be freely chosen. More precisely, sooner or later the infinite regress would have to be cut short by agreement on some focal-point-like solution. Under the circumstances, it is hard to see what other mode, besides falling back on the Articles of Confederation, could have served that purpose.

Consider next the consequences of the principle. There are two mechanisms that could be at work here. On the one hand, there is the sheer force of precedence. As Samuel Patterson asked at the convention, "If a proportional representation be right, why do we not vote so here" (1:250)? On the other hand, the equality of votes at the convention increased the voting power of the small states. Since the small states were in a minority, this could not by itself ensure their victory. However, the voting procedure at the convention increased their bargaining power for logrolling purposes.

Whatever the mechanism, we observe a deep continuity in the process. The Articles of Confederation shaped the convention. Through the convention, they also shaped the Constitution that was finally adopted.

Arguing about the Senate

A central philosophical issue in the debate over representation in the Senate was whether rights attach only to individuals, or whether a collectivity could also be the bearer of rights. Advocates of individual rights argued that states ought to be represented in the federal assembly proportionally to their population, whereas those who believed in the rights of states argued for equal representation. Samuel Patterson claimed, for example, that "There was no more reason that a great individual State contributing much should have more votes than a small one contributing little, than that a rich individual citizen should have more votes than an indigent one" (1:178). Perhaps the strongest opponent of states' rights was James Wilson: "Can we forget for whom we are forming a Government? Is it for *men* or for the imaginary beings called *States*" (1:483)?

The argument for states' rights could take the form of a claim of equal representation. However, it could and did also take the form of a claim that each state ought to have at least one representative in the Senate. John Dickinson, for instance, argued (1:159) that any scheme that would give some. states no representation in the Senate would be "unfair." Madison and others argued that any deviation from proportional representation was "unjust" (1:151). To reconcile these two claims for justice, the smallest states could be given one representative, and the larger ones a proportionally larger number. That solution would, however, give a very large Senate, which would, in Madison's eyes, be "inexpedient" (ibid.). One way of characterizing the system that was finally chosen would be to say that expediency or efficiency together with Dickinson's conception of justice won out against Madison's conception.

Below I show how representatives of the large states invoked the difference between 1776 and 1787 as a bargaining argument in their favor. That contrast was also stated in terms of justice and rights, rather than of bargaining power. According to Sherman (1:348), the time had now come to undo the inequality created at the birth of the republic.

> That the great states acceded to the confederation, and that they in the hour of danger, made a sacrifice of their interest to the lesser states is true. Like the wisdom of Solomon in adjudging the child to its true mother, from tenderness to it, the greater states well knew

that the loss of a limb was fatal to the confederation—they too, through tenderness sacrificed their dearest rights to sacrifice the whole. But the time is come, when justice will be done to their claims.

Patterson (1:250–51) turned the argument on its head. "It was observed . . . that the larger State gave up its point, not because it was right, but because the circumstances of the moment urged the concession. Be it so. Are they for that reason at liberty to take it back? Can the donor resume his gift without the consent of the donee." For some, justice requires contracts to be binding even if they are unfair. For others, justice requires contracts to be undone if they are unfair.[11]

It so happened that the arguments for equal representation came mainly from delegates from the smaller states, while delegates from the larger states demanded proportionality. As in the case of opposed opinions on proportional versus majority voting (see above), it would strain credulity to believe that this coincidence was accidental. In fact, the fit is so tight that one wonders whether these arguments made any difference at all.[12] However, not all states fell neatly into the categories of "large" and "small." If we accept the premise that ideas matter when (not necessarily only when) interest yields no clear answers,[13] arguments for justice, fairness, and efficiency may well have made an impact on the states that had little at stake in this issue.

Threats and Warnings

To explain why political actors may find it useful to substitute truth claims for credibility claims, I first need to say a few words about credible threats. If a threat has to be carried out, it is ipso facto a sign that it has not worked. The event that the threat was supposed to prevent has already happened, and cannot be undone by executing the threat. At the same time, executing it typically involves some risks or costs to the actor. A rational actor will not carry out an action that involves no benefits and accrues some costs; if he believes others to be rational, and believes them to believe him to be rational, he will not, therefore, threaten to do so either. Following Schelling, many authors have discussed various ways of overcoming this problem. Here I shall discuss strategies that amount to substituting warnings for threats, thus making the issue one of truth rather than credibility.

The idea of substituting warnings for threats can be illustrated by a look at wage negotiations. Sometimes a union leader will say things like, "If you don't give us what we ask for, I won't be able to stop my members from going on strike," or, "If you don't give us what we ask for, the morale of my members will fall and productivity will suffer." Formally, these are warnings rather than threats. Needless to say, managers will not always take them at face value. They may suspect that the effects cited in the warnings are actually within the control of the union boss. At the same time, they can't be sure that the leader doesn't have access to information that they lack. Perhaps his members are, in fact, as recalcitrant as he makes them out to be. Perhaps, indeed, he has made sure, before coming to the bargaining table, that they are so heated up that he won't be able to stop them, turning them in effect into a Doomsday Machine. Note the difference between the latter strategy and other prebargaining ploys. Often, unions invest in the *credibility of threats* by building up a strike fund, for example. Alternatively, they can invest in the *truth of warnings,* for example, by irreversibly stirring up discontent among the members.

In the debate over the representation of the states in the upper house at the Federal Convention, delegates from both the large and the small states played on the ambiguity between threats and warnings. On June 30, William Bedford asserted that "The Large States dare not dissolve the confederation. If they do the small ones will find some foreign ally of more honor and good faith, who will take them by the hand and do them justice. He did not mean by this to intimidate or alarm. It was a natural consequence; which ought to be avoided by enlarging the federal powers not annihilating the federal system" (1:492). The statement is most plausibly seen as a threat, with the reference to the "natural consequence" serving to underline its credibility.[14]

On July 5, Gouverneur Morris counterattacked:

Let us suppose that the larger States shall agree; and the smaller refuse: and let us trace the consequences. The opponents of the system in the smaller States will no doubt make a party and noise for some time, but the ties of interest, of kindred & common habits which connect them with the other States will be too strong to be easily broken. In N. Jersey particularly he was sure a great many would follow the sentiments of Pena. & N. York. This Country must be united. If persuasion does not unite it, the sword will. He begged that this consideration might have its due weight. The scenes of horror attending civil commotion cannot be described, and the conclusion of them will be worse than the term of their continuance. The stronger party will then make traytors of the weaker; and the Gallows and Halter will finish the work of the sword. How far foreign powers would be ready to take part in the confusion he would not say. Threats that they will be invited have it seems been thrown out. (1:530)

Here Morris states that he understands Bedford's statement as a threat. His own reference to the sword and the gallows is more ambiguous. It can be taken as a threat or as a mere warning. Some of the other delegates undoubtedly took it as a threat, as indicated by the following retreat by Williamson on his behalf: he "did not conceive that Mr. Govr. Morris meant that the sword ought to be drawn agst. the smaller states. He only pointed out the probable consequences of anarchy in the U.S." (1:532). In other words, Williamson sought to make it clear that Morris had been uttering a warning, not making a threat.

On the same day, Bedford also retreated, by restating as a warning what was initially made (or understood) as a threat:

> he did not mean that the small States would court the aid & interposition of foreign powers. He meant that they would not consider the federal compact as dissolved until it should be so by the acts of the large States. In this case the consequence of the breach of faith on their part, and the readiness of the small States to fulfill their engagements, would be that foreign nations having demands on this Country would find it in their interest to take the small States by the hand, in order to do themselves justice. (1:531)

In general, there are two reasons why a speaker might find it to his advantage to substitute warnings for threats. First, as emphasized above, he does not have to worry as much about credibility. Even though his adversaries know that the events referred to in the warning may in fact be within his control, they must also take account of the possibility that he may have access to relevant private information that justifies his assertion that the outcome really is beyond his control.[15] It is not unreasonable to think that the union leader knows more than the management about the state of mind of his members. Second, warnings belong to the realm of argument and hence enable the speaker to avoid the opprobrium associated with naked appeals to bargaining power. At the Federal Convention, the restatement of threats as warnings allowed the proceedings to stay within the rules of the debating game.

Inside and Outside Options

In the previous section, I referred to one line of bargaining over representation in the Senate, based on more or less well-disguised threats of civil war and the intervention of foreign powers. In addition, delegates from the large states threatened that unless they got their way they would form a separate confederation that would exclude the small states. I shall now consider the credibility of this threat.

To address this issue I first need to say something about bargaining theory in general. Bargaining concerns the division of the benefits from cooperation, compared to a permanent breakdown of cooperation. In the case of bargaining among separate states, this alternative is just the ordinary international order (or anarchy). In the case of bargaining among estates, among political parties, between civil and military institutions, or between civil and religious institutions, the noncooperative alternative is harder to specify. For reasons that will become clear later, this difficulty does not necessarily matter for bargaining theory, as its most important requirement is that we be able to specify what will happen during a *temporary* breakdown of cooperation. On that basis, the theory attempts to predict whether an efficient agreement, that is, an outcome on the Pareto frontier, will be realized and, if so, which of the many Pareto-optimal outcomes will be realized.[16]

Bargaining theory has two distinct branches. The most developed is two-person bargaining theory, as applied, for instance, to wage bargaining between capital and labor. In the following, I shall limit myself to this theory, and ignore the more adequate but less tractable n-person theory. We can, however, use two-person theory to throw some light on the n-person case. In analyzing the Federal Convention, we may to some extent talk *as if* the large states formed one actor and the small states another, and use two-person theory to understand the nature of the bargaining between them. There were, however, other, cross-cutting divisions among the states that rivaled the size issue as potential foci for coalition formation.[17] Hence, a more adequate account would have to specify the payoff structure for all possible subcoalitions of the states, and propose a theory that, on the basis of these payoffs, predicts that the grand coalition will form and the terms on which it will form. The first task is impossible for practical reasons, and the second is unresolved at the time of writing.

Let us assume that the parties to the bargaining are rational and, more specifically, that they act to maximize some set of tangible rewards. In that case, the outcome of bargaining is largely shaped by two factors. On the one hand, the outcome is constrained by the *outside options* of the parties—that is, by the rewards they would obtain if the bargaining broke down and a permanent state of noncooperation were to pertain. A rational agent will not accept an outcome that is worse than his outside option. In classical (pre-1980) bargaining theory, these outside options were seen as the exclusive determinants of the outcome.[18] In addition to serving as a floor on the outcome, these options, according to the classical theory, also determine where on the Pareto frontier the outcome will be found. Modern, post-1980 bargaining theory asserts that the outcome, although constrained by the outside options, will be determined by the *inside options* of the parties—that is, by the resources available to them while the negotiations are going on.[19] Both outside and inside options matter for the credibility of threats. An agent can credibly threaten to break off cooperation (forever) if he can get more on his own than the other offers him. He can also credibly threaten to suspend cooperation (temporarily) if he can afford to hold out for a better offer.

Rather than elaborate on the formal definitions, let me explain the idea of outside and inside options by an illustration from wage bargaining. For the workers, the outside option is set by the wage they could obtain elsewhere or their level of unemployment benefits. Their inside option is set by the size of their strike fund and what other support they might receive during a strike. The outside option of the firm is set by the resale value of the plant, while its inside option is determined by fixed costs, inventory size, and the like. Outside options constrain the wage agreement: neither the workers nor the firm will accept an outcome that is inferior to what they could get on their own. Inside options determine the credibility of strike or lockout threats if the parties do not get a certain amount over and above their outside options.[20]

The last proposition throws light on James Wilson's argument that the equality of states in the Confederation was due to "the urgent circumstances of the time" (1:179) or to "necessity" (1:343), and that the Convention ought to adopt proportional representation since "the situation of things is now a little altered" (ibid.). In a time of national danger, time is of the essence. No single state can better afford to hold out than any other; hence, bargaining power is equalized.[21] In periods of comparative calm, the larger and more self-sufficient states regain their natural bargaining advantage.

Madison suggested a different argument for the same conclusion. Addressing himself to the smaller states who wanted equal representation,

> He begged them to consider the situation in which they would remain in case their pertinacious adherence to an inadmissible plan should prevent the adoption of any plan. The contemplation of such an event was painful; but it would be prudent to submit to the task of examining it at a distance, that the means of escaping it might be

the more readily embraced. Let the union of the States be dissolved and one of two consequences must happen. Either the states must remain individually independent and sovereign; or two or more confederacies must be formed among them. In the first event would the small states be more secure against the ambition and power of their larger neighbors, than they would be under a general Government pervading with equal energy every part of the empire, and having an equal interest in protecting every part against every other part? In the second, can the smaller expect that their larger neighbours would confederate with them on the principle of the present confederacy, which gives to each member an equal suffrage; or that they would exact less severe concessions from the smaller states than are proposed in the scheme [of proportional representation]? (1:320–21)

Here Madison is characterizing various outside options of the small states, without explicitly mentioning those of the larger states. Nathaniel Gorham supplemented the argument in this respect:

The states as now confederated have no doubt a right to refuse to be consolidated, or to be formed into any new system. But he wished the small states which seemed most ready to object, to consider which are to give up most, they or the larger ones. He conceived that a rupture of the Union would be an event unhappy for all, but surely the large states would be least unable to take care of themselves, and to make connections with one another. The weak therefore were most interested in establishing some general system for maintaining order. (1:462)

These statements, taken together, imply that the small states are in a weaker bargaining position since they would have more to lose if the union broke down. However, *both* the small and the large states would be better off under *either* scheme—equal or proportional representation—than they would be on their own.[22] The outside options do not, therefore, lend credibility to the threat of the larger states to form a separate confederacy, because, to repeat, they would be worse off on their own than they would be in a union organized along the lines demanded by the small states. Madison and Gorham were simply using the wrong model of bargaining. Wilson used the right model, based on inside options, in his reference to urgency and necessity. The large states had an edge in 1787, he claimed, because they could afford to hold out longer than the small states.

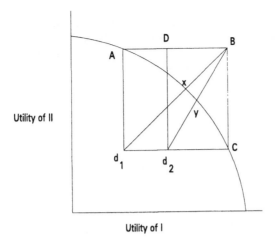

Fig. 1.   A classical bargaining theory model

To identify the fallacy behind the Madison-Gorham argument, consider figure 1.

Here, the area enclosed by the two axes and the curve represents the set of feasible agreements, measured in utility terms. The points d_1 and d_2 represent the outside options of the parties under two different arrangements. Consider first the bargaining situation in which d_1 is the outside option. Classical bargaining theories pretend to be able to predict (or prescribe) the solution on the basis of the feasible set and the location of the outside option. One of these theories (chosen here because it lends itself to easy diagrammatic exposition) asserts that the solution will be the point on the Pareto frontier that will ensure for each party a gain (compared to the outside option) that is proportional to his best possible outcome, constrained only by the need to offer the other party no less than his outside option.[23] In figure 1, the best possible outcome for I is at C, and the best possible outcome for II is at A. The theory then asserts that the solution will be found at the point x where the diagonal $d_1 B$ in the rectangle $d_1 ABC$ intersects the Pareto frontier.

Assume now that the disagreement point shifts to d_2, so as to improve the outside option for I. The theory then asserts that the outcome in the new game will be y, which is also more favorable for I. *Better outside options yield better outcomes.* This is also the intuition underlying the Madison-Gorham argument: the more you have to lose by failing to reach agreement, the less favorable for you the agreement will be that is reached. According to modern bargaining theory, however, this intuition is correct only to the extent that the outside options constrain the solution by providing a floor below which it cannot fall, which is not the case in figure 1. As the first solution x still yields a better outcome for I than the new disagreement point d_2, the shift of disagreement point should not induce a shift in the solution. To assert that it does is to assume an "action at a distance" that cannot be supported by the theory of rational behavior.

I said earlier that, in contrast to the Madison-Gorham argument for outside options, Wilson's argument for inside options for the same conclusion was formally valid. Yet, as we know, the large states did not get their way. One possible explanation is that Wilson was wrong about his facts, so that the situation was in fact perceived to be more urgent than he made it out to be. As I said earlier, the degree of crisis in the confederation in 1787 is an issue of some controversy. Although the solution adopted at the convention cannot provide evidence of the objective degree of urgency, it may perhaps indicate the urgency as *perceived* by the framers. Needless to say, I do not claim that the outcome—equal representation of all states in the Senate—can be fully explained by bargaining theory. The enhanced logrolling power that the small states obtained by virtue of the voting rules at the convention might also be part of the explanation. The normative, rights-based, and efficiency-based arguments discussed above may also have had some impact. I am not, however, trying to explain what happened at the convention, a task for which, to repeat, I have no competence. Rather, I am trying to *identify a mechanism* that may or may not have been at work at the convention, but that certainly belongs to the repertoire of patterns one might expect to observe in constitutional settings.[24]

Some readers will object to the idea that genuine argument, as distinct from paying lip service to argument, had any role to play at all. However, this objection, on reflection, is incoherent. If nobody cared about impartiality, there would be no normative pressure to appear to be impartial, nor any gains to be derived from doing so. The reasons that may force or induce self-interested speakers to adopt an impartial stance—the use of argument as precommitment, the normative pressure against overt expressions of self-interest, or the need to fool the public about what one is doing—all presuppose that some actors are genuinely committed to the ideal of impartiality. The strategic use of argument, therefore, is parasitic on the genuine, nonstrategic use.[25]

NOTES

1. Representation is not the only determinant of influence: the rules of voting also matter. In the Security Council the veto right of the permanent members

is obviously a major factor. In the Czech and Slovak Federal Republic, legislation requires a majority in both the Czech and the Slovak sections of the upper house.

2. I shall not dwell on the complex idea of proportionality used here, except to note that the rule allowed a slave to be counted as three-fifths of a free man for purposes of representation.

3. References to the proceedings at the convention will be given by the numbers 1–3 followed by a page number, corresponding to three volumes of M. Farrand (1966).

4. *Du contrat social*, 2:3. See also Manin 1987.

5. For the idea of speech acts, see J. Searle 1969, 1979. For an approach closer to my concerns here see K. Greenawalt 1989.

6. See, notably, J. Habermas 1984, 1989, and 1990.

7. The pioneering studies were made in T. Schelling 1960. More recently, noncooperative game theory has allowed the construction of a rich formal theory of credibility. For a superb nontechnical exposition, see D. Kreps 1990b. Recent surveys in the spirit of Schelling are Dixit and Nalebuff 1991 and Elster 1989.

8. P. Finkelman 1987.

9. For a more extended discussion, see Elster (forthcoming).

10. Greenawalt (1989, 251ff.) refers to "warning threats," as if an utterance could be both a threat and a warning. Schelling (1960, 123n.5) and Nozick (1969) use the distinction between warning and threat to differentiate between cases in which the actor has an incentive to carry out the announced action and those in which he does not. To tell a burglar that I will call the police unless he goes away is to warn him; to tell a girl that I will commit suicide if she does not consent to marry me is to make a threat.

11. Although one may argue that contracts made under duress are not binding if force is exercised by one party on the other or if one party exploits the exogenously caused duress of the other (Coleman and Silver 1986), it is much less clear that the same argument applies if the duress is due to external circumstances that affect both parties equally, thus undoing any natural inequalities that may exist. On this point, therefore, I believe Patterson had the better argument.

12. In my "Strategic uses of argument" I claim that impartial arguments, to have an impact, must usually deviate to some extent from the self-interest of the speaker. Of course, to serve that interest it must not deviate too much either.

13. This view is defended (in the "when and only when" version) in C. C. Jillson 1988, 16.

14. The statement, that is, may be taken as a warning in the sense of Schelling (see previous note), but not in the sense used here.

15. The point I make here is clearly related to the literature on "cheap talk" in bargaining and debating contexts; see, notably, D. Austen-Smith 1990; and J. Farrell and R. Gibbons 1989. However, I lack the competence to offer a formal model of warnings as cheap talk. Any such model would have to incorporate both the credibility of the utterance, if understood as a threat, and the probability that it is a genuine warning rather than a threat.

16. To my knowledge, the only attempt to apply bargaining theory to the constitutional process is that of D. A. Heckathorn and S. M. Maser (1987). The article is valuable in its insistence that constitution making must be seen as a bargaining issue rather than as a collective action problem with a single Pareto-optimal outcome. It relies, however, mainly on classical bargaining theory and hence does not confront the problem of the credibility of threats or the problem of "action at a distance."

17. See Jillson 1988.

18. For a nontechnical exposition, see Elster 1989, 54–68. For a full exposition, see A. Roth 1979.

19. For a nontechnical exposition, see Elster 1989, 68–82. For a semitechnical exposition, see J. Sutton 1986.

20. The exact way in which inside options determine the outcome is analyzed by a formal technique known as "backward induction." Crucial parameters include the order in which offers and counteroffers are made, the relay between the offers, the rate of time discounting of the parties, their degree of risk aversion, any fixed costs incurred during the bargaining period, and the probability that the potential benefits from cooperation might be destroyed by exogenous events.

21. The following analogy may be useful. The bargaining power of trade unions is often restricted by their limited strike funds. If, however, the state imposes compulsory arbitrations after two weeks of strike, their bargaining power is enhanced.

22. It is possible, however, that some of the states would be better off on their own than as part of the confederation. The opening debates of the convention, in which the issue was the strengthening of the national government, may well have taken place under the implicit and credible threat by some states of leaving the confederation.

23. For the original statement of this theory, see E. Kalai and M. Smorodinsky 1975. For a nontechnical discussion, see Elster 1989.

24. For the idea of a mechanism, see the Introduction to Elster 1993.

25. Again I refer to my "Strategic uses of argument" for a more extensive discussion.

The Emergence of Individual Rights

Itai Sened

Ever since Coase (1960) reminded us of the importance of property rights institutions in economic transactions, attempts have been made to construct systematic theories of the origin of property rights. Demsetz (1964, 1967), to use a notable example, suggests a neoclassical variation on Hobbes's "natural rights" theory ([1651] 1986). He argues that rights emerge from the natural inclination of human beings to control goods that are scarce enough to be valuable. Unlike Hobbes, however, Demsetz fails to recognize the implications of his argument. If humans are inclined to protect property rights over scarce resources for themselves, conflict is bound to arise. A theory of the origin of property rights must explain not only how this conflict arises, but also how it is resolved.

Umbeck (1981) follows Hobbes's argument to its logical end. He argues that, anticipating the Hobbesian "war of all against all," agents engage in contracts to establish enforcement agencies that use economies of scale in the production of law enforcement and serve as "barriers of entry" that allow members to concentrate on productive work. Umbeck shows that an agency with a monopoly over the production of law enforcement is a necessary condition for the emergence of property rights. However, he stops short of specifying the conditions under which such agencies would use their monopoly over the use of force to grant and protect individual rights.

Axiomatic theories like those suggested by Kant ([1785] 1981), Rawls (1971), or classical Utilitarianism (for a survey see Sen 1987) look for the origin of rights institutions in some "deep moral structure," or a set of fundamental moral axioms. Contemporary social-choice theory (Arrow 1951; Sen 1982) proved how problematic this position is by showing that some of the most "self-evident" moral axioms that are commonly endorsed by most Western cultures are logically inconsistent with one another (Sen 1982; Riker 1982).

The underlying premise of this chapter is that rights institutions are not constructed to satisfy abstract moral requirements, but to improve

161

ex ante expectation of agents from anticipated events (cf. Banks and Calvert 1989).

Game theorists who endorse this positive approach to the study of institutions tend to explain rights institutions as behavioral regularities—equilibria—in recurrent conflictual social interactions. Sugden (1986, 32), for example, defines a *convention* as "any stable equilibrium in a game that has two or more stable equilibria." He then goes on to argue that legal codes "merely formalize . . . conventions of behavior that have evolved out of essentially anarchic situations; . . . [and] reflect codes of behavior that most individuals impose on themselves" (1986, 5).

Like traditional economists, most game theorists systematically overlook the role of law enforcement. This chapter endorses a new approach to the study of institutions in general and rights institutions in particular that explicitly treats the role of governments in the evolution of such institutions. Many important social institutions do not emerge as equilibria in games among equal agents, but as equilibria in games among agents who control old institutions and agents who challenge such institutions with new demands. In particular, governments play a crucial role in the evolution of institutions that protect individual rights (Riker 1990; Sened and Riker 1992). Thus, we must include governments explicitly, as rational players, in any comprehensive theory of the origin of such institutions.

Governments in my model act as political entrepreneurs (cf. Frohlich, Oppenheimer, and Young 1971) who enter the business of granting rights in order to make profits (cf. Ainsworth and Sened 1993). The reason why granting rights is so lucrative was first suggested by Hobbes ([1651] 1986): without institutions, humans end up in a "war of all against all"—a very unproductive state of affairs. By granting and enforcing individual rights governments can improve productivity. Such improvements enable them to collect more tax revenues and other forms of support. This is the subject of section 1.

In section 2 I use a simple noncooperative game-theoretic model to specify conditions under which governments will grant and enforce individual rights. Surprisingly, the model provides an interesting positive explanation to the emergence of the norm of making laws public knowledge by showing that if governments did not make their law-enforcement policies public knowledge, they would not be able to benefit from their monopoly on the production of law and order. This is the subject of section 3.

The simple model explored in sections 2 and 3 assumes complete information. This assumption obscures the role of other agents—for example, economic firms and ordinary citizens—in the evolution of rights institutions. In section 4 I relax this assumption to unveil the role of individual agents in the evolution of institutions that protect individual rights. The model developed predicts that in an environment with incomplete information, governments may end up granting rights that make them poorer, or may fail to grant rights that could make them richer. This is the subject of section 5. However, both governments and ordinary agents are made better off by playing the game of petitioning for and granting rights. This final result is developed in section 6.

Thus, in this chapter, I develop a game-theoretic model of the process by which property rights are granted and enforced in a world with central governments. It turns out that this model provides an interesting rationale for the emergence of more fundamental rights institutions in modern societies, such as "the right to know your rights," "freedom of speech," and other institutional structures that allow agents to petition for new rights.

1. Public Goods, Property Rights, and the Role of Governments

A frequently invoked social dilemma is the problem of the provision of public goods (Olson 1965). The distinction between public and private goods relies on two basic features: (*a*) *Rivalry:* whatever is consumed by one agent cannot be consumed by anyone else. (*b*) *Excludability:* agents have exclusive control over the good and/or benefits that one may get from consuming it. Public goods are nonexcludable and nonrivalrous while private goods are excludable and rivalrous.[1] Providers of public goods cannot stop others from extracting utility from them. For this reason public goods are often overconsumed, undersupplied, or both (Weimer and Vining 1989, 40–44). Since anyone can enjoy the good once it is provided, agents are better off if others pay the cost of production while they consume the good as free riders.

The creation of property rights is one possible solution to the problem of public goods. Few goods are inherently nonexcludable or nonrivalrous. For example, when pollution became enough of a problem, property rights were established in pollutants (Hahn and Hester 1989). When congestion in the air, a classical example of a nonexcludable and nonrivalrous good, became a problem, property rights were established in air-slots (Sened and Riker 1992).[2] Thus, goods remain "public" only as long as property rights over them have not emerged.

One way in which public goods become private goods is when governments start protecting property rights over them. Historical evidence shows that property rights often emerge when governments impose them in order to enhance support and tax revenues (Simpson [1962] 1986; North 1981; North and Weingast 1989; Levi 1988; Sened and Riker 1992).

2. A Game-Theoretic Model with Complete Information

Consider the n-persons prisoner's dilemma—a commonly used game-theoretic conceptualization of the problem of public goods (Hardin 1982; Schofield 1985). Let $N = \{1, \ldots, n\}$ be a set of agents. Each agent pays a cost k_i to bear the duty and respect a right. For simplicity let $k_i = 1 \; \forall \, i \in N$. Each agent who respects the right increases the value of the right for any right-holder (except himself) by $0 < r/(n - 1)$, with $r > 1$.

In the "natural state," where there are no property rights institutions, each agent gets a positive payoff, $m \cdot [r/(n - 1)]$, if m agents $(0 \leq m \leq n)$ respect his rights, but would gain less if he paid the cost, k_i, of respecting their rights. I assume that no agent gets any benefit from respecting her own rights. Let $\Sigma_i = \{0,1\}$ (with $\sigma_i \in \Sigma_i$) be the set of pure strategies available to each agent where $\sigma_i = 1$ denotes that i respects the right and $\sigma_i = 0$ denotes that he does not. I assume that agents cannot discriminate among right-holders: they either respect the rights of all or respect the rights of none. Allowing for mixed strategies, the strategy space of each agent is $[0,1]$ with $p_i \equiv \mathrm{pr}(\sigma_i = 1) \in [0,1]$. Let $p = (p_1, \ldots, p_n)$ be a strategy vector with $p \in P$, and $P = [0,1]^n$. The expected payoff for every agent $j \in N$ from any $p \in P$ is:

$$u_j(p) = [r/(n - 1)] \cdot \left(\sum_{i \in N, i \neq j} p_i \right) - p_j \tag{1}$$

Regardless of what other agents do, $p_j = 0$ maximizes j's utility. The unique dominant-strategy equilibrium is $p^0 = (0, 0, \ldots, 0)$, where all agents ignore the rights of all other agents, with $u_j(p^0) = 0 \; \forall \, j \in N$. Let $p^1 = (1, \ldots, 1)$. If all players respect each other's rights, then $u_j(p^1) = [r \cdot (n - 1)/(n - 1)] - 1 = r - 1, \; \forall \, j \in N$. By assumption $r > 1 \Rightarrow r - 1 > 0$. Thus, p^1 *Pareto-dominates* the unique dominant-strategy equilibrium strategy vector p^0.

Introducing a government we get a *sequential game* Γ^g in two stages:

Stage 1: A government chooses $g \in \{0,1\}$, to enforce a right $(g = 1)$, or not $(g = 0)$.
Stage 2: All agents simultaneously choose $p \in [0,1]$.

The game form of Γ^g is a triple (D,G,F), where $D \equiv D_1 X \ldots X D_n$, with generic $d \in D$, and $d = (d_1, \ldots, d_n)$. $G = \{0,1\}$ with generic $g \in G$. A strategy $d_i \in D_i$ is an ordered pair $[(p_i \mid g = 1), (p_i \mid g = 0)] \in [0,1]^2$, specifying the probability $p_i \in [0,1]$ that agent i will respect the right, conditional on whether the government enforces the right, $g = 1$, or not,

$g = 0$. F is a mapping $F{:}DXG \rightarrow U \subseteq \mathbf{R}^{n+1}$, with $u = (u_1, \ldots, u_n, u_g) \in$ U specified by equations (2) and (3) as follows:

$$u_g(d,g) = t \cdot \left[\sum_{j \in N} [r/(n-1)] \cdot \left(\left(\sum_{i \in N, i \neq j} (p_i \,|\, g) \right) - (p_j \,|\, g) \right) \right]$$

$$- g \cdot \left(\ell \cdot \left[\sum_{j \in N} (1 - p_j \,|\, g) \right] + c_g \right) \quad (2)$$

One can think of t as a tax rate, so that the first element of the right-hand side (RHS) of equation (2) is the expected marginal payoff for the government, given g, from the improved productivity due to the fact that any number of individuals in society respect the property rights of other individuals. Such "new respect" for property rights can be interpreted as compared to the "natural state," where no rights are respected, or as respect for a new property right that was not enforced or acknowledged before.[3] The second element of equation (2) captures the costs of law enforcement. If a government decides not to enforce the right(s) then $g = 0$ and the costs of enforcement are reduced to zero. If the government decides to enforce the right, however (if $g = 1$), the government has to pay two types of costs: a fixed cost c_g, that covers things like routine patrols of police forces, and variable costs that consist of the average cost of dealing with any violation of the law, ℓ, times the number of expected violations, given g and p. To enforce the law—i.e., $g = 1$—means, in this model, to impose on every agent who disobeys the law a fine $f > 0$. Of course, if $g = 0$ then $f = 0$.[4] Equation (3) specifies the expected utility for any agent i given d and g, and accounting for government's law enforcement option:

$$u_j(d,g) = (1 - t) \cdot \left[[r/(n-1)] \cdot \left(\sum_{i \in N, i \neq j} (p_i \,|\, g) \right) - (p_j \,|\, g) \right]$$

$$- (f \,|\, g) \cdot [1 - (p_j \,|\, g)] \quad (3)$$

At that stage I assume complete information—that is, $r > 1$, n, c_g, k_i = 1, ℓ, f, and $0 < t < 1$ are common knowledge. In addition, I assume that $t + (f \,|\, g = 1) > 1$. This assumption simply means that the government is inflicting fines that are big enough to deter violation of the law.

An implicit assumption is that the strategy of granting rights dominates, for the government, the strategy of central management. A government has three basic options: (a) to take over the content of the right and manage it, ($g = 2$); (b) to grant property rights and collect taxes, ($g = 1$); or (c) to leave the good as a public good ($g = 0$) and forgo the marginal benefits from improvement in productivity due to enforcement of property rights. I assume that $(g = 2)$ is dominated by $(g = 1)$ and derive conditions under which governments would choose $g = 1$ rather than $g = 0$. This assumption can be justified on three different grounds. First, there is no reason why a government should have less hardship protecting its own rights than protecting the rights of other agents. Thus, c_g should be equal for both strategies. Second, to keep all rents from production to themselves, governments must enforce property rights without support from right-holders. Finally, private production is more efficient than centralized production. Since a government can extract, in this model, any fraction (t) of benefits it helped generate by granting a right (short of $t = 1$), it gains more by granting rights and collecting taxes than supervising centralized production.

I relax the assumption of complete information in section 4. Obviously, if $t = 0$, the government will never pay any positive cost, c_g, to enforce any right. Equation (3) implies that if $t + (f \mid g = 1) \leq 1$, then, regardless of the strategy of the government and the strategies of other agents, the strategy of ignoring the rights of others (weakly) dominates the strategy of respecting them.

As a solution concept I use the *Subgame Perfect Nash Equilibrium*, which, using the present notation, is defined as follows:

DEFINITION 1. *A strategy vector* $(\mathbf{d}^*, g^*)$ *is a Nash equilibrium iff:*

1. $u_i(\mathbf{d}^*, g^*) \geq u_i(\mathbf{d}^*_{-i}, d_i, g^*) \ \forall \ i \in N \ and \ \forall \ d_i \in D_i$.
2. $u_g(\mathbf{d}^*, g^*) \geq u_g(\mathbf{d}^*, g) \ \forall \ g \in \{0, 1\}$.

DEFINITION 2. *(Rasmusen 1989, 85) A strategy vector* $(\mathbf{d}^*, g^*)$, *is a subgame perfect Nash equilibrium (SPNE) if:*

1. It is a Nash equilibrium for the entire game.
2. Its action rules are a Nash equilibrium for every subgame.

Theorem 1 shows that in an environment defined by Γ^g, a government will grant a property right if and only if the *fixed* costs of law enforcement are smaller than the expected gains due to the enforcement of this property right.

THEOREM 1. *The following characterize all SPNE of the game* Γ^g:

i. $d_i^* = \{(p_i = 0 \mid g = 0); (p_i = 1 \mid g = 1)\} \ \forall \ i \in N$.
ii. $g^* = 0 \ if \ t \cdot n \cdot (r - 1) \leq c_g, \ g^* = 1 \ if \ t \cdot n \cdot (r - 1) \geq c_g$.

Proof. By equation (3), given that $t + (f \mid g = 1) > 1$, the unique best response (BR) to $g = 1$, $\forall\, i \in N$, is $p_i = 1$ and the BR to $g = 0$ is $p_i = 0$. Thus, the unique, dominant-strategy equilibrium, for the subgame starting following a decision by a government to enforce a right is such that all agents respect the rights of others, and the unique dominant-strategy equilibrium for the subgame starting after a government decides not to enforce the right is such that all agents do not respect the rights of others. Theorem 1 follows immediately, by backward induction. $\square$

Theorem 1 holds regardless of the value of ℓ, the cost of punishing a marginal defector, which means that the government threat to enforce the law is credible, in the technical and substantive sense, as long as the expected benefits to the government offset the fixed costs of enforcing the right and regardless of the variable costs of law enforcement. This may explain the seemingly contradictory observation that very few in society ever defy the law even though if many of them did, the cost to law enforcement agencies would be so high that no government could enforce the law. It is also notable, in this respect, that most law-enforcement systems in developed countries are based on fixed salaries. Governments usually do not pay policemen or judges any extras for prosecuting defections.

Bianco and Bates (1990) address a similar issue using the theoretical framework of repeated games. They show that if enforcement agencies can punish individual defectors discriminably—i.e., without punishing nondefectors—as the model presented here allows them to do, then they can initiate and sustain cooperation (proposition 7.b, 143). They also note that if law-enforcement agencies are rewarded with a fixed share, as in my model (t is the fixed share here), it is easier to construct "belief systems" that allow such agencies to make credible threats to enforce the law. The "belief system" that sustains the credibility of the government's threat in my model is the belief that all agents implicitly share in this model that if the government decided to enforce the law ($g = 1$), then the government would impose a fine f on any defector that satifies $t + (f \mid g = 1) > 1$.

3. Why Are Laws Made Public Knowledge?

Many democratic and nondemocratic regimes adhere to the principle that laws must be made public. Normative justifications to this maxim exist (Kant [1794] 1983, 135; Hegel [1821] 1942, § 215), but positive explanations to the commonly observed political institution are harder to come by. This principle implies that a government must make its decision whether to enforce the right or not public before agents decide whether to respect the law or not. This was the premise behind the game developed in the previous section. What would happen if governments did not publish their decisions on whether to enforce a right or not (that is, if governments and agents played this game simultaneously)? I denote this game by $\Gamma^{g'}$.

The difference between Γ^g and $\Gamma^{g'}$ is that in $\Gamma^{g'}$ agents do not know what the decision of the government was when they make their decision. Thus, agents' strategies cannot be conditional on the government's policy. The game form of $\Gamma^{g'}$ is a triple (D', G', F'), where $D' \equiv D'_1 X \ldots X D'_n$, and D'_i is the set of feasible strategies for player i. Unlike the case of Γ^g, a strategy $d'_i \in D'_i$ in $\Gamma^{g'}$ is just a probability $p_i \in [0,1]$ with which agent i will respect the right. $G' \equiv G = \{0,1\}$ and F' is a mapping F': $D' X G' \rightarrow (u_1, \ldots, u_n, u_g)$ respecified in equations (2')–(3'):

$$u_g(d,g) = t \cdot \left[\sum_{j \in N} [r/(n-1)] \cdot \left(\left(\sum_{i \in N, i \neq j} (p_i) \right) - (p_j) \right) \right]$$

$$- g \cdot \left[\ell \cdot \left(\sum_{j \in N} (1 - p_j) \right) + c_g \right] \tag{2'}$$

$$u_j(d,g) = (1 - t \cdot \left[[r/(n-1)] \cdot \left(\sum_{i \in N, i \neq j} (p_i) \right) - (p_j) \right]$$

$$- (f \mid g) \cdot (1 - p_j) \tag{3'}$$

THEOREM 2. *The unique Nash equilibrium outcome of $\Gamma^{g'}$ is one in which the government never enforces any right and all agents always ingore the rights of other agents such that* $u_g = u_i = 0 \,\forall\, i \in N$.

Proof. Equation (2') implies that the government has a dominant strategy not to enforce the right. Given that the government never enforces the right, by equation (3') $p_i^* = 0$ is the dominant strategy $\forall$ $i \in N$. □

Theorem 2 has a straightforward interpretation: without making the law of the land public knowledge, governments cannot escape from becoming themselves entangled in the $(n + 1)$-persons prisoner's dilemma. Thus, the maxim that requires that laws be made public knowledge is explained as an institutional solution adopted by governments that try to maximize their benefits as law-enforcement agencies. This institutional solution is an equilibrium solution in the sense that if governments were to decide first whether to make laws public or not, and then play Γ^g or $\Gamma^{g'}$ accordingly, they would always be better off making laws public. Thus, the institution of public law needs to be attributed not to a moral public interest, but to the fact that it is in the best interest of revenue-maximizing governments to make their laws public.[5]

Theorem 2 and the logic behind the proof point to the major problem with Sugden's premise that legal codes "merely formalize . . . conventions of behavior that have evolved out of essentially anarchic situations; . . . [and] reflect codes of behavior that most individuals impose on themselves" (1986, 5). A rational government will never spend any money on enforcing conventions that most individuals impose on themselves because the marginal benefit of stopping occasional defectors would rarely offset the costs of law enforcement.

Theorems 1 and 2 clarify an important implication of the monopoly that governments have over the use of coercive force that is often overlooked: it allows them to make credible commitments to use force against reluctant duty-bearers, which allows them to enforce the institutional structure of property rights necessary for the evolution of efficient competitive markets.

4. The Role of Ordinary Citizens

So far I have characterized, in precise terms, expectations about the behavior of rational governments facing possibilities of granting individual rights. I have assumed that they had complete information about the consequences of their decisions. The assumption of complete information, however, obscures the role of other agents in society in the evolution of individual rights.

Consider the case of a government that, based on its prior beliefs, does not expect to gain from granting a right. Agents who expect to benefit from such a right could be made better off by petitioning the government to grant the right. Let $0 < c_i < 1$ denote the cost of petitioning. Petitioning is not only costly, but it also involves a collective-action problem. As mentioned above, property rights are public goods: once they are granted all beneficiaries will benefit from the right, regardless of whether they participated in petitioning for it or not. Let $\sigma_i = 1$ denote the strategy of petitioning for the right, and $\sigma_i = 0$ denote the strategy of free riding. Let $A^1 \subseteq N$ be the set of agents who actually petition for the right, and $|A^1|$ be the cardinality of this set—i.e., the number of members in this set. Suppose there was a threshold, ω, so that if $|A^1| \geq \omega$ the government would update its beliefs and "realize" that it could benefit from granting the right, while if $|A^1| < \omega$ the government would continue to believe that the cost of enforcing the right offset the expected benefits of granting it. Lemma 7 and Corollary 1 in section 6 below show that such a threshold always exists. Theorem 1 implies that, given such a threshold, if the government observes $|A^1| \geq \omega$ it grants the right and all the agents respect it, while if the government observes $|A^1| < \omega$ it does not grant the right, no one respects the right, and no one benefits from it.

Palfrey and Rosenthal (1984, 1985) studied such participation games with the following characteristics: each agent $i \in N$ expects a payoff of $b = 1$ if a certain public good is provided. The public good is provided only if at least ω agents contribute a cost of $0 < c < 1$ each. The basic structure of this game is illustrated in table 1. Palfrey and Rosenthal show that for any threshold ω there are three types of equilibria. In the first, no one contributes. In the second, pure strategies type, exactly ω agents contribute. In this type of equilibria, however, identical agents who face the same game play different strategies. In addition, there is an implicit coordination problem since agents cannot predict who of the n agents will contribute and who will free ride. The third type of equilibria are "mixed strategy" equilibria. Of particular interest to us here is a subset of this type, namely symmetric mixed-strategy equilibria, in which all agents use the same strategy, which makes each agent indifferent between contributing and not contributing. Given this indifference, each agent may just as well use the mixed strategy that everyone else uses, which is the intuitive logic behind such equilibria. The attractive feature of "symmetric equilibria" is that each agent uses the same strategy, believing correctly that all of the other agents are using the same strategy that he is.

In these participation games, however, there is no role for a government. Once enough agents contribute, the public good is automatically provided by some implicit, benevolent provider, or by a firm that specializes in producing such goods. Here, I am concerned with governments that act as political entrepreneurs (Frohlich, Oppenheimer, and Young

TABLE 1. N-person Participation Game

We assume that	Player i's Strategies	All Players except Player i		
$b - c > 0$		Number of contributions from all		
$1 > c > 0$		players except player i		
$b = 1$		$< \omega - 1$	$= \omega - 1$	$\geq \omega$
	Contribute	$-c$	$b - c$	$b - c$
	Do Not Contribute	0	0	b

1971), providing benefits to interested agents to garner political support from them. In the next two sections, I model this interaction formally, incorporating a government with incomplete information.

5. A Model with Asymmetric Information

To introduce uncertainty about agents' preferences, I distinguish between agents who expect a positive benefit, $b_i = 1$, from the grant of the right, and agents of type $b_i = 0$, who expect no benefits from such grant. Let $S_i = \{0,1\}$ be i's pure strategy set, with $s_i \in S_i$, where $s_i = 1$ denotes "petition," and $s_i = 0$ denotes "not petition." The government and all agents have a common prior belief about a probability q that any agent is of type $b_i = 1$, $q = \mathrm{pr}(b_i = 1)$. Let $b = (b_1, \ldots, b_n)$ be a particular realization of n independent draws of $b_i \in \{0,1\}$ by the n agents, with a probability q that each draw yields $b_i = 1$. Define $B^1(b) \equiv \{i \in N \mid b_i = 1\}$. I use B^1 to denote $B^1(b)$ and β to denote $|B^1|$.

A normalized strategy σ_i is a mapping $\sigma_i: \{0,1\} \rightarrow [0,1]$ or an ordered pair $\sigma_i = [\mathrm{pr}(s_i = 1 \mid b_i = 1); \mathrm{pr}(s_i = 1 \mid b_i = 0)]$, so that agent i's normalized strategy set is $\Sigma_i = [0,1]^2$, with $\sigma_i(b_i) = \mathrm{pr}(s_i = 1 \mid b_i)$, $\sigma_i \in \Sigma_i$, and $\Sigma = \Sigma_1 X \ldots X \Sigma_n$. Let $\sigma = (\sigma_1, \ldots, \sigma_n)$, $\sigma \in \Sigma$, and $s = (s_1, \ldots, s_n)$ be a realization of σ. Let $A^1 \equiv A^1(\sigma) \equiv \{i \in N: s_i = 1 \mid s\}$ be the set of agents who petition in a particular realization s of σ, and $\alpha = |A^1|$. Let $0 < c_i < 1$ be the cost of petitioning for agent i. Assume that $c_i = c_j \ \forall \ i, j \in N \ i \neq j$.

(Re)Introducing Governments

What distinguishes this model from existing models in the literature is that I explicitly model the role that governments play in granting individual rights. A strategy for a government is a mapping $g: \{0,1\}^n \rightarrow \{0,1\}$, where $g(A^1) = 1$ denotes granting the right and $g(A^1) = 0$ denotes not granting it, after observing the group A^1 of petitioners.

Assume that government's benefits, b_g, from granting a right are a linear function of β, the number of potential beneficiaries of the right, $b_g = t \cdot \beta$. As before, $0 < t < 1$ may be interpreted as a tax rate. Recall that c_g denotes the government's costs of enforcing the right. I assume that c_g, c_i, and t are common knowledge, and that all players start with a common belief $f(\beta)$, where $f(\beta)$ is a discrete multinomial probability density function defined by q and n that assigns to every value of $k \in Z \equiv \{0, 1, \ldots, n\}$ a probability that $\beta = k$.

The game, denoted as Γ^p, is a four-stage sequential game:

Stage 1: Each agent chooses his strategy $\sigma_i \in \Sigma_i = [0,1]^2$.

Stage 2: Each agent gets from nature his type $b_i \in \{0,1\}$ and acts according to the strategy he chose in stage 1.

Stage 3: Government chooses its action $g(A^1) \in \{0,1\}$.

Stage 4: Agents decide whether to respect the right or not, given g.

Section 3 investigated the expected outcome of stage 4. Thus, we can now roll back to stage 3. In particular, by Theorem 1,[6] the payoff structure of the game can be summarized as follows:[7]

$$u_g(g) = \begin{cases} t \cdot \beta - c_g, & \text{if } g = 1 \\ 0 & \text{if } g = 0 \end{cases}$$

$$u_i = \begin{cases} (1 - t) - c & \text{if } b_i = 1, s_i = 1, \text{ and } g = 1 \\ (1 - t) & \text{if } b_i = 1, s_i = 0, \text{ and } g = 1 \\ -c & \text{if } b_i = 0, s_i = 1, \text{ and } g = 1 \\ 0 & \text{if } b_i = 0, s_i = 0, \text{ and } g = 1 \\ -c & \text{if } b_i \in \{0,1\}, s_i = 1, \text{ and } g = 0 \\ 0 & \text{if } b_i \in \{0,1\}, s_i = 0, \text{ and } g = 0 \end{cases}$$

Define $v_g(A^1,\sigma) \equiv E(u_g \mid \mu(\cdot \mid A^1,\sigma))$ where $\mu(\cdot \mid A^1,\sigma)$ denotes government's posterior beliefs about the number of beneficiaries. Define $\mu(\beta \mid A^1,\sigma)$ as:

$$\mu(\beta \mid A^1,\sigma) = \left(\frac{\text{pr}(A^1 \mid \beta,\sigma) \cdot \text{pr}(\beta \mid q,n)}{\sum_{\beta'=0}^{n} \text{pr}(A^1 \mid \beta',\sigma) \cdot \text{pr}(\beta' \mid q,n)} \right), \tag{4}$$

which says that the government uses Bayes' Rule to update its beliefs.

$$v_g(A^1, \sigma) = \begin{cases} \displaystyle\sum_{\beta=0}^{n} \beta \cdot t \cdot \mu(\beta \mid A^1,\sigma) - c_g , & \text{if } g = 1 \\ \\ 0 \text{ otherwise, i.e.,} & \text{if } g = 0 \end{cases} . \tag{5}$$

Substituting equation (4) in equation (5), we get

$$v_g(1 \mid A^1,\sigma) = t \cdot \left[\sum_{\beta=0}^{n} \left(\frac{\text{pr}(A^1 \mid \beta,\sigma) \cdot \text{pr}(\beta \mid q,n)}{\sum_{\beta'=0}^{n} \text{pr}(A^1 \mid \beta',\sigma) \cdot \text{pr}(\beta' \mid q,n)} \right) \right] - c_g \tag{6}$$

In words: the payoff the government expects, if it grants the right, is the sum, over all $\beta \in \{0, 1, \ldots, n\}$, of the payoff it expects given any β

(i.e., $t \cdot \beta$), times the probability of having β potential beneficiaries of the right, given the government posterior beliefs $\mu \left(\cdot \mid A^1, \sigma \right)$, minus the cost of enforcement, c_g.

Let $\mathfrak{N}$ be the power set of N and $W(g) = \{A^1 \in \mathfrak{N} : (g \mid A^1) = 1\}$. The expected payoff for any agent i in this game, $v_i(\sigma, g, b_i) \equiv E(u_i \mid \sigma, g, b_i)$, is

$$v_i(\sigma, g, b_i) = (1 - t) \cdot (b_i) \cdot \text{pr}(A^1 \in W(g) \mid \sigma) - c_i \cdot \sigma_i(b_i) \qquad (7)$$

Definition 3 defines the solution concept I will use to solve this model:

DEFINITION 3. *A sequential equilibrium (SE)*[8] *is a triple* $(\sigma^*, g^*, \mu(\cdot))$, *such that:*

1. $\forall \; b_i \in \{0,1\}$, $v_i(\sigma^*, g^*) \geq v_i (\sigma^*_{-i}, \sigma_i, g^*) \; \forall \; i \in N, \; \forall \; \sigma_i \in \Sigma_i$.
2. *Given* σ^*, $\forall \; A^1 \in \mathfrak{N}$, $g^*(A^1) = \underset{g \in \{0,1\}}{\text{Argmax}} \{g \cdot v_g(g = 1 \mid \mu(\cdot \; A^1, \sigma^*))\}$.
3. $\forall \; \beta \in \{0,1, \ldots, n\}$, *if* $pr(\beta \mid A^1, \sigma^*) > 0$ *then* $\mu(\beta \mid A^1, \sigma^*) =$
$$\left(\frac{pr(A^1 \mid \beta, \sigma) \cdot pr(\beta \mid q, n)}{\sum_{\beta'=0}^{n} pr(A^1 \mid \beta', \sigma) \cdot pr(\beta' \mid q, n)} \right).$$

Condition 1 says that σ_i^* maximizes i's utility, given the strategies of the government and all the other agents. Condition 2 states that g^* maximizes the government's expected utility, given its beliefs. Condition 3 says that the government's beliefs are consistent with σ^* in the sense that the government's posterior beliefs, $\mu(\cdot)$, are determined by Bayes' Rule according to its prior beliefs and the strategy vector σ^*. This definition specifies government's beliefs only along the equilibrium path. This poses a problem if a government observes an event that, according to its beliefs, occurs with probability zero. This can happen if $\sigma^* = \sigma^0 = \{\sigma \in \Sigma \mid \sigma_i(b_i) = 0, \; \forall \; b_i \in \{0,1\}, \; \forall \; i \in N\}$, but $A^1 \neq \phi$. Therefore, I use the Intuitive Criterion (IC) refinement (Cho and Kreps 1987). IC requires that government's off-the-equilibrium-path beliefs place zero probability on the likelihood that types who can only lose from defection defect. Here it implies that $\mu(b_i = 1 \mid s_i = 1) = 1$, and $\mu(b_i = 0 \mid s_i = 1) = 0$—that is, government's out-of-equilibrium beliefs put zero probability on the likelihood that a type $b_i = 0$ will petition.

6. Agents-Symmetric Equilibria

This section characterizes the set of agent-symmetric sequential equilibria [SSEs] for the game Γ^P. It is organized as follows: Lemma 1 shows that players of type $b_i = 0$ do not petition in equilibrium. I can thus limit my analysis to $\sigma_i(b_i = 1)$. Lemmas 2–6 are included mainly for the sake of completeness. Lemma 7 shows that for every strategy vector σ, if $\sigma_i(1) = \rho \in [0,1] \; \forall \; i \in B^1$, government's strategy in equilibrium must be a threshold strategy—that is, there exists an integer ω so that $g^*(\alpha) = 1$ if $\alpha \geq \omega$ and $g^*(\alpha) = 0$ if $\alpha < \omega$. Lemma 8 specifies the equilibrium strategy vector given any such threshold ω. I obtain my main result, Theorem 3, by relying on the fact that, by definition, SE requires that the value of ρ anticipated by the government and the value of the threshold, ω, that it induces in the government's best responses (BR) are consistent with the value of ρ that agents use in equilibrium anticipating ω as the threshold (proofs of Lemmas 1–8 and Theorem 3 are gathered in the appendix). Lemma 1 shows that only agents of type $b_i = 1$ ever petition in equilibrium.

LEMMA 1. *If $(\sigma^*, g^*, \mu(\cdot))$ is an SE, then $\forall \; i \in N$, $\sigma_i^*(0) = 0$.*

DEFINITION 4. *$(\sigma^*, g^*, \mu(\cdot))$ is Agents' Symmetric SE (SSE) if $\forall \; i, j \in N$ $\sigma_i^* = \sigma_j^*$.*

The attractive feature of symmetric equilibria is that they depend on the premise that each agent expects all other agents to behave in the same way he does, since they face the same payoff structure and have the same prior beliefs. Restricting attention to SSE simply means to assume that all agents play the same strategy in equilibrium.

DEFINITION 5. *Anonymity: $\forall \; A^1, A^{1'}$, with $|A^1| = |A^{1'}|$ if $A^1 \in W(g)$, then $A^{1'} \in W(g)$.*

Restricting the analysis to SSEs implies the standard assumption of anonymity—since all agents use the same mixed strategy in equilibrium, it is not an equilibrium behavior for the government to interpret the behavior of different agents as resulting from different strategies. This would violate condition 3 of the definition of SE. Thus, W.L.O.G. I use α instead of A^1 as the argument of the government's posterior beliefs $\mu(\cdot \mid \alpha, \sigma)$. Equation (8) redefines expression (6), using α instead of A^1.

$$v_g(1 \mid \alpha, \rho) = \sum_{\beta = \alpha}^{n} (t \cdot \beta - c_g) \cdot \frac{\left[\binom{n}{\beta} q^\beta (1 - q)^{n-\beta} \right] \cdot \left[\binom{\beta}{\alpha} \rho^\alpha (1 - \rho)^{\beta - \alpha} \right]}{\sum_{\beta = \alpha}^{n} \left[\binom{n}{\beta} q^\beta (1-q)^{n-\beta} \right] \cdot \left[\binom{\beta}{\alpha} \rho^\alpha (1-\rho)^{\beta - \alpha} \right]} \tag{8}$$

Lemma 2 shows that a government will grant a right if "enough" agents petition so that $\alpha > \frac{c_g}{f} \Rightarrow A^1 \in W(g^*)$. I show below that the converse is not true (i.e., $\alpha > \frac{c_g}{f}$ is sufficient but not necessary for the grant of a right).

LEMMA 2. *In an SSE satisfying IC, $\alpha > \frac{c_g}{f} \Rightarrow A^1 \in W(g^*)$*

Let $\sigma^0 = (\sigma \in \Sigma) \mid \sigma_i(1) = 0 \,\forall\, i \in N)$, $\sigma^1 = (\sigma_i \in \Sigma \mid \sigma(1) = 1 \,\forall\, i \in N)$, $\sigma^0_{-i} = (\sigma_j \in \Sigma \mid \sigma(1) = 0 \,\forall\, j \in N\, j \neq i)$, $\sigma^1_{-i} = (\sigma \in \Sigma \mid \sigma_j(1) = 1 \,\forall\, j \in N$, $j \neq i)$. Lemma 3 shows that if governments grant rights even in the absence of petitioning, then, in equilibrium, no one petitions.

LEMMA 3. *If $(\sigma^*, g^*, \mu(\cdot))$ is a sequential equilibrium and $\varnothing \in W(g^*)$, then $\sigma^* = \sigma^0$.*

Lemma 4 shows that a government will grant rights without any petitioning if and only if, by its prior beliefs, its expected benefits will exceed the costs of enforcing the right. Thus, Lemma 4 restates Theorem 1 of the complete-information model developed in section 1 as a special case of the more general model with incomplete information developed in section 4.

LEMMA 4. *If $g^*(0) = 1$, then $(\sigma^*, g^*, \mu(\cdot))$ is an SSE iff $\sigma^* = \sigma^0$, and $E(\beta) = q \cdot n \geq \frac{c_g}{f}$.*

Lemmas 5 and 6 below require one more restriction on government's out-of-the-equilibrium-path beliefs. IC implies $\mu(b_i = 1 \mid s_i = 1) = 1$ and $\mu(b_i = 0 \mid s_i = 1) = 0$. For Lemmas 5 and 6, I assume further that $\mu(b_i = 1 \mid s_j = 0, s_i = 1, \sigma^* = \sigma^0) = q$, and that $\mu(b_i = 0 \mid s_j = 0, s_i = 1, \sigma^* = \sigma^0) = (1 - q)$. Upon observing the event of probability zero where an agent petitions when no one "should," the government infers, by IC, that the petitioner must be of type $b_i = 1$. The additional restriction implies that it further infers that all other agents use their equilibrium strategy of not petitioning, regardless of their type.

Lemma 5 states that if one petitioner is necessary and sufficient to make the government grant the right, then, in equilibrium, $\sigma^* \neq \sigma^0$.

LEMMA 5. *If $g^*(0) = 0$ and $g^*(1) = 1$, then $\sigma^* \neq \sigma^0$ in an SE.*

Lemma 6 states that if more than one petitioner is necessary to convince a government to grant a right, then no one petitioning and the government not granting the right is always an SSE.

LEMMA 6. $[\sigma^* = \sigma^0,\ g^*(\alpha < 2) = 0,\ \mu(\cdot)]$ is an SSE iff $1 + [q \cdot (n - 1)] < \frac{c_g}{t}$

Lemmas 3–6 characterized all of the SSE equilibria with $\sigma^* = \sigma^0$—that is, with no participation. The triple $\{\sigma^0, g^*, \mu(\cdot)\}$ is an SSE with $g^*(0) = 1$—i.e., no one petitions and the government grants the right—iff $q \cdot n \geq \frac{c_g}{t}$ (Lemmas 3–4). $\{\sigma^0, g^*, \mu(\cdot)\}$ is an SSE with $g^*(0) = g^*(1) = 0$ (i.e., no one petitions and the government does not grant the right) iff $1 + [q \cdot (n - 1)] < \frac{c_g}{t}$ (Lemma 6). If, under the same conditions, $\omega = 1$, then $\{\sigma^0, g, \mu(\cdot)\}$ is not an SSE (Lemma 5). Thus, in the discussion that follows I am concerned only with the case where $\forall\ i \in N\ \sigma_i^*(1) = \rho \in (0,1]$, and $1 + [q \cdot (n - 1)] < \frac{c_g}{t}$.

Lemma 7 implies that the government's strategy in equilibrium is always characterized by a threshold $\omega \in Z$ such that $g^*(\alpha) = 1$ if $\alpha \geq \omega$, and $g^*(\alpha) = 0$ if $\alpha < \omega$.

LEMMA 7. $v_g(1 \mid \alpha, \rho) > 0 \Rightarrow v_g[1 \mid (\alpha + 1), \rho] > 0$.

COROLLARY 1. *Government's strategy in an SSE is always characterized by a threshold* $\omega \in Z$ *so that* $g^*(\alpha) = 1$ *if* $\alpha \geq \omega$, *and* $g^*(\alpha) = 0$ *if* $\alpha < \omega$.

Given that this is what agents anticipate from the government, we can now roll back to the first stage of the game. Lemma 8 characterizes the symmetric equilibrium response of the agents for each possible threshold strategy.

LEMMA 8. *If* $[\sigma^*, g^*, \mu(\cdot)]$ *is a mixed strategy[9] SSE, then the following must hold:*

$$c_i = (1 - t) \cdot \sum_{\gamma = \omega - 1}^{n-1} \left[\left(\begin{matrix} \gamma \\ \omega - 1 \end{matrix} \right) \rho^{\omega - 1}(1 - \rho)^{\gamma - \omega - 1} \right]$$
$$\cdot \left[\left(\begin{matrix} n - 1 \\ \gamma \end{matrix} \right) q^\gamma (1 - q)^{n - \gamma - 1} \right] \qquad (9)^{[10]}$$

Lemma 8 implies that if $c_i \geq (1 - t)$, no one petitions in equilibrium. Let h be a correspondence from the set of integers, Z, to values of $\rho \in (0,1)$—that is, $h : Z \longrightarrow (0,1)$, defined as $h(\omega) = \{\rho \in (0,1) \mid \rho$ solves for equation (9), given $\omega\}$. In this case, h assigns zero, one, or two values of ρ to every threshold value, ω. Define $y : (0,1) \to Z$, as $y(\rho) = \min$

$\{\omega \in Z \,|v_g\,[1\,|\,\mu(\cdot\,A^1,\rho),|A^1| = \omega] > 0\}$ (i.e., y assigns a threshold value, ω, to each value of ρ). This means that y and h are best-response functions. Theorem 3 characterizes the set of SSE as the intersection between y and h: the set of ordered pairs $\{\omega,\rho\}$ such that SSE = $\{(\omega,\rho)\,|\,\omega = y(\rho)$ and $\rho \in h(\omega)\}$. In other words, condition (10) of Theorem 3 guarantees that the government will use only a best-response threshold strategy, given ρ, while condition (11) guarantees that, given the threshold strategy of the government, every agent is using a mixed strategy, ρ, such that if all agents use the same strategy, each agent is indifferent between contributing and not contributing. Given this indifference, he/she may just as well use the mixed strategy that everyone else uses. This is the intuitive logic behind the proof of Lemma 8 and Theorem 3.

THEOREM 3. *The triple $\{\sigma^*,g^*,\mu(\cdot)\}$ is a mixed[11] strategy SSE iff:*

i. $\forall\,i \in N\,\sigma_i^* (0) = 0$.
ii. $\forall\,i \in N\,\sigma_i^*(1) = \rho$, $g^*(\alpha) = 1$ iff $\alpha \geq \omega$, and (ω,ρ) satisfies:

$$c_i = (1 - t)\cdot\sum_{\gamma=\omega-1}^{n-1}\left[\binom{\gamma}{\omega - 1}\rho^{\omega-1}(1 - \rho)^{\gamma-\omega-1}\right]$$
$$\cdot\left[\binom{n - 1}{\gamma}q^\gamma(1 - q)^{n-\gamma-1}\right] \tag{10}$$

$$v_g(1\,|\,\rho,\alpha) = \sum_{\beta=\alpha}^{n}(t\cdot\beta - c_g)$$
$$\cdot\frac{\left[\binom{n}{\beta}q^\beta(1 - q)^{n-\beta}\right]\cdot\left[\binom{\beta}{\alpha}\rho^\alpha(1 - \rho)^{\beta-\alpha}\right]}{\sum_{\beta=\alpha}^{n}\left[\binom{n}{\beta}q^\beta(1-q)^{n-\beta}\right]\cdot\left[\binom{\beta}{\alpha}\rho^\alpha(1-\rho)^{\beta-\alpha}\right]} \geq 0 \text{ iff } \alpha \geq \omega. \tag{11}$$

A numerical example should help readers to appreciate the implications of Theorem 3. Let $n = 10$, $q = 0.4$ $c_g = 1.0025$, $t = 0.2$, and $c_i = 0.2$. Solving for conditions (10) and (11) in 3.ii we get the set of equilibria. The three equilibrium pairs to this game in this numerical example are summarized in table 2 (Ainsworth and Sened 1993).

The first row of table 2 reports the probability that a right will be granted, given any of the three equilibria. The second row reports the probability that the government will grant the right even though, *ex post*, it would have been better off not granting it. The third row of table 2 specifies the probability that the government will grant the right and be better off by so doing, and the fourth row specifies the probability that the government will fail to grant the right even though, *ex post*, it would have been better off granting the right. The last row of table 2 specifies the expected number of petitioners, given any of the three equilibria.

Table 2 points to three important implications of Theorem 3: First, according to this model we should expect positive (at times substantial) participation rates, even when common prior beliefs indicate that the expected number of beneficiaries is not enough to justify the granting of the right—such as when $q = 0.4$, and $n = 10$, $E(\beta) = 4$, and $E(b_g - c_g) = -0.2$. In one equilibrium pair $\{\omega^* = 5, \rho^* = 0.996\}$ the expected number of petitioners, $E(\alpha) \simeq 4$, (i.e., agents of type $b_i = 1$) turn out almost with certainty. Second, we expect governments to make two types of mistakes in equilibrium: (1) they will, at times, enforce rights that make them worse off; and (2) on the other hand, they will often fail to grant rights that would make them better off. Finally, in this kind of equilibria, the number of petitioners, α, will rarely be the "efficient" number, ω. Thus, "political action" in the pursuit of individual rights is "wasteful." This, however, does not imply that political action of the kind modeled here is undesirable (cf. Lohmann 1991b). The opposite is true: Proposition 1 shows that the political action, at least as it is modeled here, makes all agents and the government better off. What drives this counterintuitive result is that in the process of petitioning for rights, ordinary citizens reveal information that is very valuable for the government's decision-making process. In this way, the model captures both the essence of the rationale behind political action, and at the same time, as discussed above, it provides valuable insights into the complexity and difficulties associated with political activism and government response to popular demands.

PROPOSITION 1. *The* ex ante *payoffs of this game are always positive for the government and for each individual agent.*

TABLE 2.   Equilibria and Expectations with $N = 10$, $q = 0.4$, $c_g = 1.0025$, and $c_i = 0.2$

Equilibrium pair $\{\omega^*, \rho^*\} \rightarrow$	$\{\omega = 3, \rho = 0.36\}$	$\{\omega = 4, \rho = 0.68\}$	$\{\omega = 5, \rho = 0.996\}$
pr(right is granted) = pr($g = 1$)	.162	.273	.363
pr(right granted but $c_{gov} < b_{gov}$) $\sum_{\beta=\omega}^{\beta=5} \text{prob}(\alpha \geq \omega \mid \beta) \cdot \text{prob}(\beta \mid q,n)$	.093	.148	.197
pr(right granted and $c_{gov} > b_{gov}$) $\sum_{\beta=6}^{\beta=n} \text{prob}(\alpha \geq \omega \mid \beta) \cdot \text{prob}(\beta \mid q,n)$	.069	.125	.166
pr(right not granted and $c_{gov} > b_{gov}$) $\sum_{\beta=6}^{\beta=n} \text{prob}(\alpha < \omega \mid \beta) \cdot \text{prob}(\beta \mid q,n)$	.097	.041	≈ 0.0
$E(\alpha)$	1.44	2.72	3.98

Proposition 1 (see appendix for the proof) has a simple substantive interpretation: governments and citizens benefit from institutions that allow agents to petition for rights. What drives the result in Proposition 1, and my "optimistic" interpretation of it, is that in the process of petitioning for new rights, ordinary citizens reveal valuable information to their government. They petition not to reveal information, but in the hope of obtaining valuable benefits from new property (and other) rights, but in the process they help the government's decision making by partially revealing their preferences.

This conclusion can be regarded as a possible explanation for the success of this type of institution in Western democracies in the last two centuries. As discussed above, the model predicts that these institutions will often yield undesired results in the short run. In the long run, however, they should have beneficial consequences for the process of the evolution of individual rights in general and property rights in particular.

Discussion

In their historical study on the evolution of rights in Western Europe, North and Thomas (1973) provide evidence that the development of property rights in England and the Netherlands, compared to the cases of France and Spain, explains the observed difference in growth rates in the sixteenth and seventeenth centuries, which were remarkable in England and the Netherlands and stagnating in Spain and France. North and Thomas explain the difference in the momentum in the development of property-rights institutions by the fact that commercial interests were politically stronger in England and the Netherlands (cf. Libecap 1989, 2–3). They overlook the fact that in both the Netherlands and England political institutions existed that allowed these interests to be heard. Such institutions were virtually absent in Spain and France.

More generally, North and Thomas (1973) show that the evolution of property rights is not a smooth progression from less to more efficient institutions of property rights. Libecap (1989, 2) describes this puzzle as follows:

> . . . a continuing puzzle is why we observe so much variety in . . . property institutions . . . studies . . . reveal that differences in property rights institutions across societies with otherwise similar resource endowments contributed importantly to observed variations in economic performance.

The model developed in this chapter provides a hint toward the solution to this puzzling diversity in property-rights institutions, inasmuch as it shows that, in equilibrium, governments make mistakes: they grant rights they "shouldn't" and fail to grant rights they "should."

More recently, North and Weingast (1989) studied institutional changes that followed the Glorious Revolution of 1688 in England. Their conclusions corroborate my theoretical model in an interesting way: North and Weingast conclude that the most important consequence of the revolution was an enhanced ability of the new institutional arrangement to secure property rights (1989, 803) and that, as a result, "not only did the government become financially solvent, but it gained access to an unprecedented level of funds" (1989, 804–5).

The model developed here constitutes only a first step toward more dynamic models of participation. Just as the government updates its beliefs based on the number of observed petitioners, a multistage dynamic model should let agents update their beliefs based on the observed number of petitioners at any stage, and act according to these updated beliefs about the support for any right in the population at large in future stages of the game.

Another extension is to introduce political entrepreneurs as intermediaries between the government and its constituency. Using an extension of the model developed here, Ainsworth and Sened (1993) show that such intermediaries can further reduce the number of equilibria and improve the efficiency of the interaction between governments and particular interests in society.

The cost of enforcing different institutional arrangements is another input factor in the production function of rights that deserves more attention. Recent work in economic history has clearly demonstrated that the cost of law enforcement is an important factor in the ability of governments to enrich themselves (and their citizens) through the manipulation of institutional structures (North and Weingast 1989; Ensminger and Rutten 1990).

Overall, the approach presented here to the study of property-rights institutions seems more realistic than previous attempts in the game-theoretic literature, inasmuch as it treats these institutions not as equilibria in games among equal agents, but as equilibria in games among players who control old institutions and agents who challenge these institutions with new demands. This approach seems to provide a richer analytical framework for the study of the evolution of individual-rights institutions to the extent that it provides an explanation to the emergence of such institutions at two different levels: it explains why property rights are granted and enforced by central governments, and, at the same time, it explains the emergence of more fundamental rights institutions, such as "the right to know your rights," and institutions that allow agents to petition for new individual rights.

According to my analysis, governments enforce such institutions not because these rights are a part of a list of "natural rights," or because they are committed to moral or economic principles. Rather, they enforce these types of institutions because they allow them to obtain, from their constituents, crucial information that helps them to improve the structure of property rights, which, in turn, makes for a more affluent society. By making society more affluent, governments increase tax revenue and enhance the support they receive from their constituents.

APPENDIX: PROOFS OF LEMMAS 1–8, THEOREM 3, AND PROPOSITION 1

LEMMA 1. *If $(\sigma^*, g^*, \mu(\cdot))$ is an SE then $\sigma_i^*(0) = 0 \; \forall \; i \in N$.*

Proof: $\forall \; i \in N$, $v_i(s_i = 1 \mid b_i = 0) = (-c) < v_i(s_i = 0 \mid b_i = 0) = 0$, regardless of σ_{-i}^*, and g^*. Thus, by condition (1) of the definition of an SE $\sigma_i^*(b_i = 0) = 0 \; \forall \; i \in N$ is a necessary condition for $\{\sigma^*, g^*, \mu(\cdot)\}$ to be an SE. □

LEMMA 2. *In an SSE satisfying IC, $\alpha > \frac{c_g}{t} \Rightarrow A^1 \in W(g^*)$.*

Proof (by contradiction):

Assume for simplicity that $\frac{c_g}{t}$ is not an integer. Suppose contrary to Lemma 2 that $\alpha > \frac{c_g}{t}$, but $A^1 \notin W(g^*)$. By condition (2) of the definition of an SE, $\underset{g \in \{0,1\}}{\text{Argmax}} \{g \cdot v_g[1 \mid \mu(\cdot \mid A^1, \sigma^*)]\} = 0$—i.e., the government's best response upon observing α petitioners is not to grant the right. By Lemma 1 and the IC refinement, the government's beliefs upon observing A^1 are $\mu(\beta \geq \alpha \mid A^1, \sigma^*) = 1$, regardless of $f(\beta)$ or σ^*, $\underset{g \in \{0,1\}}{\text{Argmax}} \{g \cdot v_g[1 \mid \mu(\cdot \mid A^1, \sigma^*)]\} = 1$, by equation (6), since $v_g[1 \mid \mu(\cdot \mid A^1, \sigma^*)] > 0$ while $v_g(0) = 0$. Thus, upon observing $\alpha > \frac{c_g}{t}$ the government is better off granting the right, a contradiction. □

LEMMA 3. *If $(\sigma^*, g^*, \mu(\cdot))$ is a sequential equilibrium and $\phi \in W(g^*)$, then $\sigma^* = \sigma^0$.*

Proof: If the government's strategy is to grant the right even if no one petitions, then it is a dominant strategy for all players not to petition, even if they are of type $b_i = 1$, since they can avoid the cost of petitioning. $\square$

LEMMA 4. *If* $g^*(0) = 1$, *then* $(\sigma^0, g^*, \mu(\cdot))$ *is an SSE iff* $E(\beta) = q \cdot n \geq \frac{c_g}{t}$.

Proof: Necessity: By condition (3) of the definition of an SE, if $\sigma^* = \sigma^0$, then upon observing A^1 of cardinality $\alpha = 0$, the government should maintain its prior beliefs $f(\beta)$, since $\mathrm{pr}(A^1 = \phi \mid B^1, \sigma^0) = 1$ for any $B^1 \subseteq N$ (substitute accordingly in the expression of Bayesian updating in condition (3) of the definition of an SE). Thus, $g^*(0) = 1$ is BR given $\mu(\cdot \mid \phi, \sigma^0)$ only if $E(\beta) = q \cdot n \geq \frac{c_g}{t}$. If $g^*(0) = 1$, by Lemma 3, any $\sigma_i > 0$ for any $i \in N$ is not BR, such that $g^*(0) = 1 \Rightarrow \sigma^* = \sigma^0$.

Sufficiency: If $E(\beta) \geq \frac{c_g}{t}$, then $g^*(\phi \mid \sigma^0) = 1$ is BR, $g^*(0) = 1 \Rightarrow \sigma_i^* = 0 \, \forall \, i \in N$ is the unique BR. Thus, $E(\beta) \geq \frac{c_{gov}}{t} \Leftrightarrow \{\sigma^* = \sigma^0, g^*(\alpha \geq 0) = 1, \mu(\cdot)\}$ is an SSE. $\square$

LEMMA 5. *If* $g^*(0) = 0$ *and* $g^*(1) = 1$, *then* $\sigma^* \neq \sigma^0$ *in an SE.*

Proof: Given the assumptions about government's beliefs and the hypothesis of Lemma 5, one petitioner is enough to convince the government to grant the right. Thus, if $\sigma^* = \sigma^0$, any agent of type $b = 1$ is better off petitioning. $\square$

LEMMA 6. *If* $g^*(0) = g^*(1) = 0$ *then* $(\sigma^0, g^*, \mu(\cdot))$ *is an SSE iff* $1 + [q \cdot (n - 1)] < \frac{c_g}{t}$.

Proof: Necessity: Lemma 5 implies that $1 + [q \cdot (n - 1)] < \frac{c_{gov}}{t}$ is necessary.

Sufficiency: If $1 + [q \cdot (n - 1)] < \frac{c_g}{t} \, (\Rightarrow q \cdot n < \frac{c_g}{t})$ then $g^*(1 \mid \sigma^0) = g^*(0 \mid \sigma^0) = 0$ is BR for the government given the out-of-equilibrium beliefs specified above. If $\sigma_{-i}^* = \sigma_{-i}^0$, and $g^*(0) = g^*(1) = 0$, $v_i^0[\sigma^*, g, \mu(\cdot)] = 0$ while $v_i^0(\sigma_{-i}^*, \sigma_i > 0, g^*, \mu(\cdot))\} = -\sigma_i \cdot c$. $\square$

LEMMA 7. $v_g(1 \mid \alpha, \rho) > 0 \Rightarrow v_g[1 \mid (\alpha + 1), \rho] > 0$.

Proof: By equation (8) reproduced below:

$$v_g(1 \mid \alpha, \rho) = \sum_{\beta = \alpha}^{n} (t \cdot \beta - c_g) \cdot \frac{\left[\binom{n}{\beta} q^{\beta}(1 - q)^{n - \beta} \right] \cdot \left[\binom{\beta}{\alpha} \rho^{\alpha}(1 - \rho)^{\beta - \alpha} \right]}{\sum_{\beta = \alpha}^{n} \left[\binom{n}{\beta} q^{\beta}(1 - q)^{n - \beta} \right] \cdot \left[\binom{\beta}{\alpha} \rho^{\alpha}(1 - \rho)^{\beta - \alpha} \right]} \quad (8)$$

we have to prove that

$$v_g(1 \mid \alpha,\rho) = \sum_{\beta=\alpha}^{n} (t \cdot \beta - c_g)$$

$$\cdot \frac{\left[\binom{n}{\beta}q^{\beta}(1-q)^{n-\beta}\right]\cdot\left[\binom{\beta}{\alpha}\rho^{\alpha}(1-\rho)^{\beta-\alpha}\right]}{\sum_{\beta=\alpha}^{n}\left[\binom{n}{\beta}q^{\beta}(1-q)^{n-\beta}\right]\cdot\left[\binom{\beta}{\alpha}\rho^{\alpha}(1-\rho)^{\beta-\alpha}\right]} > 0 \quad (12)$$

implies $v_g[1 \mid (\alpha + 1),\rho] = \sum_{\beta=\alpha+1}^{n} (t \cdot \beta - c_g)$

$$\cdot \left(\frac{\left[\binom{n}{\beta}q^{\beta}(1-q)^{n-\beta}\right]\cdot\left[\binom{\beta}{\alpha+1}\rho^{\alpha+1}(1-\rho)^{\beta-\alpha-1}\right]}{\sum_{\beta=\alpha+1}^{n}\left[\binom{n}{\beta}q^{\beta}(1-q)^{n-\beta}\right]\cdot\left[\binom{\beta}{\alpha+1}\rho^{\alpha+1}(1-\rho)^{\beta-\alpha-1}\right]} \right) > 0, \quad (13)$$

To prove that (12) implies (13) it is enough to prove that

$$\sum_{\beta=\alpha}^{n} (t \cdot \beta - c_g) \cdot \left[\binom{n}{\beta}q^{\beta}(1-q)^{n-\beta}\right]\cdot\left[\binom{\beta}{\alpha}\rho^{\alpha}(1-\rho)^{\beta-\alpha}\right] > 0 \quad (14)$$

implies $\sum_{\beta=\alpha+1}^{n} (t \cdot \beta - c_g) \cdot \left[\binom{n}{\beta}q^{\beta}(1-q)^{n-\beta}\right]$

$$\cdot \left[\binom{\beta}{\alpha+1}\rho^{\alpha+1}(1-\rho)^{\beta-\alpha-1}\right] > 0. \quad (15)$$

But (15) can be rewritten as

$$\frac{\rho}{(\alpha+1)\cdot(1-\rho)}\left\{ \sum_{\beta=\alpha}^{n} (t \cdot \beta - c_{gov})(\beta - \alpha)\left[\binom{n}{\beta}\right] \right.$$

$$\left. \cdot \left[\binom{\beta}{\alpha}\rho^{\alpha}(1-\rho)^{\beta-\alpha}\right]\right\} > 0 \quad (16)$$

Thus, we only have to prove that (14) implies (16). Let β^0 be the largest value of the index in equation (14) for which $t \cdot \beta - c_{gov} \leq 0$. Then (14) implies:

$$\sum_{\beta=\alpha}^{\beta^0} (t\beta - c_g) \cdot \left[\binom{n}{\beta}q^{\beta}(1-q)^{n-\beta}\right] \cdot \left[\binom{\beta}{\alpha}\rho^{\alpha}(1-\rho)^{\beta-\alpha}\right]$$

$$< \sum_{\beta=\beta^0+1}^{n} (t\beta - c_g) \cdot \left[\binom{n}{\beta}q^{\beta}(1-q)^{n-\beta}\right] \cdot \left[\binom{\beta}{\alpha}\rho^{\alpha}(1-\rho)^{\beta-\alpha}\right]. \quad (17)$$

Multiplying each summand on each side by $(\beta - \alpha)$ leaves inequality (17) true, since the RHS is increased more than the left-hand side (LHS). Multiplying both sides by $\rho/(\alpha + 1)(1 - \rho) > 0$ does not alter the relation in the inequality either. We get:

$$\frac{\rho}{(\alpha+1)(1-\rho)} \left\{ \sum_{\beta=\alpha}^{\beta^0} (t \cdot \beta - c_g) \cdot (\beta - \alpha) \cdot \left[\binom{n}{\beta} q^\beta (1-q)^{n-\beta} \right] \left[\binom{\beta}{\alpha} \rho^\alpha (1-\rho)^{\beta-\alpha} \right] \right\}$$
$$< \frac{\rho}{(\alpha+1)(1-\rho)} \left\{ \sum_{\beta=\beta^0+1}^{n} (t \cdot \beta - c_g) \cdot (\beta - \alpha) \cdot \left[\binom{n}{\beta} q^\beta (1-q)^{n-\beta} \right] \left[\binom{\beta}{\alpha} \rho^\alpha (1-\rho)^{\beta-\alpha} \right] \right\},$$

$$(18)$$

which, rearranging terms, yields (16).   □

COROLLARY 1. *Government's strategy in an SSE is always characterized by a threshold* $\omega \in \mathbf{Z}$ *so that* $g^*(\alpha) = 1$ *if* $\alpha \geq \omega$, *and* $g^*(\alpha) = 0$ *if* $\alpha < \omega$.

Proof: Since we consider only SSEs, if $\rho \in (0,1]$ then Lemma 7 and conditions (2) and (3) of the definition of SE (in equilibrium the government uses a best response, and there is a consistency of beliefs) imply Corollary 1. If $\rho = 0$, Corollary 1 follows from Lemma 4, given the assumed "out-of-equilibrium beliefs."   □

LEMMA 8. *If* $[\sigma^*, g^*, \sigma(\cdot)]$ *is a mixed strategy SSE, then the following must hold:*

$$c_i = (1 - t) \cdot \sum_{\gamma=\omega-1}^{n-1} \left[\binom{\gamma}{\omega-1} \rho^{\omega-1}(1-\rho)^{\gamma-\omega-1} \right] \cdot \left[\binom{n-1}{\gamma} q^\gamma (1-q)^{n-\gamma-1} \right]$$

Proof: To play mixed strategies in equilibrium, agents must be indifferent between contributing and not contributing. Thus $\forall\, i \in N$, equation (19) below must hold:

$$(1 - t) \cdot pr(g = 1 \mid \rho_i = 0) = (1 - t) \cdot pr(g = 1 \mid \rho_i = 1) - c_i. \quad (19)$$

By Lemma 1, in equilibrium only agents of type $b_i = 1$ ever contribute. Every agent, $i \in N$, upon observing that he is of type $b_i = 1$, updates his beliefs such that: $pr(|B^1| = \beta \mid b_i = 1) = \left[\binom{n-1}{\beta-1} q^{\beta-1}(1-q)^{n-\beta} \right]$. He thus believes that:

$$\text{pr}(g = 1 \mid \rho_i = 1) = \sum_{\alpha = \omega - 1}^{n-1} \sum_{\gamma = \alpha}^{n-1} \left[\binom{\gamma}{\alpha} \rho^\alpha (1 - \rho)^{\gamma - \alpha} \right]$$

$$\cdot \left[\binom{n-1}{\gamma} q^\gamma (1 - q)^{n - \gamma - 1} \right], \tag{20}$$

$$\text{and pr}(g = 1 \mid \rho_i = 0) = \sum_{\alpha = \omega}^{n-1} \sum_{\gamma = \alpha}^{n-1} \left[\binom{\gamma}{\alpha} \rho^\alpha (1 - \rho)^{\gamma - \alpha} \right]$$

$$\cdot \left[\binom{n-1}{\gamma} q^\gamma (1 - q)^{n - \gamma - 1} \right] \tag{21}$$

Thus, (19) can be rewritten as:

$$\left\{ \sum_{\alpha = \omega - 1}^{n-1} \sum_{\gamma = \alpha}^{n-1} \left[\binom{\gamma}{\alpha} \rho^\alpha (1 - \rho)^{\gamma - \alpha} \right] \right.$$

$$\left. \cdot \left[\binom{n-1}{\gamma} q^\gamma (1 - q)^{n - \gamma - 1} \right] \right\} - \left[c_i / (1 - t) \right] \tag{22}$$

$$= \sum_{\alpha = \omega}^{n-1} \sum_{\gamma = \alpha}^{n-1} \left[\binom{\gamma}{\alpha} \rho^\alpha (1 - \rho)^{\gamma - \alpha} \right] \cdot \left[\binom{n-1}{\gamma} q^\gamma (1 - q)^{n - \gamma - 1} \right].$$

Subtracting $\sum_{\alpha = \omega}^{n-1} \sum_{\gamma = \alpha}^{n-1} \left[\binom{\gamma}{\alpha} \rho^\alpha (1 - \rho)^{\gamma - \alpha} \right] \cdot \left[\binom{n-1}{\gamma} q^\gamma (1 - q)^{n - \gamma - 1} \right]$ from both sides of (22) above and multiplying by $(1 - t)$ and adding c_i to both sides we get:

$$c_i = (1 - t) \cdot \sum_{\gamma = \omega - 1}^{n-1} \left[\binom{\gamma}{\omega - 1} \rho^{\omega - 1} (1 - \rho)^{\gamma - \omega - 1} \right] \cdot \left[\binom{n-1}{\gamma} q^\gamma (1 - q)^{n - \gamma - 1} \right].$$

THEOREM 3. *A triple $\{\sigma^*, g^*, \mu(\cdot)\}$ is a mixed strategy SSE iff:*

i. $\forall i \in A \; \sigma_i^* (0) = 0.$

ii. $\forall i \in N \; \sigma_i^*(1) = \rho, \; g^*(\alpha) = 1 \text{ if } \alpha \geq \omega, \text{ and } g^*(\alpha) = 0 \text{ if } \alpha < \omega,$
and (ω, ρ) satisfies:

$$c_i = (1 - t) \cdot \sum_{\gamma = \omega - 1}^{n-1} \left[\binom{\gamma}{\omega - 1} \rho^{\omega - 1} (1 - \rho)^{\gamma - \omega - 1} \right]$$

$$\cdot \left[\binom{n-1}{\gamma} q^\gamma (1 - q)^{n - \gamma - 1} \right] \tag{10}$$

$$v_g(1 \mid \rho, \alpha) = \sum_{\beta = \alpha}^{n} (t \cdot \beta - c_g)$$

$$\cdot \frac{\left[\binom{n}{\beta} q^\beta (1 - q)^{n - \beta} \right] \cdot \left[\binom{\beta}{\alpha} \rho^\alpha (1 - \rho)^{\beta - \alpha} \right]}{\sum_{\beta = \alpha}^{n} \left[\binom{n}{\beta} q^\beta (1 - q)^{n - \beta} \right] \cdot \left[\binom{\beta}{\alpha} \rho^\alpha (1 - \rho)^{\beta - \alpha} \right]} \gtreqless 0 \text{ iff } \alpha \gtreqless \omega. \tag{11}$$

Proof: Sufficiency: If equation (11) holds, then, by Lemma 7, g^*, as specified in (ii) is BR for the government, satisfying condition (2) of the definition of an SE. By Lemma 8, equation (10) characterizes the equilibrium response to g^*. If both (10) and (11) hold simultaneously, then the government's beliefs are consistent with the strategies of the agents, satisfying condition (3) of the definition of an SE, and the agents are playing a best response satisfying condition (1) of the same definition.

Necessity: Lemma 8 implies that condition (10) is necessary. By Lemma 7 and Corollary 1, the only strategy that the government ever uses, in equilibrium, is a threshold strategy. If the threshold, ω, that defines such a strategy does not satisfy condition (11), then g^* is not a BR, since it would grant a right expecting negative payoffs, or not grant it expecting positive payoffs, which violates condition (2) of the definition of an SE. Thus, (11) is necessary. If (10) and (11) do not hold simultaneously, condition (3) of the definition of an SE is violated. Thus, condition (ii) is a necessary for $(\sigma^*, g^*, \mu(\cdot))$ to be an equilibrium. Finally, (i) is necessary by Lemma 1. $\square$

PROPOSITION 1. *The* ex ante *payoffs of this game are always positive for the government and for each individual agent.*

Proof: Assuming that every player plays a strategy corresponding to the same equilibrium, the *ex ante* expected payoff for the government, $E^a(v_g)$, is:

$$E^a(v_g) = \sum_{\alpha=\omega}^{n} \sum_{\beta=\alpha}^{n} (t \cdot \beta - c_g) \cdot \left[\binom{\beta}{\alpha} \rho^\alpha (1-\rho)^{\beta-\alpha} \right] \cdot \left[\binom{n}{\beta} q^\beta (1-q)^{n-\beta} \right] \quad (23)$$

By Condition (11) of Theorem 3 and by Lemma 7, $E^a(v_g)$ is always nonnegative in equilibrium. Let ∇b_i denote "net benefit to agent i." The *ex ante* expected payoff for each agent $i \in N$ in this game is:

$$E^a(v_i) = [(1-q) \cdot E(\nabla b_i \mid b_i = 0) + q \cdot E(\nabla b_i \mid b_i = 1)]. \quad (24)$$

By construction and Lemma 1 (agents for type $b_i = 0$ never petition) the first term of this equation is always zero, such that:

$$E^a(v_i) = q \cdot E(\nabla b_i \mid b_i = 1) = q \cdot [\rho \cdot E(\nabla b_i \mid b_i = 1, s_i = 1)$$
$$+ (1-\rho) \cdot E(\nabla b_i \mid b_i = 1, s_i = 0)] \quad (25)$$

$$\Rightarrow E^a(v_i) = (1-t) \cdot q \cdot [\rho \cdot (\text{pr}(g = 1 \mid s_i = 1) - c_i] + (1-\rho)$$
$$\cdot [\text{pr}(g = 1 \mid s_i = 0)]. \quad (26)$$

Thus, by Lemma 8, $[\mathrm{pr}(g = 1 \mid s_i = 1) - c_i] = \mathrm{pr}(g = 1 \mid s_i = 0)$, in equilibrium:

$$E^a(v_i) = (1 - t) \cdot q \cdot [\mathrm{pr}(g = 1 \mid s_i = 0], \tag{27}$$

which is always nonnegative.

NOTES

This project was inspired by the late William H. Riker. My debt to his advice can hardly be exaggerated. I thank Randall L. Calvert, David Austen-Smith, and Jeffrey S. Banks for their advice and thorough critiques of different stages of this paper, Simon Jackman, David L. Weimer, Barry R. Weingast, and Susanne Lohmann for important comments. I am the only one to blame for all remaining errors. Finally, I gratefully acknowledge the financial support of the John M. Olin Foundation.

1. A third distinctive feature of public goods is the absence of *free disposal:* if a public good is provided, agents don't have the freedom not to consume it.

2. The emergence of property rights is often presented as a solution to the problem of excludability, but it often solves the problem of rivalry as well. A favorite example for rivalrous goods is air. Sened and Riker (1992) report how air became a rivalrous good when the government decided to enforce property rights in air-slots. Hahn and Hester (1989) provide other examples of how the creation of property rights turned nonrivalrous into rivalrous goods.

3. Two interesting examples of "new" property rights are property rights in pollutants (Hahn and Hester 1989), and air-slots (Sened and Riker 1992).

4. A comprehensive model should treat f as a function of ℓ and c_g and compliance as function of f. Since compliance in such a model is a function of the resources that the government invests in law enforcement, the government decision will not be whether to enforce the right or not but rather to what extent to enforce the right. It all comes down to treating ℓ, c_g, and f as endogenous, while treating them as exogenously fixed.

5. It is of some interest to cite from Hegel's discussion of this principle: "**215.** if laws are to have a binding force, it follows that . . . they must be made universally known. . . . Rulers who have given a national law to their people in the form of a well-arranged and clear-cut legal code . . . have been the greatest benefactors of their peoples and have received thanks and praise for their beneficence. But the truth is that their work was at the same time a great act of justice" ([1821] 1942, 138). See also proposition 1 in the text. This result also captures Kant's justification for his categorical imperatives, inasmuch as it shows that if the law was not made public knowledge, there would be no law enforcement.

6. Technically we have to assume that the payoff 0 that agents of type $b_i = 0$ get takes into account the fact that they pay the cost of respecting the right of others.

7. I rely on Theorem 1 in that, first, by Theorem 1, if the government enforces the right all agents respect it, so that any agent $i \in B^1$ gets $b_i = (1 - t) \cdot (r - 1) = 1$ as a payoff and the government gets a payoff of $t \cdot \beta$ as tax revenues given any $B^1 \subseteq N$. Second, I drop the term $g \cdot \ell \left[\Sigma_{j \in N}(1 - p_j \mid g) \right]$ from the payoff structure because if $g = 0$ this term obviously drops out and, by Theorem 1, $(p_j \mid g = 1) + 1$ in equilibrium implying $(1 - p_j^* \mid g = 1) = 0$ so that if $g = 1$ this term drops out as well.

8. The classical reference is Kreps and Wilson 1982. More penetrable discussions are found in Cho 1987, Cho and Kreps 1987, and Banks and Sobel 1987. The definition I use is adopted from Banks's (1991, 7) definition of a sequential equilibrium of a signaling game. It is easy to see that the game I am analyzing here can be reinterpreted as a signaling game with the government being the receiver (R), each agent $i \in N$ being a sender (S) with two types $b_i \in \{0,1\}$ and two messages $M\{0,1\}$, where 0 is the message of not petitioning and 1 the message of petitioning. I stop short of using this terminology in the text to save on notations and technicalities that are not needed for the sake of the argument.

9. For completeness, the case of $\rho = 1$ is covered in fn. 11.

10. For every value of ω there exist zero, one, or two solutions to the symmetric equilibrium condition characterized by Lemma 8. This follows immediately from Lemma 8, and Proposition 2 & Corollary 2.1 in Palfrey and Rosenthal 1984.

11. By mixed strategy SSE we mean $\rho \in (0,1)$; thus, the case of $\rho = 1$ is left out. For completeness, I state without proof Theorem 3' for the case of $\rho = 1$, i.e., $\sigma^* = \sigma^1$:

THEOREM 3'. *The triple* $\{\sigma^1, g^*, \mu(\cdot)\}$ *is an SSE iff:*

i. $\forall\, i \in N\, \sigma_i^*(b_i = 0) = 0.$
ii. $\forall\, i \in N\, \sigma_i^*(b_i = 1) = p,\ g^*(\alpha \geq \omega) = 1,\ and\ g^*(\alpha < \omega) = 0,\ and\ the\ pair$ $\{\omega, \rho\}$ *solves simultaneously:*

$$c_i = \binom{n-1}{\omega-1} q^\omega (1 - q)^{(n-\omega-1)},$$

and

$$\omega = min\{k \in \mathbf{Z} \mid k \cdot t \geq c_g\}$$

Democratic Stability

Norman Schofield

At its most general, political economy is the theoretical and substantive study of collective decision making. In this sense it is more general than economics, which after all is the examination of how individuals choose in economic environments governed by scarce resources. The discipline also embraces politics, since political theory includes an examination of how voters choose politicians and of the choices politicians then make.

The roots of the discipline go back at least to Condorcet, who is credited with the first intuition of what we now call the Condorcet Jury Theorem—that uncertain individuals can improve their chances of making a valid choice if they agree to abide by majority rule. Condorcet also noted that individuals whose preferences are well behaved (i.e., transitive) may nonetheless give rise to badly behaved collective preferences.

Much of the modern discussion in social-choice theory is concerned with the question of the existence of equilibria in voting mechanisms. It should be emphasized that the formal theory is best developed for the case of direct democracy or committees, where one can assume that voters vote directly on issues. In this domain the results generally indicate that voting can be badly behaved, in the sense of possessing no voting equilibrium. These results lead Tullock (1981) to ask why there is so much stability in democratic institutions. In some sense, Tullock's response was inappropriate.

Democratic institutions are typically representative voting systems, where politicians intrude between electoral preferences and political outcomes. A fully developed theory of representative democratic institutions is not currently available, so that it is not yet possible to give unequivocal answers to the question of democratic stability.

This chapter will address the general theoretical results that have been obtained on the operation of direct democracy. After reviewing the so-called instability results, the argument is presented that, for large electorates, the operation of direct democracy is *well behaved.*

More precisely, the model that is proposed is one in which a sample f of size n is drawn from an underlying distribution on a space W of voter characteristics. Some simple assumptions are made about how a generic voter will behave on the basis of the sampled characteristics. For a society N of size n, an $\alpha(n)$ rule is adopted, specifying how many voters must agree in order to have an outcome adopted. Our concern is with whether there exists an outcome that is unbeaten under the $\alpha(n)$ rule. Such an equilibrium outcome is called a core point. With respect to the distribution, f, and the rule $\alpha(n)$, a technique is presented that allows computation of the probability $p(f,\alpha,n)$ that the core exists. The result shows that the class of rules bifurcates—in one subset the probability of a core approaches zero as n approaches infinity, and for a second subset the probability approaches 1 in the limit. The characteristic that distinguishes the two classes of rules can be thought of as friction. One might use the metaphor of a frictionless oscillator (for example, a spherical pendulum), where most initial states result in nonstationary orbits or cycles, in contrast to an oscillator with friction, where all initial states converge to a stationary outcome, namely an equilibrium.

The same form of argument is then used to show that, even for finite n, the set of possible outcomes under direct democracy will lie in a restricted set, which is "centrally located" with respect to the distribution of voter preferred points. This set is termed the *electoral heart*.

The political economy literature over the last fifty years may be thought of as veering from an emphasis on instability to one on stability, and back again. The question, after all, is quite fundamental. Are we to believe that democratic institutions are fundamentally flawed, in the sense that no equilibrium in preferences is likely to occur, so that the outcomes of the political process are no more than accidental consequences of institutions or personalities? Or is there some reason to hope that there is an underlying rationality to what goes on? It is difficult to draw immediate conclusions from looking at the world. It is now true that democracy is coming to life in Eastern Europe and what was the Soviet Union. However, the fragmentation of the USSR into many independent republics, and the extent of nationalistic, cultural, and linguistic antagonisms must make one doubt that there can possibly exist a process of convergence to an equilibrium.

To be able to deal with the problem of stability in a representative democracy, it is necessary to model, in appropriately complex detail, the nature of the electoral system, the motivations of politicians, the formation of parties, and so on. The concluding part of the chapter will present a model of representative democracy based on the notion of a *political heart*. Stability of a representative democracy will be interpreted in terms of the extent of convergence to the political heart. This notion also suggests the possibility that the degree of "representativeness" of the democracy can be described in terms of the coincidence of the electoral and political hearts.

Stability or Instability in Direct Democracy with a Finite Electorate

In 1944, von Neumann and Morgenstern published the *Theory of Games and Economic Behavior*. One situation that they studied in detail was that of a constant-sum game, or problem of division. Suppose some simple majority of more than half, but less than all, of the society can enforce its will. Then, no division is stable. Moreover, any division can occur. Indeed, one can show that from any initial division, x_0, it is possible to construct a trajectory $\{x_1, x_2, \ldots, x_r\}$, say, for any final division x_r whatsoever, such that each position on the trajectory beats the preceding point. Even more alarming is the observation that if one does not impose the requirement that all decisions are optimal (use all resources), then there is, in principle, no reason why the final division need not be as close as one wishes to the zero distribution. In case this seems preposterous, consider the situation in Lebanon in these terms. The solution proposed to this problem by Von Neumann and Morgenstern was elegant but did not really solve the fundamental problem regarding the stability of the game. It was clear that the nonexistence of a core—or voting equilibrium, in this game—was the fundamental source of the problem.

In the late 1960s a new solution to the problem in constant-sum games was proposed in a series of papers by Aumann, Peleg, and Rabinowitz (1965); Davis and Maschler (1967); Peleg (1967); and Billera (1970). The idea was to assign to each winning coalition in the game a set of payoffs that was in some sense stable with respect to defection by members of that coalition. From this theory one could infer that if a particular coalition came into being, then in the constant-sum game there would be a stable payoff for that particular coalition. Clearly this was only a partial solution, since no attempt was made to solve the question of coalition formation.

On the instability side, Arrow's (1951) celebrated impossibility theorem seemed to demonstrate that there was a profound trade-off in all social choice procedures between stability and the concentration of power. Any mechanism that aggregates individual preferences (which are transitive in both strict preferences and indifference) and results in a social preference of the same kind must be dictatorial. In particular, voting mechanisms such as majority rule that are nondictatorial must sometimes result in social decisions that violate transitivity. Later results in this area (Gibbard 1969; Brown 1973, for example) concentrated on whether or not the social preference was acyclic. A preference P is acyclic if and only if there exists no sequence of alternatives, $\{x_1, \ldots, x_r\}$, say, such that $x_i P x_{i+1}$ (x_i preferred to x_{i+1}) for $i = 1, \ldots, r - 1$ yet $(x_r P x_1)$. When the set of alternatives, W is finite or a compact subset of a topological space then the acyclicity of P is sufficient to guarantee that P has a choice, or *core*, namely a point x such that yPx for no $y \in W$.

Although Arrow's Theorem effectively demonstrated that social choice mechanisms *could be* cyclic, it certainly did not show that such mechanisms were necessarily cyclic. In the succeeding years much effort was devoted to considering restrictions of various kinds sufficient to guarantee acyclicity. For example, consider a mechanism called a q/n-rule, where any coalition of size at least q out of the society of size n can enforce its will. If W is finite, of cardinality no greater than $n/(n - q)$, then no social cycle can occur (Ferejohn and Grether 1977). Nakamura (1979) later extended this result to arbitrary voting games.

The most general form of a voting rule is a specification of a family, $\mathcal{D}$, of winning, or decisive coalitions. Call this a $\mathcal{D}$-rule. A member of $\mathcal{D}$ is a winning coalition, M. If all members of M prefer alternative x to alternative y, then x beats y. The core is the set of unbeaten alternatives. If there is a nonempty group K that belongs to every M in $\mathcal{D}$, then $\mathcal{D}$ is called *collegial*. The Nakamura number of $\mathcal{D}$, labeled $v(\mathcal{D})$, is defined in this case to be infinity, and the largest such group, K, is called the *collegium* of $\mathcal{D}$, and written $K(\mathcal{D})$. If $\mathcal{D}$ is noncollegial, then the Nakamura number of $\mathcal{D}$ is the cardinality of the smallest subfamily of $\mathcal{D}$, which is still noncollegial. By definition, if $\mathcal{D}'$ is a subfamily of $\mathcal{D}$ with cardinality $v(\mathcal{D}) - 1$, then there must be a collegium for $\mathcal{D}'$. To illustrate, suppose $N = \{1,2,3,4\}$ and $\mathcal{D}$ is the three-fourths rule consisting of all coalitions with at least three members. Then $\mathcal{D}' = \{1,2,3\}, \{2,3,4\}, \{1,2,4\}, \{1,3,4\}$ has empty intersection. Thus, $v(\mathcal{D}) = 4$. Nakamura showed that if W is finite, with $|W| \leq v(\mathcal{D}) - 1$, then the $\mathcal{D}$-rule had no cycles and thus a core. Note that if $\mathcal{D}$ is collegial then there is a core, irrespective of the cardinality of W.

To illustrate this result for a general weighted voting game, consider the qualified majority rule used by the European Council of Ministers. Table 1 sets out the voting weight of the twelve ministers. The supramajority of fifty-four out of seventy-six is generally required for a decision. To calculate the Nakamura number, we note that the following four coalitions are all decisive:

M_1 = {FRA,ITA,UK,GER,BEL,GRE,NET}, weight 55

M_2 = {SPA,BEL,GRE,NET,POR,DEN,IRE,FRA,ITA}, weight 54

M_3 = {UK,GER,SPA,POR,DEN,IRE,FRA,NET}, weight 54

M_4 = {GER,ITA,UK,SPA,BEL,GRE,POR,LUX}, weight 55.

Clearly M_1, M_2, M_3 have an intersection, the collegium {FRA,NET}, but neither France nor the Netherlands belongs to M_4.

Thus the Nakamura number for this rule is $v(\mathscr{D}) = 4$. Consequently, any decision involving three alternatives must have a core, since a group such as {FRA,NET} will have an effective veto on this three-alternative choice.

Notice that to have an effective veto in general a "blocking" group must control twenty-three weighted votes. Recent discussions over the enlargement of the European Union to include Scandinavian countries and Austria became quite heated because of the proposal to increase the required blocking size to 27. Under the current rules, Britain together with, say, Germany and Ireland could block decisions. Under the pro-

TABLE 1. Voting Weights in the European Council of Ministers

	Label	Weight
France	FRA	10
Germany	GER	10
Italy	ITA	10
United Kingdom	UK	10
Spain	SPA	8
Belgium	BEL	5
Greece	GRE	5
Netherlands	NET	5
Portugal	POR	5
Denmark	DEN	3
Ireland	IRE	3
Luxembourg	LUX	2
Total		76
Supramajority		54
Majority		39

posed new system, the blocking group would have to include another country, such as Portugal. Evidently, the "numerics" of voting can give rise to quite severe disagreement.

A somewhat different attempt to "induce stability" by Sen (1970), Inada (1969), and others was to restrict preferences, rather than the cardinality of W. The essential idea was to forbid the occurrence of so-called Condorcet cycles. A Condorcet cycle is simply a triple $\{x,y,z\}$ of alternatives, with preferences among three individuals $\{i,j,k\}$ of the form:

i	j	k
x	y	z
y	z	x
z	x	y

Clearly, if the two-thirds rule is applied to this profile then the resulting social preference is a cycle $xPyPzPx$.

If no Condorcet cycle occurs in a preference profile then majority rule is well behaved. Note that this is not a necessary condition: majority rule can be acyclic even though Condorcet cycles exist. The profile:

i	j	k	l
x	y	z	z
y	z	x	x
z	x	y	y

gives a social preference $zPxPy, zIy$ (where I is social indifference). Alternative z is the core.

As an application, suppose that W is a compact subset of the real line. Suppose further that each individual, i, has a *bliss point*, x_i, in W and Euclidean preference P_i of the form xP_iy iff $\|x - x_i\| < \|y - x_i\|$, where $\| \ \|$ is the usual norm on $\Re$. Such preferences are clearly single-peaked, so there cannot exist any Condorcet cycles. It follows that no voting cycles can exist. Since W is compact, there must exist a voting equilibrium or core. Indeed, it is easy to see that this core must be at the *median voter position*. A bliss point x_i is at the median if on neither side of the point is there a majority of the voters. Downs (1957) used this *one-dimensional* model to argue that two-party competition should result in an equilibrium where both parties converge to the same equilibrium position. (See fig. 1, where m represents the median.)

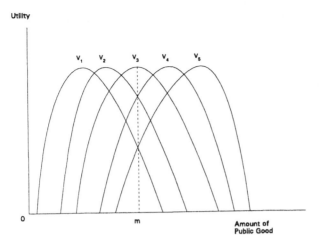

Fig. 1. The median voter in a one-dimensional model

To make the jump from a result on direct democracy to an inference about representative democracy is, of course, invalid if there is no attempt to model politicians' motives. For example, if politicians are concerned with policy outcomes rather than simply gaining office, then convergence to the median need not occur (Wittman 1977).

Attempts to extend this model to two or more dimensions had to contend with two instability theorems, by Plott (1967) and Kramer (1973). Plott's result concerned the symmetry conditions necessary for a point x to be a core point under majority rule. The situation is simpler to discuss when n is odd ($n = 2k + 1$) and a majority ($k + 1$) is required. For convenience, suppose $n = 5$ and all individuals have Euclidean preferences. Let x be a candidate for a core, and suppose no individual has a bliss point at x. Let $h(x)$ be an arbitrary hyperplane through x. If three or more bliss points lie in one of the open half-spaces defined by $h(x)$, then x must be beaten by a point y near x and on the *heavy* side of $h(x)$. Clearly this is a condition that cannot be satisfied for every hyperplane. Thus, there must be a bliss point at x, so let us assume that player 1 has a most preferred point at x, which we relabel as x_1. Now consider another arbitrary hyperplane $h(x)$. If $h(x)$ contains precisely one other bliss point, x_2, then there must be at least two more bliss points, x_3 and x_4, on one side of $h(x)$. Then $h(x)$ can be perturbed to $h'(x)$, with three points $\{x_2, x_3, \text{and } x_4\}$ on one side of $h'(x)$. Thus x_1 is beaten, since the three players $\{2,3,4\}$ prefer some point, y, to x_1. (See fig. 2.) Consequently, if a bliss point x_2 is on $h(x)$ then there must be exactly one other bliss point x_3 on $h(x)$, but on the other side of x_1 from x_2.

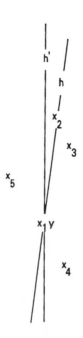

Fig. 2. *y* is nearer to x_2, x_3, x_4 than is x_1

Another way of expressing the *Plott symmetry condition* is to note that the direction gradients $du_2(x)$ of 2 at x and $du_3(x)$ of 3 at x must satisfy a linear relationship $du_2(x) + \lambda du_3(x) = 0$ for $\lambda > 0$. In just the same way the remaining two gradients must satisfy a similar relationship: $du_4(x) + \alpha du_5(x) = 0$. Note also that $du_1(x) = 0$. (The direction gradient of player i at x is simply the vector pointing from x toward x_i, the most preferred direction of i.) The core point obtained in this way is structurally unstable, since small perturbations are sufficient to destroy the occurrence of this symmetry condition at any point at all. Another way of expressing this, in general, is to identify the set of Euclidean profiles with $(\mathfrak{R}^w)^n$, where $\mathfrak{R}^w$ is the space of outcomes. Then under majority rule (n odd), the set of profiles in $(\mathfrak{R}^w)^n$ that have a nonempty core is of measure zero, as long as $w \geq 2$. In common parlance, the probability of obtaining a core point must be zero. For majority rule (n odd), the integer 2 is termed the *instability dimension*.

To consider the case of majority rule with n even ($= 6$) consider figures 3 and 4. Figure 3 shows the situation in two dimensions where no individual has a bliss point at x. The direction gradients satisfy the Plott symmetry condition at x, but again this core point is structurally un-

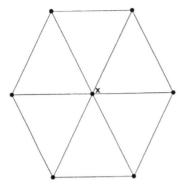

Fig. 3. Plott symmetry at a structurally unstable core for majority rule in two dimensions

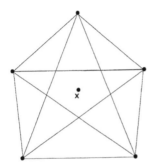

Fig. 4. A structurally stable core for majority rule (*n* even) in two dimensions

stable. On the other hand, in figure 4, the point x is a bliss point of a player, and indeed is a core point. To see this note that no line through x has more than three bliss points in either of its two open half-spaces. A structurally stable core can therefore exist in two dimensions under majority rule (*n* even). With some effort it can be shown that the instability dimension for majority rule (*n* even) is, in fact, three (Schofield 1983). This result was later generalized to cover an arbitrary noncollegial voting rule $\mathcal{D}$, and techniques for computing the instability dimension, $w(\mathcal{D})$, were developed (Schofield 1980; McKelvey and Schofield 1986). For example, if $\mathcal{D}$ is a q/n-rule (with $q < n$) then the instability dimension can be shown to be $2q - n + 1$. These results hold for any noncollegial rule, and can be summed up in the following theorem.

INSTABILITY THEOREM (McKelvey and Schofield 1986). *Let $\mathfrak{D}$ be a noncollegial voting rule, with Nakamura number $v(\mathfrak{D})$ for a finite population N of size n. Then there is an instability dimension $w(\mathfrak{D}) \in [v(\mathfrak{D}) - 1, n - 1]$ that characterizes $\mathfrak{D}$ in the following sense. If $w \geq w(\mathfrak{D})$ and if preferences are Euclidean, then there is an open dense set V in $(\mathfrak{R}^w)^n$ such that for any profile $x = (x_1, \ldots, x_n) \in V$, the core of the voting rule, $Core_{\mathfrak{D}}(x)$, at x is empty. For any q/n-rule the instability dimension is equal to $2q - n + 1$. In particular, for majority rule the instability dimension is 2 or 3, depending on whether n is odd or even.*

More briefly, this theorem asserts that the core of the rule, $\mathfrak{D}$, is generically empty above the instability dimension. One inference from the theorem is that if voter preferences are Euclidean, and the bliss points are sampled using any continuous distribution f, then the probability that a core exists for the $\mathfrak{D}$-rule must be zero, at least in dimension $w(\mathfrak{D})$. In the theorems discussed below, we shall restrict attention to the case of Euclidean preferences. However, it is possible that versions of these results can be obtained for arbitrary smooth preferences (see Banks 1994).

The second class of instability theorems developed from a result by Kramer (1973) that focused on the possibility of cycles. To illustrate his result, consider a situation with three individuals {1,2,3} whose direction gradients at a point, x, are $\{du_i(x) : i = 1,2,3\}$. Suppose one of the following conditions is satisfied at x. Either

1. $\{du_i(x) : i = 1,2,3\}$ are linearly independent; or
2. $\{du_i(x) : i = 1,2,3\}$ are strictly positively dependent. That is, there exists $\lambda_1 > 0$, $\lambda_2 > 0$ such that

$$du_1(x) + \lambda_1 du_2(x) + \lambda_2 du_3(x) = 0.$$

There then exist three points $\{a,b,c\}$ such that the preferences of {1,2,3} on $\{a,b,c\}$ form a Condorcet cycle.

Further analysis shows that in any neighborhood U of x there exist three points $\{a,b,c\}$ with a *cyclic trajectory* connecting a to b to c to a. (See fig. 5.) Thus for example there exists a smooth curve from b to c with both players 1 and 2 preferring each point along the curve to b. To generalize this idea, consider any Euclidean profile $x = (x_1, \ldots, x_n)$ where $x_1, \ldots, x_n$ are the bliss points. Let $\mathfrak{D}$ be the voting rule. Say a point y belongs to the *Cycle* set, $Cycle_{\mathfrak{D}}(x)$, iff for any neighborhood U of y there exists a voting cycle containing y that is inside U. Write *Cycle* for this set when $\mathfrak{D}$ and x are fixed.

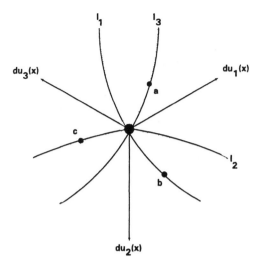

Fig. 5. Existence of a Condorcet Cycle {*a,b,c*} at a point where the direction gradients are positively dependent

Cycle can be thought of as the set of all possible outcomes from the voting process. Indeed, the larger *Cycle* is, the greater the potential for agenda manipulation. To see this suppose y and z both belong to a component of *Cycle*, and let C be *any* path from y to z inside *Cycle*. For any neighborhood U of C in *Cycle*, it is possible to construct a voting trajectory from y to z that stays inside U.

The McKelvey-Schofield (1986) Chaos Theorem asserts that *Cycle* can be almost everything, when the dimension is sufficiently large.

CHAOS THEOREM. *Let $\mathcal{D}$ be a noncollegial voting rule with instability dimension* $w(\mathcal{D})$. *If* $w \geq w(\mathcal{D}) + 1$ *then there is an open dense set* V *in* $(\mathcal{R}^w)^n$ *such that for any profile* x $\in$ V *the set* Cycle$_\mathcal{D}$(x) *contains an open dense subset of* $\mathcal{R}^w$.

The Chaos Theorem suggested that if majority rule were employed with a finite population on a policy space W of dimension at least 4, then continuous manipulation of the process could lead to almost anything.

In the case of majority rule with n odd in two dimensions, the generic nonexistence of the core implies that *discontinuous* manipulation or agenda control (McKelvey 1979) can lead almost anywhere. However, these discontinuities require moves that traverse the Pareto set. (Here the Pareto set is simply the convex hull of the voter preferred points.) Various experiments performed by Fiorina and Plott (1978), McKelvey, Ordeshook, and Winer (1978), and Laing and Olmstead (1978) gave no indication that this occurred. It remains an open question whether almost anything can happen in three dimensions. We return to this question below.

These two results do appear relevant for two-party competition, however. No matter what the voting procedure, if parties are concerned about winning, then there is absolutely no reason to expect convergence if the underlying dimension is at least $w(\mathfrak{D}) + 1$.

In the instability theorem, the restriction $w(\mathfrak{D}) > v(\mathfrak{D}) - 1$ is necessary. This follows from a result by Greenberg (1979), which developed the idea of Ferejohn and Grether (1977) and Nakamura (1979) on restricting the cardinality of the set of alternatives. The extension to the Euclidean profile we shall term the Stability Theorem.

STABILITY THEOREM I (Greenberg 1979; Schofield 1984). *Let $\mathfrak{D}$ be a voting rule (possibly collegial) with Nakamura number $v(\mathfrak{D})$ and finite population n.*

Suppose preferences are Euclidean on a compact subset of $\mathfrak{R}^w$.

1. *If $w \leq v(\mathfrak{D}) - 2$, then for any profile $x \in (\mathfrak{R}^w)^n$, $Core_{\mathfrak{D}}(x)$ is nonempty.*
2. *If $w \geq v(\mathfrak{D}) - 1$ then there exists a profile $x \in (\mathfrak{R}^w)^n$ such that $Core_{\mathfrak{D}}(x)$ is empty and $Cycle_{\mathfrak{D}}(x)$ is nonempty.*

The *stability dimension* is the largest integer, v, that satisfies $v \leq v(\mathfrak{D}) - 2$, and for a q/n-rule this is the largest integer that is strictly less than $q/(n - q)$.

To illustrate for majority rule with n odd, $n \geq 3$, the Nakamura number is 3, so $v = 1$.

This theorem can be generalized in a number of ways. Note first that if preferences are Euclidean and the core is nonempty, then the cycle set must be empty. This need not be the case for more general preferences. However, it can be shown that when W is compact then an empty cycle set is a sufficient condition for a nonempty core. The Stability Theorem can be generalized by showing that when $w \leq v(\mathfrak{D}) - 2$ then the cycle set is empty. Just above the stability dimension (when $w = v(\mathfrak{D}) - 1$), the cycle set must belong to the Pareto set, *Pareto(x)*, of the profile (i.e., the set of unanimously preferred outcomes). In higher dimensions this need not be so. The results can be summed up in the second Stability Theorem. We suppose preferences are continuous and convex, rather than simply Euclidian, and write $Core_{\mathfrak{D}}(u)$, $Cycle_{\mathfrak{D}}(u)$, and *Pareto(u)* for the various sets defined by the profile u.

STABILITY THEOREM II (Schofield 1986). *Let $\mathfrak{D}$ be a voting rule (possibly collegial) with Nakamura number $v(\mathfrak{D})$ and finite population* n. *For a profile* u *and policy space* W *of dimension* w:

1. *if* w ≤ $v(\mathfrak{D})$ − 2, *then* $Cycle_{\mathfrak{D}}(u)$ *is empty;*
2. *if* w = $v(\mathfrak{D})$ − 1 *then* $Cycle_{\mathfrak{D}}(u)$ *is a subset of* Pareto(u);
3. *if* w ≥ $v(\mathfrak{D})$ *then there exists a Euclidean profile* x *such that* $Cycle_{\mathfrak{D}}(x)$ *contains points that do not belong to* Pareto(x).

As we know, a core can only be guaranteed in one dimension for majority rule. For supramajority q/n-rules there is a dimension range $[q/(n − q), 2q − n + 1]$ within which both structurally stable cores and nonempty cycle sets can occur. As an illustration, in cases of multiparty competition where no single party gains a majority, it is possible that a structurally stable core can occur in two-dimensional policy spaces. In general, however, such a core position must be at the bliss point of the largest (or dominant) party. (See Schofield 1995, for the technical definition of dominant party, and the proof of this assertion.) When this occurs one would expect that party to form a government without the formal allegiance of other parties. Analysis of multiparty government in European political systems (Laver and Schofield 1990) suggests that this is a reasonable explanation of the regular occurrence of minority governments in the Scandinavian countries.

To give a more general illustration of these two stability theorems, consider the example of the European Council of Ministers. We showed earlier that the Nakamura number of this system of weighted majority rule is $v(\mathfrak{D}) = 4$. Thus, any policy decision involving just two dimensions must have a core. To illustrate, consider figure 6, which represents European political geography. Positions of the countries are based on underlying policy cleavages of north against south and east against west. The north-south axis is based on agricultural protection, the east-west on the problem of enlargement. The lines labeled $\mathfrak{D}$-median lines are obtained by counting votes until the supramajority is reached. The shaded area spanned by these $\mathfrak{D}$-medians defines the core. It is important to note how the core is computed. Each $\mathfrak{D}$-median defines a "heavy" half-space containing a supramajority (of fifty-four out of seventy-six). The intersection of all such heavy half-spaces defines the core. Note in particular that the points for France and Germany belong to this supramajority core. Centrally located countries can exercise veto power in the Council

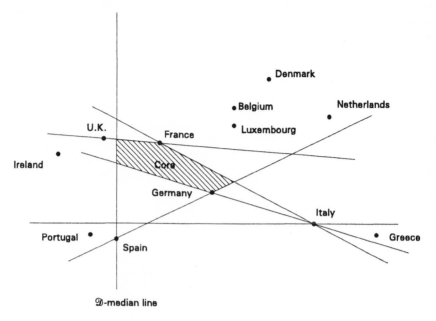

𝒟-median line

Fig. 6. The 𝒟-core for the European Council of Ministers under the supramajority rule

of Ministers. The general argument is true no matter what the nature of the underlying policy space and what the preferences are.

Suppose, however, that the Council used weighted majority rule, using a majority of thirty-nine out of the seventy-six weighted votes. The relevant half-median lines are drawn in figure 7. It should be clear that the heavy half-spaces, defined in figure 7, do not intersect, so the majority core is empty.

Note, however, that the half-median lines span a small set (shaded in fig. 7). Earlier work has formally defined this set, and termed it the *heart* (Schofield 1993a). Under quite general conditions the heart is nonempty, is contained within the Pareto set, and is "continuous" with respect to the preferences of the voters. In a sense the heart is a geometric version of the "uncovered set" (see McKelvey 1986; Cox 1987). Negotiation between the parties will lead into this small set (Schofield 1993b). Note that Germany's position is on the boundary of the heart. While Germany cannot actually veto all proposals, in this particular

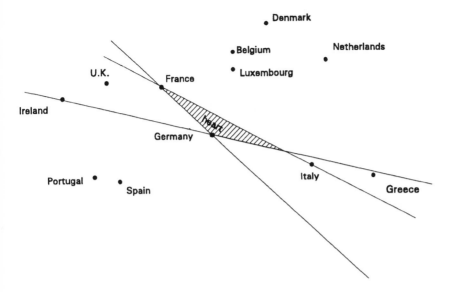

Fig. 7.   The heart for the European Council of Ministers under majority rule

game it almost has an effective veto. A different situation would arise if the German position were displaced slightly to the north in figure 7. In this case the heavy half-spaces would intersect in the German position. Just as in figure 4, the German position would be a core point, and Germany would be in a position to exercise a veto. It is entirely possible that the Council of Ministers adopted a supramajority rule precisely to avoid the possibility of effective veto power by a single country. However, if this reasoning is even approximately valid, it is plausible that the choice of a supramajority rule gives both France and Germany effective veto power. That is, although France and Germany cannot exercise formal veto power, even together (since the blocking size is twenty-three), it is reasonable that they can coordinate their activities to constrain decisions in the areas that are most important to them, namely agriculture (the CAP) and monetary union.

In the next section we introduce the notion of the heart in large legislative bodies using majority rule. The same concept could be used in this context to evaluate the likely policy outcomes resulting from dispersed political preferences in a legislative institution such as the European Parliament. In principle, the relationship between the supramajority Council heart and the majority Parliamentary heart can give insight into the pattern of political bargaining between council and Parliament, or indeed within any bicameral political forum.

Another point should be emphasized. As we have shown, there must be a core in two dimensions in the supramajority council decision. In three dimensions, the core need not exist, but the heart will. It is difficult to compute the instability dimension for this rule, but my estimate is that $w(\mathfrak{D}) = 7$. Below the instability dimension a core is possible, but in some sense the probability that a core can occur will drop as the dimension increases. Above the instability dimension, chaos is possible. However, if negotiation is *efficient,* in the sense formally described in Schofield (1993a), then coalition outcomes will lie within a "centrally located" political heart.

The theory that emerges has the following features. The formal political institutional rules allow computation of the core or heart, as long as this dimension is below the institutionally determined instability dimension. Above this dimension chaos can occur, but also can be avoided if the political agents adopt normative rules in negotiation that allow them to search "efficiently" for compromise. In this case, outcomes will lie in a heart, or in another centrally located domain of compromise that is determined by the structure of these rules.

These inferences are based on a model of committee decision making involving a relatively small number of political agents. To more fully understand the behavior of representative democracy, it is necessary to apply the model to the case of a large electorate. The next section presents some results on this topic.

Stability in Large Electorates

At the same time that the Plott-Kramer results were circulating, Tullock (1967) wrote an article directed against the relevance of the Arrow Impossibility Theorem. His intuition was that although cycles would be likely they would nonetheless be constrained to the Pareto set. As we have noted, for Euclidean preferences the Pareto set is simply the convex hull of the bliss points of the electorate. From the previous results the stability dimension for majority rule with a finite electorate (other than $n = 4$) is $v = 1$. By the second Stability Theorem, the cycle set is a subset of the Pareto set only in two dimensions, and in three dimensions "cycle" points can be far from the Pareto set. Tullock's general supposition is therefore invalid. However, the two-dimensional example that Tullock (1967) analyzed in some detail involved a large number of voters (namely

999,999). In fact, his analysis mixed two different cases. In the first case it was assumed that there was a continuous distribution, say f, of voter "bliss" points (in fact, f was taken to be uniform), while in the second case a finite sample, of size n, say, of voters was taken from f. The results in these two cases are somewhat different but there is a formal connection. To pursue these two cases, let us suppose that all preferences are Euclidean. In the first case, let us assume that electoral preferences are represented by a distribution f on a compact subset W of $\Re^w$. What conditions on f are sufficient to guarantee the existence of a core for majority rule, or for an arbitrary rule $\mathcal{D}$? Because the population is infinite in this case we have to be careful about how to define $\mathcal{D}$. We may define an α-rule by saying a subset M of W is winning iff it contains at least a proportion α of the electorate (where of course, $\alpha > \frac{1}{2}$); $Core_\alpha(f)$ is then the core of the α-rule so defined. A limiting case is plurality rule, where M is winning as long as it contains strictly more than half the electorate. The core under plurality rule is written $Core_{1/2}(f)$.

For such an α-rule, an α-median is a hyperplane with a proportion α of the population on one side (the heavy side) and $1 - \alpha$ on the other (the light) side. If x is a candidate for an α-core, then any hyperplane through x must be an α'-median for some $\alpha' \leq \alpha$, with $\alpha' \geq \frac{1}{2}$. For a point to belong to $Core_{1/2}(f)$ it is evident that some symmetry must be exhibited by f. Enough symmetry on f will be sufficient to guarantee existence of a core.

DISTRIBUTION THEOREM I (Arrow 1969). *Let* W *be a disc in* $\Re^2$ *and let* f *be the uniform distribution on* W *representing voter preferences. Then* $Core_{1/2}(f)$ *is nonempty.*

It is evident that at the origin x of the disc every line through x has exactly half the mass of f on either side, so x must be a core point. Of course the assumption that f is spherically symmetric is an extremely strong assumption. To see the effect of weakening this assumption, consider the uniform distribution f_1 on the equilateral triangle $\triangle$ in $\Re^2$. (See fig. 8.) For reasons of symmetry, identify the origin x of the distribution as the barycenter (the intersection of the perpendicular bisectors of the sides). As before, define median lines to be lines that have half the mass of the distribution on either side. Some easy arithmetic shows that the median lines divide the sides of the triangle in the ratio $1 : 2^{1/2} + 1$. Thus the horizontal median line is below the barycenter and x cannot be a core point. The three median lines parallel to the sides of the triangle define a small triangle X similar to the large triangle. The ratio of the area of X to the Pareto set (namely $\triangle$) is $0.0147 : 1$.

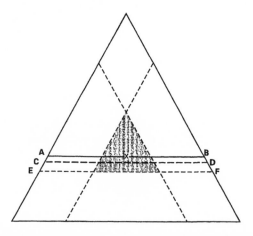

Fig. 8. Median lines for various rules and distributions on the triangle in $\mathfrak{R}^2$**. The heart for majority rule with the uniform distribution on the boundary is the shaded small triangle.** $\overline{AB}$ **is the 5⁄9 median for uniform distribution on the triangle;** $\overline{CD}$ **is the ½ median for uniform distribution on the triangle; and** $\overline{EF}$ **is the ½ median for uniform distribution on the boundary.**

For a second illustration let f_2 be the uniform distribution on the *boundary* of $\triangle$. In this case the median lines divide the sides in the ratio 1 : 3 so the relative area of the triangle, Y, bounded by the three median lines, to the area of $\triangle$ is 1 : 16 or 0.0265 : 1.

Two geometric objects have been proposed as "descriptors" of the voting distribution. Figure 9 shows the yolk (McKelvey 1986) or the smallest circle that intersects the three median lines. To compute the second object, consider all median lines generated by the distribution f_2. These define a family of three curves, which in turn define the three-pointed star in figure 9. This star can be shown to be the heart, introduced earlier. The ratio of the area of the heart to that of $\triangle$ is approximately 1 : 10.

It is evident that the relative area of the heart gives some idea of the extent to which the distribution departs from perfect spherical symmetry. A second way of characterizing this is in terms of the min-max value $\alpha_m(f)$ of the distribution. In the case of the distribution on $\triangle$, consider any line through x. It is clear that on the heavy side of this line the mass can be no more than 5⁄9. (See the line AB in fig. 8.) This maximum we call the min-max value of f.

In fact, Caplin and Nalebuff (1988) show that in dimension w, as

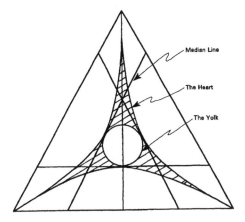

Fig. 9. The heart and the yolk for the boundary distribution on the triangle

long as the distribution f satisfies a condition known as *log-concavity* then

$$\alpha_m(f) \le \alpha_m(w) \text{ where } \alpha_m(w) = 1 - [w/(1 + w)]^w.$$

Many standard distributions (the uniform, normal, etc.) are log-concave.

In the case of the uniform distribution on $\triangle$, a rule that requires at least a proportion of $\frac{5}{9}$ of the population must have a core point at x. More generally, if f is any log-concave distribution in w dimensions, then for any α-rule satisfying $\alpha \ge \alpha_m(w)$, the core $Core_\alpha(f)$ must be nonempty. Note also that $lim_{\alpha \to \infty} 1 - [w/(1 + w)]^w = 1 - \frac{1}{e}$ where e is the exponential. Since $1 - \frac{1}{e} \cong 0.64$, the following distribution theorem can be obtained.

DISTRIBUTION THEOREM II (Caplin and Nalebuff 1988, 1991). *Let f be a log-concave distribution on a compact convex set in $\Re^w$. Then the core, Core$_\alpha$(f), is nonempty as long as $\alpha \ge \alpha_m(w)$. In particular if $\alpha \ge 0.64$ then Core$_\alpha$(f) is nonempty irrespective of w.*

Note that the cycle set for the α-rule must also be empty under these conditions.

While the two distribution theorems are interesting, they shed only partial light on the existence of a core for a large electorate. To illustrate the problem of application consider figure 10, which presents data

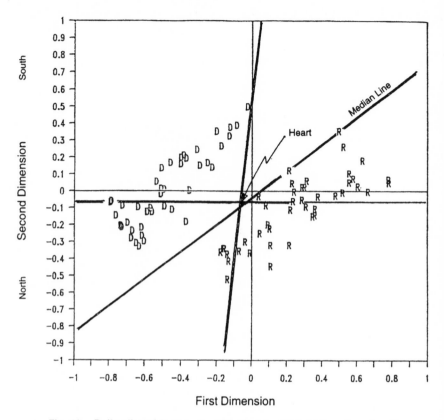

First Dimension

Fig. 10. Roll-call positions in the U.S. Senate, 1985. (Taken from fig. 10 of Poole and Rosenthal 1991.)

obtained by Poole and Rosenthal (1991) on U.S. Senate positions in 1985. The data are obtained by multidimensional scaling of roll-call votes. While it is not directly evident that these data directly represent senator preferences, nonetheless they do give an indication of the distribution of senator positions. Let us assume that each symbol (*R* for Republican and *D* for Democrat) represents the bliss point of a senator. Three of the median lines are drawn in figure 10. It is consistent with the instability theorem that these median lines do not intersect, so the core is empty. On the other hand, the area spanned by these lines (namely *the Senate heart*) is a tiny fraction of the Pareto set. The distribution of senator bliss points is not precisely spherically symmetric since the core is empty. However, the distribution does satisfy some weak symmetry conditions, since the min-max value must be very close to ½. This example suggests that if a large sample of voter bliss points is obtained from a symmetric distribution, then the probability of a core existing must approach 1. We shall show that this is *not* true for majority rule, but it is true for an α-rule (with $\alpha > \frac{1}{2}$). Thus what appears a trivial difference between majority and a *supramajority* α-rule turns out to be significant in the limit.

As we noted earlier, a generalization of the core is the yolk, namely the smallest sphere that intersects all median hyperplanes (or hypersurfaces in high dimensions). Clearly with Euclidian preferences, if the core is nonempty then the yolk is a point, and so has radius zero. If the core is empty, the median hyperplanes do not intersect, and the yolk radius is nonzero. Tovey (1991a, 1991b) has recently explored the connection between the yolk radius for a sample of size n and the yolk radius for the underlying distribution.

For the Senate example of figure 10 it is evident that the yolk radius is extremely small in relation to the size of the Pareto set. This suggests that there is a degree of symmetry in the underlying distribution from which the Senate positions are sampled. It is possible that this is reflected in the symmetry of the underlying distribution of voter preferences.

Since the following results concern the limiting properties of voting rules as n approaches infinity, it is convenient to reinterpret the idea of an α-rule. Say a coalition M is *winning* under $\alpha(n)$rule iff $|M| \geq \alpha(n)$ where $\alpha(n) = \frac{1}{2} + k(n)$. Thus majority rule is defined simply by taking $k(n) = \frac{1}{2}$ or 1 depending on whether n is odd or even. On the other hand an α-rule was defined by requiring $|M| \geq \alpha n$ for some $\alpha > \frac{1}{2}$. Letting $\alpha = \frac{1}{2} + \epsilon, \epsilon > 0$, allows us to interpret an α-rule as an $\alpha(n)$-rule with $k(n) = \epsilon n$, for $\epsilon > 0$. We consider situations where we sample an electorate of size n from a population distribution f. Under the α-rule we obtain estimates for the probability that the core is empty or nonempty. To adopt our notation let us now write $Core_{\alpha(n)}(f)$ and $Yolk_{\alpha(n)}(f)$ for the core and yolk under $\alpha(n)$ rule, with distribution f of bliss points.

The various conditions on the probability distribution f on $\mathfrak{R}^w$ that we impose are as follows:

1. f is *nonsingular* iff the mass of f on any lower dimensional hyperplane in $\mathfrak{R}^w$ is zero;
2. f is *sign-invariant* iff $f(x) = f(-x)$ for any $x \in \mathfrak{R}^w$;
3. f is *weakly centered* on a point $x \in \mathfrak{R}^w$ iff for every hyperplane h passing through x, the mass of f on each of the two open half-spaces defined by h is less than or equal to $\frac{1}{2}$.

The following two theorems on the core have recently been obtained by Schofield and Tovey (1992) and Tovey (1992).

SAMPLING THEOREM I. *Let* f *be a nonsingular sign-invariant distribution on* $\mathfrak{R}^2$. *Let* x *be the origin of* f *and let* $\{x_1, \ldots, x_{n-1}\}$ *be a sample drawn independently from* f.

1. *If* n *is even and* ≥ 6, *then the probability that* x *belongs to the majority rule core is* $(\frac{1}{2})^{n-2}$.
2. *For an* $\alpha(n)$-*rule if* $k(n)/n^{1/2} \to \infty$ *as* n $\to \infty$, *then the probability that* x *belongs to* $\text{Core}_{\alpha(n)}(f)$ *approaches 1 as* n *approaches* ∞.

Note that the Instability Theorem showed that the instability dimension for majority rule is two for *n* odd. As we have noted, we can infer that the probability of existence of a core for majority rule, *n* odd, and any sample from a nonsingular distribution must be zero. The first part of the Sampling Theorem effectively shows that the probability of a majority rule core for any sample of even size ($n \neq 4$) drops to zero as *n* increases.

To interpret part (2) we may regard $k(n)$ as the extent of the supramajority required of a coalition to win. As we have noted for an α-rule, $k(n) = \epsilon n$ for some small $\epsilon > 0$. Clearly $\epsilon n/n^{1/2} \to \infty$ and so the probability of a core approaches 1.

The stability aspect of this theorem can be developed further in the more general *w*-dimensional case.

SAMPLING THEOREM II. *Let* f *be a nonsingular distribution on* $\mathfrak{R}^w$ ($w > 1$), *is weakly centered at the origin. Let* $\{x_1, \ldots, x_n\}$ *be a sample drawn independently from* f.
Suppose that the limit of $\xi[w, n, k(n)] \to 0$ *as* n $\to \infty$, *where*

$$\xi[w, n, k(n)] = 2n^{w-1} \, exp\left[\frac{-2[k(n) - 1(w - 1)]^2}{n - w - 1} \right]$$

Then the probability that the origin of f *is a core point converges to 1 as* n *approaches* ∞.

We can apply this theorem directly to the case where *f* is log-concave with a min-max value of $1 - \left(\frac{w}{w+1}\right)^w = \alpha_m(f)$. Consider an $\alpha(n)$ rule of the form $\alpha(n) = n\alpha_m(f) + \epsilon n$, where $\epsilon > 0$. Then the probability that the origin of *f* is a core point converges to 1 as the sample size, *n*, approaches ∞.

In these two theorems we may think of $k(n)$ as the institutionalized political *friction* that has to be overcome in order to put together a winning coalition. The theorems imply that if $k(n)$ is sufficiently large then a core must almost surely exist under direct democracy as the sample size increases, as long as there is sufficient electoral symmetry. No country appears to use a direct democratic system of this kind. However, any indirect or representative democracy based on constituencies must have an inbuilt friction. In two-party systems the probability must be vanishingly small that one party obtains a majority of the seats as a consequence of having a majority of one electoral vote. It is plausible that politicians use a rule of thumb that an electoral majority of 4–6 percent is generally sufficient to guarantee a parliamentary majority. This suggests that $k(n)$ is of the order $5n/100$.

To be more explicit, in two-party political systems based on first-past-the-post elections with single member constituencies, there must always be a great deal of uncertainty. If the degree of uncertainty in the election results can be expressed as a percentage of the number of constituencies, then the effective voting rule can be expressed as an $\alpha(n)$-rule. With some degree of symmetry in the characteristics of the constituencies, then the expression in Sampling Theorem II may, in principle, be used to estimate the probability of an unbeaten party position.

Other results by Tovey (1990) can also be used to estimate the relationship between the symmetry properties of f, the number of constituencies, and the expected yolk radius. It is also possible that these relationships could throw light on the size of the political heart.

The Electoral and Political Heart

The theorems discussed in the previous section attempt to characterize the possibility of electoral equilibrium with a large voting population. Even though we assume that underlying electoral preferences are distributed over a policy space of some kind, we can never completely tabulate these preferences. However, it is possible, in principle, to sample from the electoral population to gain some idea of the nature of this distribution. Even when the true distribution is not weakly centered at an origin, the Sampling Theorems suggest that the median voter lines will span a small set. Just to illustrate, consider figure 11, which represents the allocation of electoral college votes to the individual states in the United States of America. The dark-shaded states are those that returned a plurality for Clinton in 1992. It is evident that the distribution of such states is not random. Indeed, it is clear that there are voter correlations within the Republican states of the central west (Texas, Oklahoma, Kansas, Nebraska, etc.) and the southeast (Florida, Georgia, South

The Presidential Race, County by County

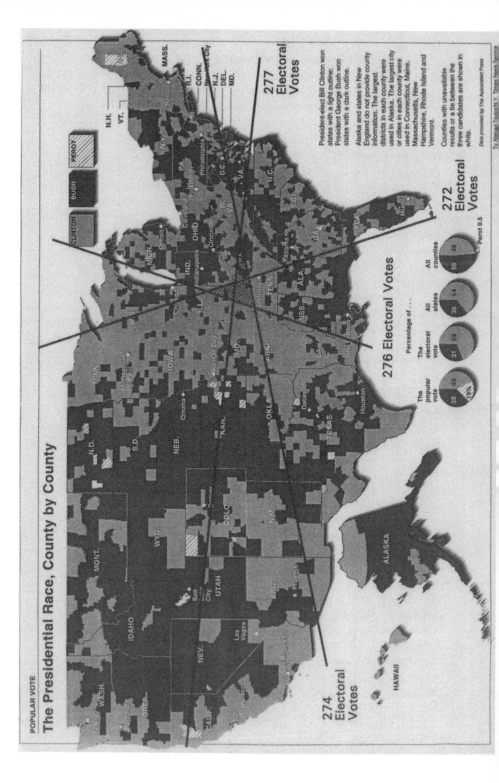

CLINTON   BUSH   PEROT

274 Electoral Votes

276 Electoral Votes

Percentage of . . .

	The popular vote	The electoral vote	All states	All counties
	43	69	64	69
	38	31	36	46
	19%			16

Perot 0.5

272 Electoral Votes

277 Electoral Votes

President-elect Bill Clinton won states with a light outline; President George Bush won states with a dark outline.

Alaska and states in New England do not provide county information. The largest districts in each county were used in Alaska. The largest city or cities in each county were used in Connecticut, Maine, Massachusetts, New Hampshire, Rhode Island and Vermont.

Counties with unavailable results or a tie between the three candidates are shown in white.

Data provided by The Associated Press

The New York Times News Service

Carolina, etc.) and within the Democratic states of the northeast, midwest, and the Pacific coast. One can infer that there is an essential political geography to political preferences.

Let us make the extremely simplifying assumption that each state has political preferences based on Euclidian distance centered at its own geographical position, and has political weight given by its electoral college vote. Four of the resulting median lines are drawn in figure 11.

These lines are only meant to give an approximate idea of the nature of the distribution of the electoral distribution. The heart of the electoral college is a triangular figure approximately based on southern Illinois/Indiana. (Note that the population "center" of the United States is a few hundred miles to the west in Missouri.) Even though the population density is not symmetrically distributed, we might expect that the area of the population yolk and heart would be very small. By the "population heart," we mean, of course, the heart generated by median lines defined by the underlying population density.

In principle the relationship between the population heart and electoral-college heart can be used as a technique for judging the representativeness of the electoral college. Moreover, if one could transform the Senate roll-call data of figure 10 to the underlying space of the appropriate political geography, then it would be possible, by comparing the Senate heart and population heart, to judge the degree of representativeness of the Senate.

This metaphor gives us a thought experiment with which to examine the nature of two-party representative democracy and to compare it with parliamentary democracy. Suppose the two presidential candidates are uninterested in policy per se, but compete in the manner proposed by Downs (1957) to secure electoral college votes. Logic would oblige them to enter the electoral-college heart. Once there, it would be a matter of luck which candidate would win, but in any case presidential competition necessarily leads to a form of Downsian convergence. Suppose now the candidates represent specific geographic interests, R in Texas and D in Massachusetts. Standard models of political competition under electoral uncertainty (Cox 1984, for example) suggest the existence of a Nash equilibrium with R declaring position R' (in Oklahoma City perhaps!) and D declaring position D' (in Pittsburgh, say). Convergence in declared positions occurs, but is weaker than Downsian convergence. At the election, one of these two positions (say R') wins. A first-term president might be credibly committed to position R', but a second-term winner might be expected to defect back to position R. An obvious consequence of this reasoning is that R, or even R', can be far in policy terms from the Senate heart, the population heart, and the electoral-college heart.

The same logic applies in the more general situation of a multi-dimensional policy space on a complex, nongeographically based pattern of electoral preferences. The technical difficulty here is to define the heart in an abstract fashion, and to show that it always belongs to the underlying Pareto set (Schofield 1993a). In this general case the winner of a two-candidate presidential race may adopt a position far from the Senate and Congress hearts. Since the president can veto congressional bills, so-called gridlock can occur.

Notice that a presidential candidate who is less tied to specific geographical interests is more likely to approach the electoral-college heart. Because the electoral-college heart and congressional heart can be expected to be close to one another, such a successful presidential candidate is likely to choose a declared position that is compatible with a congressional majority.

To pursue the thought experiment further, suppose that preferences were aggregated using a method of proportional representation. Because of the political geography implicit in this thought experiment, one might expect five or six parties to come into being (the northeast, southeast, midwest, Texas, the Rocky Mountain states, and the Pacific Coast). Under a parliamentary system, coalitions between these regions would be necessary to implement majority government.

Previous work (Laver and Schofield 1990; Schofield 1993b) has emphasized the importance of a core party in controlling a parliamentary government. By definition, such a party must be centrally located and control the largest number of seats. However, the logic of this thought experiment is the conflict between east and west, as well as between north and south. In such a situation, a dominant core party could not develop. The resulting fragmentation could lead to fission.

Although these suggestions are made in a highly speculative way, it is obvious that recent elections in Russia (in 1992) and Italy (in 1993) involved strong elements of political geography, or regionalism. It remains to be seen whether such political phenomena will lead to fission.

Conclusion

The general argument presented here is that direct democracy may lead to centrist outcomes if the tendency toward voting chaos can be avoided, by using particular representative institutions appropriate to the underlying distribution of electoral preferences. Thus, the more the political game resembles a zero-sum situation, then the more likely is it that such voting chaos can occur. However, if the distribution of electoral preferences is symmetrically balanced and there is friction in the process of political choice, then political equilibrium becomes more probable in large electorates.

Even given electoral equilibrium, the structure of representative democracy can be very different depending on the nature of electoral rules and norms of political behavior.

A thought experiment based on political geography gives some insight, perhaps, into the complicated balance of power and preference between Congress and the president. The experiment suggests that, were the United States to have a multiparty parliamentary system based on proportional representation, then political fission could well occur. It is interesting to speculate on whether this may be the underlying reason for political fission in so many of the new states in Eastern Europe and the Commonwealth of Independent States and Russia.

NOTE

This material is based on work supported by NSF Grant No. SES-88-20845. Presented at the Ecole des Hautes Etudes Commercial, Montreal, Canada and the International Political Science School, Tallinn, Estonia, October 1991.

Bibliography

Abreu, Dilip; Paul Milgrom; and David Pearce. 1991. Information and Timing in Repeated Partnerships. *Econometrica* 59:1713–33.

Abreu, Dilip, and David Pearce. 1991. "A Perspective on Renegotiation in Repeated Games." In R. Selten, ed., *Game Equilibrium Models*. Vol. 2: *Methods, Morals and Markets*. Heidelberg: Springer.

Abreu, Dilip; David Pearce; and Ennio Stacchetti. 1986. "Optimal Cartel Equilibria with Imperfect Monitoring." *Journal of Economic Theory* 39:251–69.

Abulafia, David. 1985. "Catalan Merchants and the Western Mediterranean, 1236–1300: Studies in the Notarial Acts of Barcelona and Sicily." *Viator* 16:209–42.

Ainsworth, Scott, and Itai Sened. 1993. "The Role of Lobbyists: Entrepreneurs with Two Audiences." *American Journal of Political Science* 37(4): 834–66.

Alchian, Armen A. 1950. "Uncertainty, Evolution and Economic Theory." *Journal of Political Economy* 58:211–21.

Arrow, Kenneth. 1951. *Social Choice and Individual Values*. New Haven, CT: Yale University Press.

———. 1969. "Tullock and an Existence Theorem." *Public Choice* 6:105–111.

Arthur, Brian. 1989. "Competing Technologies, Increasing Returns, and Lock-In by Historical Events." *Economic Journal* 99:116–31.

Aumann, Robert; B. Peleg; and P. Rabinowitz. 1965. "A Method for Computing the Kernel of n-Person Games." *Mathematics of Computation* 19:531–51.

Austen-Smith, David. 1990. "Credible Debate Equilibria." *Social Choice and Welfare* 7:75–93.

Axelrod, Robert. 1981. "The Emergence of Cooperation among Egoists." *American Political Science Review* 75:305–18.

———. 1986. "An Evolutionary Approach to Norms." *American Political Science Review* 80:1095–1112.

Bachrach, Samuel B., and Edward J. Lawler. 1981. *Bargaining: Power, Tactics and Outcomes*. San Francisco: Jossey-Bass Publishers.

Bairoch, Paul; Jean Batou; and Pierre Chevre, eds. 1988. *The Population of European Cities from 800 to 1850*. Geneva: Center of International Economic History.

Banks, Jeffery S. 1991. *Signaling Games in Political Science*. Forthcoming.

———. 1994. Singularity Theory and Core Existence in the Spatial Model. Manuscript: University of Rochester.

Banks, Jeffrey S., and Randall L. Calvert. 1989. "Communication and Efficiency in Coordination Games." Working Paper No. 196, Department of Political Science, University of Rochester.

Banks, J. S., and J. Sobel. 1987. "Equilibrium Selection in Signaling Games." *Econometrica* 55:647–61.

Baron, David P. 1989. "A Noncooperative Theory of Legislative Coalitions." *American Journal of Political Science* 33:1048–84.

———. 1991. "Majoritarian Incentives, Pork Barrel Programs, and Procedural Control." *American Journal of Political Science* 35:57–90.

Baron, David P., and John A. Ferejohn. 1989. "Bargaining in Legislatures." *American Political Science Review* 83:1181–1206.

Barzel, Yoram. 1989. *Economic Analysis of Property Rights.* Cambridge: Cambridge University Press.

Bates, Robert H. 1989. *Beyond the Miracle of the Market: The Political Economy of Agrarian Development in Kenya.* Cambridge: Cambridge University Press.

Berman, Harold J. 1983. *Law and Revolution.* Cambridge, MA: Harvard University Press.

Bernheim, Douglas, and Debraj Ray. 1989. "Collective Dynamic Consistency in Repeated Games." *Games and Economic Behavior* 1:295–326.

Bianco, William T., and Robert H. Bates. 1990. "Cooperation by Design: Leadership, Structure, and Collective Dilemma." *American Political Science Review* 84:496–97.

Bien, David. 1987. "Offices, Corps, and a System of State Credit: The Uses of Privilege under The Ancien Regime." In K. Baker, ed., *The French Revolution and the Creation of Modern Political Culture,* 1:89–114. Oxford: Pergamon Press.

Billera, L. J. 1970. "Existence of General Bargaining Sets for Cooperative Games without Side Payments." *Bull Am Math Soc* 76:375–97.

Bliss, C., and B. Nalebuff. 1984. "Dragon-slaying and Ballroom Dancing: The Private Supply of a Public Good." *Journal of Public Economics* 25:1–12.

Brennan, Geoffrey, and James Buchanan. 1985. *The Reason of Rule.* Cambridge: Cambridge University Press.

Brentano, Lujo. 1870. *English Guilds: The Original Ordinances of More Than One Hundred Early English Guilds.* London: N. Trubner and Company.

Brown, D. J. 1973. Acyclic Choice. Mimeo. Yale University: Cowles Foundation.

Buchanan, James M., and Gordon Tullock. 1962. *The Calculus of Consent.* Ann Arbor: The University of Michigan Press.

Calvert, Randall, L. 1989. "Reciprocity among Self-Interested Actors: Uncertainty, Asymmetry, and Distribution." In Peter C. Ordeshook, ed., *Models of Strategic Choice in Politics.* Ann Arbor: University of Michigan Press.

———. 1991. "Leadership and Its Basis in Problems of Social Coordination." *International Political Science Review* 13:7–24.

Caplin, Andrew, and Barry Nalebuff. 1988. "On 64% Majority Rule." *Econometrica* 56:787–814.

———. 1991. "Aggregation and Social Choice: A Mean Voter Theorem." *Econometrica* 59:1–24.

Carus-Wilson, E. M. 1967. *Medieval Merchant Venturers.* London: Butler and Tanner.

Cho, In-koo. 1987. "A Refinement of Sequential Equilibrium." *Econometrica* 55:1367–89.

———, and David Kreps. 1987. "Signaling Games and Stable Equilibria" *The Quarterly Journal of Economics* 102:179–221.

Clark, Andrew. 1989. *Microcognition.* Cambridge, MA: MIT Press.

Coase, Ronald H. 1960. "The Problem of Social Cost." *Journal of Law and Economics* 3:1–44.

Coleman, James. 1990. *The Foundations of Social Theory.* Cambridge, MA: Harvard University Press.

Coleman, Jules, and Charles Silver. 1986. "Justice in Settlements." *Social Philosophy and Policy* 4:102–44.

Colvin, Ian D. 1971. *The Germans in England, 1066–1598.* London: Kennikat Press.

Cox, Gary. 1984. "An Expected Utility Model of Electoral Competition." *Quality and Quantity* 18:337–49.

———. 1987a. "Electoral Equilibrium under Alternative Voting Institutions." *American Journal of Political Science* 31:81–108.

———. 1987b. "The Uncovered Set and the Core." *American Journal of Political Science* 31:408–22.

———. 1990. "Centripetal and Centrifugal Incentives in Electoral Systems." *American Journal of Political Science* 34:903–35.

Crawford, Vincent P., and Hans Haller. 1990. "Learning How To Cooperate: Optimal Play in Repeated Coordination Games." *Econometrica* 58:571–95.

David, Paul. 1985. "Clio and the Econometrics of QWERTY." *American Economic Review* 75:332–37.

———. 1988. "Path Dependence: Putting the Past into the Future of Economics." Technical Report No. 533, IMSSS California, Stanford University.

Davis, Michael, and Michael Maschler. 1967. "Existence of Stable Payoff Configurations for Cooperative Games." In Martin Shubik, ed., *Essays in Mathematical Economics,* 39–52. Princeton: Princeton University Press.

Dawes, Robyn M.; Alphons J. C. van de Kragt; and John M. Orbell. 1990. "Cooperation for the Benefit of Us—Not Me, or My Conscience." In Jane J. Mansbridge, ed., *Beyond Self-Interest.* Chicago: University of Chicago Press.

Day, W. Gerald. 1988. *Genoa's Response to Byzantium, 1155–1204.* Urbana, IL: University of Illinois Press.

De Roover, Raymond. 1948. *Money, Banking and Credit in Mediaeval Bruges.* Cambridge, MA: The Mediaeval Academy of America.

———. 1965. The Organization of Trade. *Cambridge Economic History of Europe.* Vol. 3. Cambridge: Cambridge University Press.

Demsetz, Harold. 1964. "The Exchange and Enforcement of Property Rights." *Journal of Law and Economics* 7:11–26.

———. 1967. "Toward A Theory of Property Rights." *American Economic Review* 57:347–59.

————. 1982. *Economic, Legal, and Political Dimensions of Competition.* Amsterdam: North Holland.

Dixit, Avinash, and Barry Nalebuff. 1991. "Making Strategies Credible." In R. Zeckhauser, ed., *Strategy and Choice,* 161–84. Cambridge, MA: MIT Press.

Dollinger, Philippe. 1970. *The German Hansa.* Stanford, CA: Stanford University Press.

Downs, Anthony. 1957. *An Economic Theory of Democracy.* New York: Harper and Row.

Durkheim, Emile. [1895] 1938. *The Rules of the Sociological Method.* 8th ed. Edited by George E. G. Catlin. Translated by Sarah A. Solovay and John H. Mueller. Chicago: University of Chicago Press.

Easterlin, Richard. 1981. "Why Isn't the Whole World Developed?" *The Journal of Economic History* 41:1–20.

Eggertsson, Thrainn. 1990. *Economic Institutions and Behavior.* Cambridge: Cambridge University Press.

Elster, Jon. 1989. *The Cement of Society.* Cambridge: Cambridge University Press.

————. Forthcoming. "Strategic Uses of Argument." In K. Arrow et al., eds., *Barriers to Conflict Resolution.* New York: Norton.

————. 1993. *Political Psychology.* Cambridge: Cambridge University Press.

English Historical Documents (EHD). 1975. Vol. 3, for the years 1189–1327. Edited by Harry Rothwell. London: Eyre and Spottiswoode.

Ensminger, Jean. 1992. *Making a Market: The Institutional Transformation of an African Society.* Cambridge: Cambridge University Press.

Ensminger, Jean, and Andrew Rutten. 1990. "The Political Economy of Changing Property Rights: Dismantling a Kenyan Commons." Political Economy Working Paper No. 146, Center in Political Economy, Washington University in St. Louis.

Farrand, Max, ed. 1937 (1966). *The Records of The Federal Convention of 1787.* 3 vols. New Haven, CT: Yale University Press.

Farrell, Joseph, and Robert Gibbons. 1989. "Cheap Talk Can Matter in Bargaining." *Journal of Economic Theory* 48:221–37.

Farrell, Joseph, and Eric Maskin. 1989. "Renegotiation in Repeated Games." *Games and Economic Behavior* 1:327–60.

Ferejohn, John, and David Grether. 1977. "On a Class of Rational Decision Procedures." *Journal of Economic Theory* 8:471–82.

Finkelman, P. 1987. "Slavery and the Constitutional Convention: Making a Covenant with Death." In R. Beeman, S. Botein, and E. C. Carter II, eds., *Beyond Confederation: Origins of the Constitution and American National Identity.* Chapel Hill: University of North Carolina Press.

Fiorina, Morris P., and Charles R. Plott. 1978. "Committee Decisions under Majority Rule: An Experimental Study." *American Political Science Review* 72:575–98.

Frank, Robert H. 1985. *Choosing the Right Pond.* New York: Oxford University Press.

———. 1988. *Passions within Reason: The Strategic Role of the Emotions.* New York: W.W. Norton.

Frohlich, Norman; Joseph A. Oppenheimer; and Oran R. Young. 1971. *Political Leadership and Collective Goods.* Princeton: Princeton University Press.

Games and Economic Behavior. 1991. Vol. 3.

Gibbard, Alan. 1969. "Intransitive Social Indifference and the Arrow Dilemma." Mimeo. University of Michigan: Department of Philosophy.

Goodall, Jane. 1986. *The Chimpanzees of Gombe: Patterns of Behavior.* Cambridge: Harvard University Press.

Green, Edward, and Robert Porter. 1984. "Noncooperative Collusion Under Imperfect Price Information." *Econometrica* 52:87–100.

Greenwalt, Kent. 1989. *Speech, Crime, and the Uses of Language.* New York: Oxford University Press.

Greenberg, Joseph. 1979. "Consistent Majority Rules over Compact Sets of Alternatives." *Econometrica* 41:285–97.

Greif, Avner. 1989. "Reputation and Coalitions in Medieval Trade: Evidence on the Maghribi Traders." *Journal of Economic History* 59:857–82.

———. 1991. "Cultural Beliefs as a Common Resource in an Integrating World: An Example from the Theory and History of Collectivist and Individualist Societies." Stanford University. Mimeo.

———. 1992a. "Institutions and Commitment in International Trade: Lessons from the Commercial Revolution." *American Economic Review, Papers and Proceedings* 82(40): 128–33.

———. 1992b. "Institutional Infrastructure and Economic Development: Reflections from the Commercial Revolution." In Michael Kaser, ed. *Proceedings of the Tenth World Congress of the International Economic Association.* London: Macmillan.

———. 1992c. "Cultural Beliefs and the Organization of Society: Historical and Theoretical Reflection on Collectivist and Individualist Societies." Stanford University. Mimeo.

———. 1993a. "Contract Enforceability and Economic Institutions in Early Trade: The Maghribi Traders' Coalition." *American Economic Review* 83: 525–48.

———. 1993b. "On the Nature and Evolution of Political and Economic Institutions: Commitment, Reputation, and Self-Enforcing Institutions in Late Medieval Genoa." Working Paper, Stanford University.

Greif, Avner; Paul Milgrom; and Barry Weingast. 1990. "The Merchant Guild as a Nexus of Contracts." Working Papers in Political Science P-90-9, Hoover Institution, Stanford University.

Gross, Charles. 1890. *Gild Merchant.* Oxford: Clarendon Press.

Gufstafsson, Bo. 1987. "The Rise and Economic Behavior of Medieval Craft Guilds: An Economic-Theoretical Interpretation." *The Scandinavian Economic History Review* 35(1):1–39.

Habermas, Jürgen. 1984. *The Theory of Communicative Action.* Vol. 1. Boston: Beacon Press.

———. 1989. *The Theory of Communicative Action.* Vol. 2. Boston: Beacon Press.

———. 1990. *Moral Consciousness and Communicative Action.* Cambridge, MA: MIT Press.

Hahn, Frank. 1987. "Information, Dynamics and Equilibrium." *Scottish Journal of Political Economy* 34:321–34.

Hahn, R. W., and G. L. Hester. 1989. "Marketable Permits: Lessons for Theory and Practice." *Ecology Law Quarterly* 16:361–406.

Hardin, Russel. 1982. *Collective Action.* Baltimore: Johns Hopkins University Press.

———. 1990. "The Social Evolution of Cooperation." In Karen Schweers Cook and Margaret Levi, eds., *The Limits of Rationality.* Chicago: University of Chicago Press.

Hayek, F. A. 1967. "Notes on the Evolution of Systems of Rules of Conduct." In *Studies in Philosophy, Politics, and Economics.* Chicago: University of Chicago Press.

Hechter, Michael. 1990a. "The Emergence of Cooperative Social Institutions." In Michael Hechter, Karl-Dieter Opp, and Reinhardt Wippler, eds., *Social Institutions: Their Emergence, Maintenance, and Effects.* New York: Aldine de Gruyter.

———. 1990b. *Principles of Group Solidarity.* Berkeley: University of California Press.

Hechter, Michael; Karl-Dieter Opp; and Reinhardt Wippler, eds. 1990. *Social Institutions: Their Emergence, Maintenance and Effects.* New York: Aldine de Gruyter.

Heckathorn, Douglas D. 1993. "Collective Action and Group Heterogeneity: Voluntary Provision versus Selective Incentives." *American Sociological Review* 58:329–50.

Heckathorn, Douglas D., and Steven M. Maser. 1987. "Bargaining and Constitutional Contracts." *American Journal of Political Science* 31:142–68.

Hegel, G. W. F. [1821] 1942. *Hegel's Philosophy of Right.* Translated by T. M. Knox. New York: Oxford University Press.

Heiner, Ronald. 1983. "The Origins of Predictable Behavior." *American Economic Review* 73:560–95.

Hickson, Charles R., and Earl A. Thompson. 1991. "A New Theory of Guilds and European Economic Development." *Explorations in Economic History* 28:127–68.

Hirst, Francis W. 1948. *The Stock Exchange: A Short Study of Investment and Speculation.* London: Oxford University Press.

Hobbes, Thomas. [1651] 1986. *Leviathan.* New York: Penguin Classics.

Hoffman, Philip. 1989. "Taxes, Fiscal Crises, and Representative Institutions: The Case of Early Modern France." Center for the History of Freedom, Washington University, St. Louis.

Holland, John; Keith Holyoak; Richard Nisbett; and Paul Thagard. 1986. *Induction.* Cambridge, MA: MIT Press.

Hume, David. 1978. *A Treatise of Human Nature.* 2d ed. Oxford: Oxford University Press.

Inada, K. 1969. "On the Simple Majority Decision Rule." *Econometrica* 37:490–506.

Jillson, C. C. 1988. *Constitution Making: Conflict and Consensus in the Federal Convention of 1787*. New York: Agathon Press.

Johnson, James D. 1990. "On the Cultural Dimensions of Rational Choice Theory." Paper presented at the Midwest Political Science Association annual meetings, Chicago, IL.

Kalai, E., and M. Smorodinsky. 1975. "Other Solutions to Nash's Bargaining Problem." *Econometrica* 43:513–18.

Kandori, Michihiro. 1992. "Social Norms and Community Enforcement." *Review of Economic Studies* 59(January): 61–80.

Kant, Immanuel. [1785] 1981. *Grounding the Metaphysics of Morals*. Indianapolis: Hackett.

———. [1794] 1983. *Perpetual Peace and Other Essays*. Indianapolis: Hackett.

Kedar, Benjamin A. 1976. *Merchants in Crisis*. New Haven, CT: Yale University Press.

Knight, Jack. 1992. *Institutions and Social Conflict*. Cambridge: Cambridge University Press.

Koford, Kenneth J., and Jeffrey B. Miller. 1991. *Social Norms and Economic Institutions*. Ann Arbor: University of Michigan Press.

Kramer, Gerald H. 1973. "On a Class of Equilibrium Conditions for Majority Rule." *Econometrica* 41:285–97.

Krehbiel, Keith; Kenneth A. Shepsle; and Barry R. Weingast. 1987. "Controversy: Why are Congressional Committees Powerful?" *American Political Science Review* 81:929–45.

Kreps, David M. 1990a. *A Course in Microeconomic Theory*. Princeton, NJ: Princeton University Press.

———. 1990b. *Game Theory and Economic Modeling*. Oxford: Oxford University Press.

Kreps, David M., and Robert Wilson. 1982. "Sequential Equilibria." *Econometrica* 50:1003–37.

Kreuger, Anne. 1991. "The Political Economy of Controls: American Sugar." *NBER Reprint No. 1657*.

Krueger, Hilmar C. 1932. "The Commercial Relations between Genoa and Northwest Africa in the Twelfth Century." Ph.D. diss., University of Wisconsin.

———. 1933. "Genoese Trade with Northwest Africa in the Twelfth Century." *Speculum* 6:377–95.

Laing, J. D., and S. Olmstead. 1978. "An Experimental and Game Theoretic Study of Committees." In P. Ordeshook, ed., *Game Theory and Political Science*. New York: New York University Press.

Lane, C. Frederic. 1973. *Venice*. Baltimore: The Johns Hopkins University Press.

Laver, Michael, and Norman Schofield. 1990. *Multiparty Government: The Politics of Coalition in Europe*. Oxford: Oxford University Press.

Ledyard, John O. 1984. "The Pure Theory of Large Two-Candidate Elections." *Public Choice* 44:43–47.

Levi, Margaret. 1988. *Of Rule and Revenue*. Berkeley: University of California Press.

Lewis, David. 1969. *Convention: A Philosophical Study*. Cambridge, MA: Harvard University Press.

Libecap, Gary. 1989. *Contracting for Property Rights*. Cambridge: Cambridge University Press.

Lloyd, T. H. 1991. *England and the German Hansa, 1157–1611*. Cambridge: Cambridge University Press.

Lohmann, Susanne. 1991a. "Information Aggregation through Costly Political Action." Stanford University, Graduate School of Business Research Paper No. 1130.

———. 1991b. "Can Costly Political Action Be Oversupplied?" Paper presented at the Conference on Political Economy: Institutions, Information, Competition and Representation, Washington University, St. Louis.

Lopez, Robert Sabatino. 1943. "European Merchants in the Medieval Indies: The Evidence of Commercial Documents." *Journal of Economic History* 3:164–84.

Lopez, Robert Sabatino. 1976. *The Commercial Revolution in the Middle Ages, 950–1350*. Cambridge: Cambridge University Press.

Luce, R. D., and Howard Raiffa. 1957. *Games and Decisions*. New York: Wiley.

Manin, Bernard. 1987. "On Legitimacy and Political Deliberation." *Political Theory* 15(3):338–68.

March, James G., and Johan P. Olsen. 1989. *Rediscovering Institutions: The Organizational Basis of Politics*. New York: Free Press.

Margolis, Howard. 1982. *Selfishness, Altruism, and Rationality: A Theory of Social Choice*. Chicago: University of Chicago Press.

Maynard Smith, John. 1982. *Evolution and the Theory of Games*. Cambridge: Cambridge University Press.

McKelvey, Richard. 1976. "Intransitivities in Multi-Dimensional Voting Models and Some Implications for Agenda Control." *Journal of Economic Theory* 12:472–82.

———. 1979. "General Conditions for Global Intransitivities in Formal Voting Models." *Econometrica* 47:1085–1111.

McKelvey, Richard D. 1986. "Covering, Dominance and Institution-Free Properties of Social Choice." *American Journal of Political Science* 30: 283–314.

McKelvey, Richard; Peter Ordeshook; and M. D. Winer. 1978. "The Competitive Solution for N-Person Games without Transferrable Utility, with an Application to Committee Games." *American Political Science Review* 72:599–615.

McKelvey, Richard, and Norman Schofield. 1986. "Structural Instability of the Core." *Journal of Mathematical Economics* 15:179–98.

Michael, M. 1965. "The Archives of Naharay ben Nissim, Businessman and Public Figure in Eleventh Century Egypt." Ph.D. diss., The Hebrew University, Jerusalem.

Milgrom, Paul R.; Douglass North; and Barry R. Weingast. 1990. "The Role of Institutions in the Revival of Trade: The Medieval Law Merchant, Private Judges, and the Champagne Fairs." *Economics and Politics* 1:1–23.

Miller, Gary. 1992. *Managerial Hierarchies.* Cambridge: Cambridge University Press.

Moore, Ellen Wedemeyer. 1985. *The Fairs of Medieval England.* Toronto: Pontifical Institute of Medieval Study.

Nakamura, K. 1979. "The Vetoers in a Simple Game with Ordinal Preferences." *International Journal of Game Theory* 8:55–61.

Nelson, Richard R., and Sidney G. Winter. 1982. *An Evolutionary Theory of Economic Change.* Cambridge, MA: Harvard University Press.

Niemi, Richard, and Herbert Weisberg. 1968. "A Mathematical Solution for the Probability of the Paradox of Voting." *Behavioral Science* 13:317–23.

North, Douglass C. 1981. *Structure and Change in Economic History.* New York: Norton.

———. 1990. *Institutions, Institutional Change and Economic Performance.* Cambridge: Cambridge University Press.

———. 1991. "A Transaction Cost Theory of Politics." *The Journal of Theoretical Politics* 3:355–68.

North, Douglass C., and Robert Paul Thomas. 1973. *The Rise of the Western World.* Cambridge: Cambridge University Press.

North, Douglass C., and Barry R. Weingast. 1989. "Constitutions and Commitment: The Evolution of Institutions Governing Public Choice in Seventeenth-Century England." *The Journal of Economic History* 49:803–32.

Nozick, Robert. 1969. "Coercion." In S. Morgenbesser et al., eds., *Philosophy, Science and Method.* New York: Macmillan.

Oberschall, Anthony, and Eric M. Leifer. 1986. "Efficiency and Social Institutions: Uses and Misuses of Economic Reasoning in Sociology." *American Review of Sociology* 12:233–53.

Olson, M. 1965. *The Logic of Collective Action.* Cambridge: Harvard University Press.

Osborne, Martin J., and Ariel Rubenstein. 1990. *Bargaining and Markets.* San Diego: Academic Press, Inc.

Ostrom, Elinor. 1990. *Governing the Commons.* Cambridge: Cambridge University Press.

Palfrey, Thomas, and Howard Rosenthal. 1984. "Private Incentives in Social Dilemma: The Effects of Incomplete Information and Altruism." *Journal of Public Economics* 28:171–93.

Palfrey, Thomas, and Howard Rosenthal. 1985. "Voter Participation and Strategic Uncertainty." *American Political Science Review* 79:62–78.

Parker, Geoffrey. 1990. *The Military Revolution (1500–1800).* Cambridge: Cambridge University Press.

Pearce, David. 1987. "Renegotiation-Proof Equilibria: Collective Rationality and Intertemporal Cooperation." Yale University. Mimeo.

Peleg, Bezalel. 1967. "Existence Theorem for the Bargaining Set." In Martin Shubik, ed., *Essays in Mathematical Economics.* Princeton: Princeton University Press.

Plott, Charles. 1967. "A Notion of Equilibrium and its Possibility under Majority Rule." *American Economic Review* 57:787–806.

Pollock, Frederick, and Frederic William Maitland. 1968. *The History of the English Law before the Time of Edward I.* Vols. 1 and 2. 2d ed. Cambridge: Cambridge University Press.

Poole, Keith, and Howard Rosenthal. 1991. "Patterns of Congressional Voting." *American Journal of Political Science* 35:228–78.

Posner, Richard A. 1980. "A Theory of Primitive Society, with Special Reference to Law." *Journal of Law and Economics* 23:1–53.

Postan, Michael. 1973. "The Economic and Political Relations of England and the Hansa from 1400 to 1475." In *Medieval Trade and Finance.* Cambridge: Cambridge University Press.

———. 1987. "The Trade of Medieval Europe: The North." *Cambridge Economic History of Europe.* Vol. 2, *Trade and Industry in the Middle Ages.* Cambridge: Cambridge University Press.

Raiffa, Howard. 1982. *The Art and Science of Negotiation.* Cambridge, MA: Harvard University Press.

Rashdall, Hastings. 1936. *The Universities of Europe in the Middle Ages.* Vol. 1. Edited by F. M. Powicke and A. B. Emden. Oxford: Oxford University Press.

Rasmussen, Eric. 1989. *Games and Information.* Cambridge: Basil Blackwell.

Rawls, John. 1971. *A Theory of Justice.* Cambridge, MA: Harvard University Press.

Riker, William H. 1956. "The Senate and American Federalism." *American Political Science Review* 49:452–69.

———. 1957. "Dutch and American Federalism." *The Journal of the History of Ideas* 18:495–521.

———. 1980. "Implications from the Disequilibrium of Majority Rule for the Study of Institutions." *American Political Science Review* 74:432–46.

———. 1982. *Liberalism against Populism.* San Francisco: Freeman.

———. 1987. *The Development of American Federalism.* Boston: Kluwer Academic Publishers.

———. 1988. "The Place of Political Science in Public Choice." *Public Choice* 57:247–57.

———. 1990. "Civil Rights and Property Rights." In E. F. Paul and H. Dickman, eds., *Liberty, Property, and the Future of Constitutional Development.* Albany, NY: SUNY Press.

Root, Hilton L. 1989. "Tying the King's Hands: Credible Commitments and Royal Fiscal Policy during the Old Regime." *Rationality and Society* 1:240–58.

Rorig, Fritz. 1967. *The Medieval Town.* Berkeley: University of California Press.

Roth, Alvin, 1979. *Axiomatic Bargaining Theory.* New York: Springer.

Rousseau, Jean-Jacques. 1964. *Du Contrat Social.* Paris: Gellimard.

Rubenstein, Ariel. 1982. "Perfect Equilibrium in a Bargaining Model." *Econometrica* 50:97–109.

Rutland, Richard, ed. 1975. *The Papers of James Madison.* Vol. 9. Chicago: University of Chicago Press.

———. 1977. *The Papers of James Madison.* Vol. 10. Chicago: University of Chicago Press.

Salzman, L. F. 1928. "A Riot at Boston Fair." *The History Teachers' Miscellany* 6:2–3.

Samuelson, Larry. 1991. "Limit Evolutionarily Stable Strategies in Two-Player, Normal Form Games." *Games and Economic Behavior* 3:110–28.

Schelling, Thomas C. 1960. *The Strategy of Conflict.* Cambridge, MA: Harvard University Press.

———. 1978. *Micromotives and Macrobehavior.* New York: W.W. Norton & Company.

Schildhauer, Johannes. 1985. *The Hansa History and Culture.* Leipzig: Edition Leipzig.

Schofield, Norman. 1980. "Generic Properties of Simple Bergson-Samuelson Welfare Functions." *Journal of Mathematical Economics* 7:175–92.

———. 1983. "Generic Instability of Majority Rule." *Review of Economic Studies* 50:695–705.

———. 1984. "Social Equilibrium and Cycles on Compact Sets." *Journal of Economic Theory* 33:59–71.

———. 1985a. "Anarchy, Altruism, and Cooperation." *Social Choice and Welfare* 2:207–19.

———. 1985b. *Social Choice and Democracy.* Berlin and Heidelberg: Springer Verlag.

———. 1986. "Existence of a *Structurally Stable* Equilibrium for a Non-Collegial Voting Rule." *Public Choice* 51:267–84.

———. 1991. *A Theory of Coalition Government in a Spatial Model of Voting.* Center in Political Economy, Washington University in St. Louis.

———. 1993a. "Party Competition in a Spatial Model of Coalition Formation." In William Barnett, et al., eds., *Political Economy.* Cambridge: Cambridge University Press.

———. 1993b. "Political Competition in Multiparty Coalition Governments." *European Journal of Political Research* 23:1–33.

———. 1995. "Coalition Politics: A Formal Model and Empirical Analysis." *Journal of Theoretical Politics* 7:245–81.

Schofield, Norman, and Craig Tovey. 1992. "Probability and Convergence for Supra-Majority Rule with Euclidean Preferences." *Mathematical and Computer Modelling* 16:41–58.

Schotter, Andrew. 1981. *The Economic Theory of Social Institutions.* Cambridge: Cambridge University Press.

Scitovsky, Tibor. 1971. *Welfare and Competition.* Homewood, IL: Richard D. Irwin.

Searle, John. 1969. *Speech Acts.* Cambridge: Cambridge University Press.

———. 1979. *Expression and Meaning.* Cambridge: Cambridge University Press.

Selten, Reinhardt. 1983. "Evolutionary Stability in Extensive Two-Person Games." *Mathematical Social Sciences* 5:269–363.

Sen, Amartya K. 1970. *Collective Choice and Social Welfare.* Amsterdam: North Holland.

———. 1982. *Choice, Welfare, and Measurement.* Cambridge, MA: MIT Press.

———. 1987. *On Ethics and Economics.* New York: Blackwell.

Sened, Itai. 1990. "A Political Theory of the Evolution of Rights: A Game with Asymmetric Information." PoliSci Working Paper No. 147, Washington University, St. Louis.

Sened, Itai, and William H. Riker. 1992. "Common Property and Private Property: The Case of Air Slots." Working Paper. University of Rochester: Rochester, NY.

Shepsle, Kenneth A. 1979. "Institutional Arrangements and Equilibrium in Multidimensional Voting Models." *American Journal of Political Science* 23:27–59.

———. 1986. "Institutional Equilibrium and Equilibrium Institutions." In Herbert F. Weisberg, ed., *Political Science: The Science of Politics.* New York: Agathon Press.

———. 1991. "Discretion, Institutions and the Problem of Government Commitment." In Pierre Bourdieu and James Coleman, eds., *Social Theory for a Changing Society.* Boulder, CO: Westview Press.

Shepsle, Kenneth, and Peter Ordeshook. 1982. *Political Equilibrium.* Boston: Kluwer-Nijhoff.

Shepsle, Kenneth, and Barry Weingast. 1987. "The Institutional Foundations of Committee Power." *American Political Science Review* 81:85–104.

Simon, Herbert. 1986. "Rationality in Psychology and Economics." In Robin Hogarth and Melvin Reder, eds., *The Behavioral Foundations of Economic Theory. The Journal of Business* (Supplement) 59(4, Part 2): 209–24.

Simpson, A. W. B. [1962] 1986. *A History of the Land Law.* Oxford: Oxford University Press.

Sinclair, Barbara. 1989. *The Transformation of the U.S. Senate.* Baltimore: Johns Hopkins University Press.

Smith, Adam. 1976. *An Inquiry into the Nature and Causes of the Wealth of Nations.* Indianapolis: Liberty Classics.

Sobel, Robert. 1970. *The Curbstone Brokers: The Origins of the American Stock Exchange.* New York: Macmillan.

Strayer, Joseph R., ed. 1985. *Hanseatic League.* Vol. 6 of the *Dictionary of the Middle Ages.* New York: Charles Scribners' Sons.

Sugden, Robert. 1986. *The Economics of Rights, Co-operation and Welfare.* Oxford: Basil Blackwell.

Sutton, John. 1986. "Non-cooperative Bargaining Theory: An Introduction." *Review of Economic Studies* 53:709–24.

Taylor, Michael. 1976. *Anarchy and Cooperation.* London: John Wiley.

———. 1987. *The Possibility of Cooperation.* Cambridge: Cambridge University Press.

Thrupp, Sylvia L. 1963. "The Gilds." In M. M. Postan, E. E. Rich, and Edward Miller, eds., *The Cambridge Economic History of Europe.* Vol. 3. Cambridge: Cambridge University Press.

Tovey, Craig. 1990. *The Almost Surely Shrinking Yolk.* School of Industrial and Systems Engineering, Georgia Institute of Technology, Atlanta.

————. 1991a. *A Critique of Distributional Analysis in Social Choice.* Naval Postgraduate School Technical Report No. 91-16. Monterrey, California.

————. 1991b. *The Instability of Instability.* Naval Postgraduate School Technical Report No. 91-15. Monterrey, California.

————. 1992. "The Probability of an Undominated Central Voter in Two Dimensional Spatial Majority Voting." *Social Choice and Welfare* 9:43–48.

Trivers, R. L. 1974. "Parent-Offspring Conflict." *American Zoologist* 14:249–64.

Tsebelis, George. 1990. *Nested Games.* Berkeley: University of California Press.

Tullock, Gordon. 1967. "The General Irrelevance of the General Impossibility Theorem." *Quarterly Journal of Economics* 81:256–70.

————. 1981. "Why So Much Stability?" *Public Choice* 37:189–202.

Ullman-Margalit, Edna. 1977. *The Emergence of Norms.* Oxford: Oxford University Press.

Umbeck, John R. 1981. *A Theory of Property Rights.* Ames: University of Iowa Press.

Veitch, John M. 1986. "Repudiations and Confiscations by the Medieval State." *Journal of Economic History* 46:31–36.

Von Neumann, John, and Oscar Morgenstern. 1944. *Theory of Games and Economic Behavior.* Princeton, NJ: Princeton University Press.

Weimer, D. L., and A. R. Vining. 1989. *Policy Analysis: Concepts and Practice.* Englewood Cliffs, NJ: Prentice Hall.

Weiner, A. 1932. "The Hansa." In *The Cambridge Medieval History.* Vol. 7. Edited by J. R. Tanner, C. W. Previte-Orton, and Z. N. Brooke, 216–69. Cambridge: Cambridge University Press.

Weingast, Barry R. 1981. "Regulation, Reregulation, and Deregulation: The Political Foundations of Agency-Clientele Relations." *Law and Contemporary Problems* 44:147–77.

————. 1992. "Institutional Foundations of the 'Sinews of Power': British Financial and Military Success Following The Glorious Revolution." Hoover Institution, Stanford University.

Weingast, Barry R., and William Marshall. 1988. "The Industrial Organization of Congress: Or Why Legislatures, Like Firms Are Not Organized As Markets." *Journal of Political Economy* 96:132–63.

Williamson, Oliver. 1975. *Markets and Hierarchies.* New York: The Free Press.

————. 1985. *The Economic Institutions of Capitalism.* New York: The Free Press.

Wittman, Donald. 1977. "Candidate Motivation: A Synthesis of Alternative Theories." *American Political Science Review* 77:142–57.

Young, H. Peyton. 1993. "The Evolution of Conventions." *Econometrica* 61:57–84.

Zald, Mayer N. 1987. "Review Essay: The New Institutional Economics." *American Journal of Sociology* 93:701–8.

Contributors

Randall L. Calvert, University of Rochester

Jon Elster, Columbia University

Avner Greif, Stanford University

Jack Knight, Washington University in St. Louis

Paul Milgrom, Stanford University

Douglass C. North, Washington University in St. Louis

William H. Riker, University of Rochester (deceased)

Norman Schofield, Washington University in St. Louis

Itai Sened, Tel Aviv University

Barry Weingast, Stanford University

Index

Alchian, Armen, 3–4
Arrow, Kenneth, 191–92
Arrow's Theorem, 191–92
Arthur, Brian, 21
Articles of Confederation, 123–27, 135–36, 139, 149–50

Bargaining, 4–5, 8, 77, 81, 110, 119n.5; inside options, 155–58; outside options, 154–57; theory, 109, 119n.4, 154–57, 160n.16; theory of institutional emergence, 97, 99–101, 107–10, 117–18
Bargaining power, 109–10, 114–15, 145, 150, 153, 160n.21; and institutions, 19, 97, 118n.3
Bayes' Rule, 172–73
Belgium: Flanders, 31, 35, 37–40
Beliefs, 10, 167–77, 180–87; cultural, 25, 26n.2; see also social expectations
Britain, 53, 54n.17, 179–80; dual monarchy, 123, 144n.1; influence on constitutions, 125, 129; merchants, 29, 31, 35, 37–38
Bureaucracy. See Organization
Byzantine Empire, 31

Cartels, of merchant guilds, 30, 34, 52
Champagne fairs, 28
Coalitions, 191–93; collegiality of, 192, 197–200; decisiveness of, 192–93
Coercion. See Sanctions
Cognitive science, 6, 20, 24–25,

26n.5, 122–23; and mental models, 15, 17, 25
Collective action, 1, 4, 30, 41, 53, 100, 146; and commitment, 29; and enforcement, 70; thresholds, 169–71
Collective benefits. See Public goods
Commitment: credible, 6, 22–23, 27–29, 33, 37–38, 41–42, 72, 109–10, 147, 151, 153, 159n.7, 159n.15, 167, 169
Committees, 189
Communication, 8, 146; centralized, 61, 66, 68; claims to credibility, 147; claims to validity, 147; costly, 66–74; endogenous, 46; informal, 46; multilateral, 63–66; organized, 47; slow, 33
Competition, 4, 97, 104, 117, 118n.3, 119n.7; conditions for, 107; evolutionary, 106; among merchants, 43; of organizations, 15–16; political markets, 23; as a selection mechanism, 106, 113–15
Complementarities, 15, 22
Condorcet Jury Theorem, 189
Congress: United States, 23, 75–80, 127, 142, 146–58; United States Continental, 123–24, 128, 130, 140
Connecticut Compromise, 141
Constitutional Convention, United States, 82, 125–30, 132–44, 146–58, 160n.22
Constitutions, 4–5, 121; internal consistency, 121–22, 130–31; state,

lemma, 7, 59–73, 84–92, 100; pure coordination, 80; repeated, 28, 32, 42–44, 48, 82, 84–92, 97, 100, 103, 111, 167; repeated cooperation, 57–69; sequential, 164–73; signaling, 188n.8
Game theory: and cooperation, 20; evolutionary, 80, 82, 94n.18, 109, 118n.2
Germany: Bundesrat, 145; Hansa, 38–42, 52–53, 55n.29, 56n.46; Kontor, 39–41, 55n.26; merchants, 35, 37, 38–41, 56n.39; merchant guilds, 30, 51
Greek Leagues, 123, 144n.1
Guilds: craft, 29, 54n.3; merchant, 6, 27–53, 54n.5, 55nn.19,26, 56n.4, 79

Habermas, Jurgen, 147–48
Hahn, Frank, 17
Hayek, F. A., 3
Hechter, Michael, 81
Hierarchy, 122

Ideology, 23–24, 26n.4
Incentives, 15, 17, 20, 30, 37, 50, 105
Informal institutions, 5, 10, 15, 26n.2, 57, 75, 161–62; as an equilibrium, 63, 73; as framework for social interactions, 11; information provision, 11; and organizations, 16; and path dependence, 22; violations of, 11; *see also* Norms; Social conventions
Information, 9, 28, 103, 162–63; asymmetric, 33, 171–73; complete, 61, 63, 167–69, 175; diffusion of, 45–46; imperfect, 38; incomplete, 169–77; and institutions, 24, 74, 81–82; and organizations, 36, 47; perfect, 61, 63
Inheritance, 122
Institutional emergence, 1–2, 4–5, 7, 80, 95–118; bargaining theory, 2, 4–5, 7, 97, 99–101, 107–10, 117–18, 145–58; evolutionary emer-

gence of social conventions, 7, 97, 99–104, 112–13, 118; intentional design, 3, 4, 7, 81; market theories of exchange and selection through competition, 3, 7, 97, 99–101, 104–7, 113–18; spontaneous emergence, 2–3, 7, 80–82, 98
Institutions: cross-cutting, 112–13; and change, 2, 15, 18, 95, 97; as constraints (or rules of the game), 7, 15, 18, 58, 66, 75, 98; contract-enforcement, 28; convergence of, 12–13; for coordination, 33; definition of, 15, 18, 57, 75, 98–99; in economic history, 1; emergence of, 1–2, 80, 95–118; as equilibrium behavior, 7, 58–83; evolution of, 12–13, 25, 97, 103; and exogenous change, 16; as features of individual preferences, 58; general characteristics of, 116–17; inefficient, 2, 83; internal consistency of, 8, 121–22, 130–31; and mental models, 25, 26n.2; and organizations, 1, 16; and path dependence, 18, 22, 25; in philosophy, 1; in political science, 1; as separate from organizations, 15; in sociology, 1; *see also* Formal institutions; Informal institutions; Institutional emergence
Interpretation: of fact, 33; of models, 7, 95–98, 111
Islam: Muslim merchants, 35
Italy, 214; city-states in, 31–32, 35–36, 41–42, 54n.1, 56n.39; merchants in, 35–36

Judicial review, 139, 141
Justice, 8, 145, 150

Kinship, 122
Knowledge: accumulation of, 16; and economic performance, 18–21; and incentives, 17
Krehbiel, Keith, 75–79